GLOBAL MEDIA LITERACY IN A DIGITAL AGE

CRITICAL ISSUES FOR LEARNING AND TEACHING

Shirley R. Steinberg
General Editor

Vol. 16

The Minding the Media series is part of both
the Peter Lang Education list and the Media and Communication list.
Every volume is peer reviewed and meets
the highest quality standards for content and production.

PETER LANG
New York • Bern • Frankfurt • Berlin
Brussels • Vienna • Oxford • Warsaw

GLOBAL MEDIA LITERACY IN A DIGITAL AGE

teaching beyond borders

EDITED BY BELINHA S. DE ABREU & MELDA N. YILDIZ

PETER LANG
New York • Bern • Frankfurt • Berlin
Brussels • Vienna • Oxford • Warsaw

Library of Congress Cataloging-in-Publication Data
Names: De Abreu, Belinha S. | Yildiz, Melda N., editor.
Title: Global media literacy in a digital age: teaching beyond borders /
edited by Belinha S. De Abreu, Melda N. Yildiz.
Description: New York: Peter Lang, [2015] | Series: Minding the media:
critical issues for learning and teaching, ISSN 2151-2949; v. 16 |
Includes bibliographical references and index.
Identifiers: LCCN 2015029778 | ISBN 9781433128455 (hardcover: alkaline paper) |
ISBN 9781433128448 (paperback: alkaline paper) | ISBN 9781453917282 (e-book)
Subjects: LCSH: Mass media in education—Cross-cultural studies. |
Media literacy—Cross-cultural studies. | Educational technology—Cross-cultural studies. |
Computer-assisted instruction—Cross-cultural studies. |
Education and globalization—Cross-cultural studies.
Classification: LCC LB1043 .G565 2015 | DDC 374/.26—dc23
LC record available at http://lccn.loc.gov/2015029778

Bibliographic information published by **Die Deutsche Nationalbibliothek**.
Die Deutsche Nationalbibliothek lists this publication in the "Deutsche
Nationalbibliografie"; detailed bibliographic data are available
on the Internet at http://dnb.d-nb.de/.

The paper in this book meets the guidelines for permanence and durability
of the Committee on Production Guidelines for Book Longevity
of the Council of Library Resources.

Table of Contents

Part 3 Practice, Assessment, Action

Part 4 Take Action

Foreword

It is with great anticipation that I look to *Global Media Literacy in a Digital Age*, an exploration that is both timely and prescient. Political divides across the globe are as sharp as ever, but economic and cultural divides are softening more and more as the global village that Marshall McLuhan envisioned in 1962 permeates our lives. Youth throughout the world have more in common with each other than they do with their elders, as mobile phones and headsets become mandatory accessories. The generational technology divide affects individual and organizational prospects as much if not more than political divides, with just as many tribes with self-interest at stake.

We are living through the establishment of a new world order, where information—previously valued as scarce—is now plentiful. And as the scarce becomes plentiful, business models and organizational structures alike continue to topple. Education is no exception, and in fact, schools and libraries are no longer seen as temples of learning to be visited regularly, with attendant wise men and women, and rituals. Education is a pillar of society subject to radical change, and in today's context, education is even subject to a needed revolution, moving from a factory-based model to an information-based model.

What to do, what to do? It is a simple call to recognize that the basic tenets of education must change, but no simple task to channel the change. Information is now infinitely available and subjects are infinitely variable, making the previous content silos irrelevant and, indeed, an impediment to problem solving. Yet effective information filters are scarce and opaque. When students journey through cyberspace, they no longer have adults selecting information to be shared, helping evaluate that information, and guiding them with the degree of control in the past; no one accompanies youth minute-by-minute through their journeys in the global village.

But young people still need filters (and more!) for all kinds of purposes, from Internet safety to having the ability to select credible information sources. They (and we) need a mindset to go with the headset—an internalized filtering system that can be used anytime, anywhere; that is commonly shared; and that transcends cultural and national boundaries. We need algorithms for our brains, to use as we are both consuming and producing media and participating in a globalized society.

Algorithms have become the holy (and golden) grails that form the basis of search and sorting tools; they are constants applied to the infinite variety of information available. These self-contained, step-by-step sets of software operations perform calculations, data processing, and automated reasoning in exactly the same way each time; but each algorithm also has a different goal, a different value, and a different approach. We trust algorithms to identify pertinent information in response to our Internet queries, to adjust street lights to changing traffic conditions, and even to allocate our retirement savings through "robo-advisors." Yet at the end of the day, an algorithm must fit the task at hand to enable the most effective output; judgment is still indispensible.

In a sense, media literacy is an algorithm for the brain—a consistent way of filtering and processing the infinite information available to us. Currently, the heuristic process skills of media literacy are indeed scarce and scarcely being taught, because these skills are not yet valued as highly in educational institutions as access to content knowledge. The current valuing of content knowledge at the expense of process skills creates a misalignment between education attainments and education outcomes. Rather than teach the skills citizens need to be successful in the future, an education system rooted in the past ignores what is truly important, and subsequently focuses on irrelevant outcomes to value and to measure.

This is not to say that content knowledge is unimportant—quite the contrary—but media literacy skills in the global village are needed as the central tools through which to contextualize, acquire, and apply content knowledge. Like algorithms, media literacy skills are "constants" used in deconstructing and constructing communication through a process of inquiry. Content knowledge is "variable," with an infinite number of subjects. Having media literacy—a consistent, heuristic process of inquiry that is internalized—enhances the ability to communicate and share ideas through a common vocabulary that transcends subject areas as well as geographic boundaries. Thus, there are no "silos" within this method for teaching critical thinking, because the media literacy skills are cross-cultural, cross-curricular, and common to all. It is through this process of inquiry that students acquire and master content knowledge, but both media literacy skills and content knowledge rest on a continuum of knowledge that can always be expanded and deepened.

The Aspen Institute issued a 2014 report called *Learner at the Center of a Networked World*, which recognized that media literacy and social/emotional literacies should be at the heart of education—not at the periphery. It is this recognition of the importance of media literacy—indeed, the global imperative to provide media literacy education—that is driving an international quest to explore what media literacy education is and how to deliver it effectively: better, faster, and cheaper.

National races to elevate human capital, now seen as *the* competitive key to economic success, are the modern-day equivalents of the race to the South Pole or the race to space. Such modern-day quests include media literacy, and media literacy missions have taken me to places far and near. When I visited China with an education-focused delegation sponsored by the College Board and Hanban in 2013, I was struck by road-side banners in Beijing advertising a conference on innovation and creativity, which in certain Chinese provinces are now being emphasized in an education system primarily based on rote learning. With its emphasis on critical thinking and on media construction (whether print, audio, video, or social media), media literacy is ideally suited to play a central role in the education revolution. Indeed, Finland, a country noted for its leadership in education, now has a national strategy for media literacy, called "Good Media Literacy," adopted in 2013. And so what was outside the mainstream now comes inside.

Countries who prepare their citizens to live in the global village as well as their local villages are equipping their citizens with the discretionary, creative, and participatory skills they need to influence their destinies. The stakes are high. A 2015 open letter sponsored by the Future of Life Institute, and signed by luminaries such as Stephen Hawking and Elon Musk, asserts that Artificial Intelligence (AI) could spell the end of the human race, as humans come to be dominated by robots. Yet must we be cowed by algorithms of our own making? Having media literacy skills empowers people to declare their independence, yet enables them to contribute to their communities and to the spirit of humanity as well. This book enables an understanding of how to be a citizen of the world—the world of today and tomorrow: the global village.

Each chapter in *Global Media Literacy in a Digital Age* applies a media literacy filter to a variety of topics pertinent around the world: literacy, technology, the environment, terrorism and violence, religion and culture, activism, and the education system itself. The list of topics could be endless, but rather, the discretion and judgment of these outstanding authors and editors provide a meaningful and useful curation that is a hallmark of, as the Finns say, "good media literacy." I invite you to take advantage of this carefully prepared banquet, and to savor this moment when media literacy is poised to enjoy the global recognition and adoption that we on the edges have long espoused. It is with confidence and hope that we continue this journey to bring media literacy to the world.

Tessa Jolls
President and CEO, Center for Media Literacy
Director, Consortium for Media Literacy
Los Angeles, CA

Introduction

Belinha S. De Abreu
Melda N. Yildiz

Are we a globally literate society? Do we consider the world around us when we view the media, or are we segmented according to the geographical area we inhabit each night? The idea of global media literacy is not so much an innovation as it is a necessity to a world that is being shaped daily by trends. These trends are carried very quickly through technological spaces and places via social networks, news sites, and so much more.

Pulitzer Prize winner Thomas Friedman stated "the world is flat," referring to how technology has changed our world and made us into a more global, conglomerate society, since we are connected via phone wires, Internet lines, and much more. Is he wrong? No, not necessarily, but the issue is that many more connections still need to be made, especially in the world of education. In schools across the United States, the recognition that more critical digital learning is needed is taking shape through the induction of 21st-century learning skills. Media literacy education has always been considered more advanced and prevalent in other countries. However, the sweep of new digital technology has created a shared apprehension and impasse surrounding how media literacy needs to be used within the context of these new tools. When the Internet became the medium for disseminating information simultaneously around the world, the transmission of information became faster and the verification of information became questionable. These shifting sands of digital technologies generated another conversation regarding media literacy education. It was inclusive of all these new technologies and opened further international dialogue for how media literacy needed to be used in a global context. The worry is expressed best by David Buckingham in the United Kingdom, that the rhetoric of today may actually be problematic for media literacy education. He argued that it has become so saturated with the discussion of digital technology, digital footprints, and digital infrastructure that the capacity for understanding and learning has been set adrift by good intentions (Buckingham, 2010; De Abreu & Mihailidis, 2014; Jenkins, 2014). At least in the United Kingdom and in the European Union, policymakers have made media literacy education a priority and overall welcomed the idea of growing this type of literacy. In addition, they have demonstrated this further positive appeal by providing government resources to develop curriculum and ideas.

In the United States, the struggle for growing media literacy continues, along with the understanding that world literacy and global knowledge is lacking despite having a variety of technology sources and digital access points available. The *National Geographic* and Roper Public Affairs 2006 Geographic Literacy Study assessed the geographic knowledge of young American adults between the ages of 18 and 24. The results demonstrated that their world knowledge was lacking. The survey asked respondents how much they think they know about geography and other global and national subjects. Their views on the importance of geographic, technological, and cultural knowledge were also assessed. The results showed several areas of limitations, from understanding world events to general knowledge of important events from around the globe; even national events were not well known by young Americans (National Geographic Society, 2006).

This book addresses some of these concerns while considering questions such as: How do we connect with one another in a mediated society? How do the media portray different cultures and beliefs? What messages are often omitted from media? How do we connect what we see in the worldwide media to the classroom? This book will serve to answer many of these questions by providing a three part look at how media literacy education has become a global and interconnected dialogue brought about by the evolution of technology.

In Part 1, the first three chapters of the book, authored by Belinha S. De Abreu from Fairfield University, provide some historical background on media literacy education, and how literacy has progressed globally. Each of these chapters will look at how this form of literacy has grown to a worldwide audience through organizations such as UNESCO and the Alliance for Civilizations. These organizations have taken up the cause of bringing this literacy to all parts of the world. This section will also cover the global theorists who have been a voice in moving media literacy education forward in other locations such as the United Kingdom, China, and the Middle East.

Through thematic examples, Part 2 focuses on strategies for decoding what we know about issues of global importance and their rise to global prominence. In this section, we have a series of authors from around the globe contributing further to the consideration of what happens in the local context when an issue becomes globalized. In Chapter 4, Richard Hornik, Director of the Overseas Partnership Programs for the Center for News Literacy, Stony Brook University; Masato Kajimoto, PhD, Assistant Professor, University of Hong Kong; and Jennifer Fleming, PhD, Associate Professor, California State University, Long Beach collaborated on writing "Creating a Global Community of News Literacy Practice." This chapter blends action research and reflective practice principles in the exploration of how and why a news literacy curriculum, devised and developed at the School of Journalism at Stony Brook University in New York, has organically spread to numerous countries overseas. News literacy is a specialized approach to media literacy in the sense that it shares many of the same analytic goals of media literacy education, such as teaching students how to access, analyze, and evaluate media messages. Lessons and activities in news literacy classrooms focus exclusively on news texts and images—how to identify them, how to analyze them, and how to deconstruct them. In recent years, the definition of news in news literacy has been broadened to include reliable, verified information that comes from non-traditional news sources, particularly social media.

In Chapter 5, Michael RobbGrieco, Director of Curriculum and Technology Integration at Windham Southwest Supervisory Union in Vermont, writes a piece entitled "Digital Remix for Global Media Literacy." This chapter uses participant observation and action research to show how engaging learners in digital remix practice supports global media literacy development and helps educators resolve some of the persistent struggles in media literacy pedagogy. Digital remix involves selection, manipulation, and recombination of elements from source texts either to create new media texts or to produce altered and repurposed versions of the source texts. Remix culture involves global information flows, global memes, and cross-cultural transformations of meaning, as artists play with media artifacts, identities, and representations from all over the world. The chapter concludes with a discussion of how the success of using digital remix practice to support media literacy development depends on five factors of instructional design: clear articulation of apt learning purposes and goals; choice of remix tools in relation to learners' technical skills and experience, source texts, content access, and/or requirements; critical group dialogue about phases of source text curation and analysis, production process, and product assessment; and degree of student choice over form and content.

Kristine Scharaldi from Unite to Educate continues this discussion with Chapter 6, "Fostering Global Competencies and 21st-Century Skills through Mobile Learning." This chapter shares ideas and strategies for educators to help foster global and 21st-century competencies while utilizing mobile digital technologies. This chapter will includes examples of how educators are incorporating culturally-aware pedagogies while providing learning opportunities that engage students in thoughtful and relevant themes in the contexts of collaborative, trans-disciplinary, inquiry- and project-based approaches, as well as student engagement with digital content in varied learning environments and contexts.

From Bosnia and Herzegovina, Vanja Ibrahimbegović-Tihak, Media Literacy and Communications Director at Internews, authors Chapter 7, "Enhancing Media Literacy in Bosnia and Herzegovina: Toward Utilization of IT Tools in Teaching Media and Digital Literacy," discussing how media literacy education for the 21st century should be about teaching citizens to be active participants in the society, by being critical, analytical thinkers able to evaluate, re-think and question, as well as create media content. This chapter also includes the discussion of utilizing new technologies in the learning process, which poses challenges to the current education system. In the education system in Bosnia and Herzegovina, media literacy is hardly a part of curricula. Moreover, there is a severe lack of research and empirical data in B-H on almost all media literacy issues including different age groups' media habits, evaluation of the media literacy educational programs in order to improve and update it, utilization of new IC technologies in the learning process and education system, social networks and youth/adults/seniors, etc. This chapter advocates for an up-to-date media and digital literacy curricula in B-H, utilizing digital technologies as a part of the learning process.

In Chapter 8, Kelly McNeal from William Paterson University focuses her chapter on "Contextualizing Global Media Literacy in the Standards-Based Classroom: Moving Beyond the Culture of the Dichotomous 'Like.'" Her work takes us through the issues faced in a digital world, including the idea that students are in fact polarized in the digital culture. Students enter classrooms believing that to discuss an issue, person, or event means to "like," agree, or disagree with it. Polarization of any topic undermines students' ability to question and learn different perspectives about the topic. The National Core Curriculum Standards in the United States mandates the idea of comprehending complex texts, assessing point of view, evaluating diverse media formats, and evaluating arguments and validity of claims while citing sufficient evidence. This chapter discusses how Bloom's Taxonomy can be utilized, educating teachers and students in how to use international media sources such as the BBC's and Al Jazeera's websites and resources in order to investigate global perspectives about controversial topics such as ISIS, the Palestine conflict, and the fighting in the Middle East.

Looking at the idea of activism in the area of media literacy education is Chapter 9, authored by Rob Williams, PhD, Founding President of ACME, entitled "Project Censored: Building a Global 'Networked Fourth Estate' in a Digital Age." In the chapter, Williams discusses teaching media education as a way of fostering citizen activism. It is a provocative pedagogical approach to media literacy practice in classrooms and communities. As the world witnesses social movements with worldwide significance, how are teachers, students, and community organizers using media education and networked story production platforms like blogging, Twitter, YouTube, and Facebook supposed to facilitate social change? This chapter explores how schools and community organizations are using media education and emergent media tools to organize and share information in the service of citizen activism.

Chapter 10 takes us to Germany and focuses on "Developing Students' Pedagogical Media Competencies and Intercultural Competencies through a U.S.-German Partnership." The authors of this chapter—Silke Grafe, PhD, and Jennifer Tiede, PhD candidate, from the University of Würzburg, Germany, Maria Boos, PhD, from the University of Cologne, and Petra Hesse, PhD, from Wheelock College—worked collaboratively to present a chapter demonstrating the intercultural development of media literacy education. The authors present a pilot research project of two institutions of higher education in Germany and the United States. The main goal of this project was to develop the pedagogical media competencies and intercultural competencies of pre-service teachers. To achieve this goal, a semester-long seminar was developed for students in Germany, which focused on pedagogical media competencies. Additionally, a collaboration with an American researcher and her class on children's media was initiated via two online conferences, in order to help students from both countries develop intercultural competencies. The chapter presents their results and findings from this global project.

Returning back to the United States is Chapter 11, which looks at the ideas of universal design as a window to the world. Victoria Brown, EdD, Florida Atlantic University, writes the chapter, "Breaking Down Barriers: Digital Media and Universal Design." Connecting to the world through the use of various technologies allow classrooms to become transparent windows into cultures around the world. Through these windows, children develop a global understanding of issues they will one day be involved in solving. Through the discussion of the principles of universal design, Brown demonstrates how the form of learning complements the technology used to expand the children's world beyond the classroom walls.

In Part 3, the next three chapters of the book, authored by Melda N. Yildiz, present ideas, case studies, educational perspectives, and assessment opportunities for bringing global media literacy into the classroom. This section of the book focuses more on the practitioner and his or her role in creating lessons and curricula designed to provide global awareness to students in the educational setting here and abroad.

Part 4 of the book has the theme of "Take Action." This section provides readers with resources and opportunities for growing global media literacy education in whatever part of the world they teach, work, or wish to become active in, in this field.

In conclusion, the main goal of this book is to draw on the natural links between global education and media literacy, and their crucial role in shaping the educators, activists, and citizens of the world. The authors as a whole have explored how global media literacy education provides a praxis for investigating the world, recognizing perspectives, and communicating ideas that lead to taking action, promote social justice and multicultural education, and prepare educators, researchers, and others to be inclusive as well as culturally and linguistically responsive.

References

Buckingham, D. (2010). The future of media literacy in the digital age: Some challenges for policy and practice. *Media Education Journal, 47*, 3–10.

De Abreu, B. and Mihailidis, P. (2014). *Media literacy education in action: Theoretical and pedagogical perspectives.* New York, NY: Routledge.

Jenkins, H. (2014, December 1, 3, and 6). Media literacy in action: An interview with Belinha S. De Abreu and Paul Mihailidis (3 parts). *Confessions of an ACA-fan: The official web blog of Henry Jenkins.* Retrieved from http://henryjenkins.org/2014/12/media-literacy-in-action-an-interview-with-belinha-de-abreu-and-paul-mihailidis-part-one.html

National Geographic Society. (2006). Final report: *National Geographic*-Roper Public Affairs 2006 geographic literacy study. *The National Geographic Education Foundation.* Washington, DC: National Geographic Society. Retrieved from http://www.nationalgeographic.com/roper2006/pdf/FINALReport2006GeogLitsurvey.pdf

Part 1
Media Literacy Education Framework and Brief History

1. Media Literacy: Global Connections

Belinha S. De Abreu

"The globalization of education marches on inexorably as the integration of economies has created complex webs of capital, trade, information, currencies, services, supply chains, capital markets, information technology grids and technology platforms that form a more intricate, multifaceted system than a model of simple economic competition among nations. The competition for industries to attract talent and for citizens to obtain high-skill, high wage jobs—as well as the need to cooperate on the most pressing issues of our time, such as terrorism, water shortages, environmental changes and pandemic diseases—has moved beyond national boundaries, with stakes for success higher than ever."
—Vivian Stewart, *World Class Education*, 2012

The world is globalized. We exist in a time when the connections we make with each other go beyond the everyday person-to-person and extend to whom we connect with through media. The media are the hub for these connections. They are the conduits and the influencers, the messengers, the producers, the innovators, and the creators. As people, we live within the frames developed by the media, and we have become the communicators as encoders, decoders, and even methods of delivery. The media have become an augmentation of our person. Our distinction that separates us from the media as a tool is our ability to discern and consider the media as a platform, vehicle, tool, and representation. We are in essence where literacy, language, and learning come together. These associations are the significance of global media literacy. The exchanges and interchanges that link us all have expanded our thinking and our understanding of ourselves and the world around us.

Media literacy education gives us each the ability to think, process, evaluate, understand, and produce the media in all forms. The Center for Media Literacy in the United States defines "media literacy" as follows:

Media Literacy is a 21st century approach to education. It provides a framework to access, analyze, evaluate, create and participate with messages in a variety of forms—from print to video to the Internet. Media literacy builds an understanding of the role of media in society as well as essential skills of inquiry and self-expression necessary for citizens of a democracy. (Center for Media Literacy, 2002)

The Canadian International Development Agency states that,

Media literacy is the practice of developing critical thinking skills regarding the media we consume. It builds the capacity of young people to identify, analyze, and evaluate media and media messages. Media literate children are better equipped to participate effectively in society today and throughout their lives. Media literacy is not one unit of study—it is a life-long learning process. (Halliday & Blackburn, 2003)

Much of the development of their work came from the media literacy educator and pioneer Barry Duncan who in 1989 provided the Ministry from Ontario with a theoretical paper with eight key concepts for media literacy.

Eight Key Concepts for Media Literacy

1. **All media are constructions.** The media do not present simple reflections of external reality, nor are they a clear window to the world. Rather, they present carefully crafted constructions that have been selected. Media literacy works towards deconstructing these constructions and taking them apart to show how they are made.
2. **The media construct reality.** The media are responsible for the majority of the observations and experiences from which we build up our personal understandings of the world and how it works. Much of our view of reality is based on media messages that have been pre-constructed and have attitudes, interpretations, and conclusions already built in. Thus, the media, to a great extent, give us our sense of reality.
3. **Audiences negotiate meaning in media.** If the media provide us with much of the material upon which we build our picture of reality, each of us finds or "negotiates" meaning according to individual factors: faith perspectives; personal needs and anxieties; the pleasures or troubles of the day; racial and sexual attitudes; family and cultural background; gender; and so forth. At the same time, this negotiation is limiting because it happens on both the sub-conscious and conscious levels.
4. **Media have commercial implications**. Media literacy aims to encourage an awareness of how the media are influenced by commercial considerations, and how they impinge on content, technique, and distribution.

Most of media production is a business, and therefore media often operate to make a profit for some. Questions of ownership and control are central: a relatively small number of individuals control what a relatively large number of people watch, read, and hear in the media.

5. **Media contain ideological and value messages.** There is no such thing as objective reporting. Everything has a bias because it is written or stated from a person's (or group of persons') perspectives. Much of mainstream media is advertising, and much of media proclaims values and ways of life. The mainstream media convey, explicitly or implicitly, ideological messages about issues such as the virtue of consumerism, the role of women, the acceptance of authority, and unquestioning patriotism.

6. **Media have social and political implications.** The media have a great influence in politics and informing social change. Television can greatly influence the election of a national leader on the basis of image. The media involve us in concerns such as civil rights issues, famines in Africa, and the HIV/AIDS epidemic. They give us an intimate sense of national issues and global concerns so that we have become what media expert Marshall McLuhan calls the "global village." However, the mainstream media often fail to involve us in certain major world events, such that significant occurrences take place with little notice from the media.

7. **Form and content are closely related in the media.** As Marshall McLuhan noted, each medium has its own grammar and codifies reality in its own particular way. Different media will report the same event, but create different impressions and messages, depending on who is reporting.

8. **Each medium has a unique aesthetic form.** Just as we notice the pleasing rhythms of certain pieces of poetry or prose, so we ought to be able to enjoy the pleasing forms and effects of the different media. People of different backgrounds and ages may be more attracted to one form of media over another.

Source: Duncan (1989)

Len Masterman from the United Kingdom in 1989 came up with a series of principles that has been used widely in the UK for teaching and learning as related to media education. It is important to note that media education and media literacy are terms that are interchanged widely in this study.

Media Awareness Education: Eighteen Basic Principles

1. Media Education is a serious and significant endeavor. At stake is the empowerment of individuals, especially minorities, and the strengthening of society's democratic structures.
2. The central unifying concept of Media Education is that of representation. The media mediate. They do not reflect but re-present the world. The media, that is, are symbolic sign systems that must be decoded. Without this principle no media education is possible. From it, all else flows.
3. Media Education is a lifelong process. High student motivation, therefore, must become a primary objective.
4. Media Education aims to foster not simply critical intelligence, but critical autonomy.
5. Media Education is investigative. It does not seek to impose specific cultural or political values.
6. Media Education is topical and opportunistic. It seeks to illuminate the life-situations of learners. In doing so it may place the "here-and-now" in the context of wider historical and ideological issues.
7. Content, in Media Education, is a means to an end. That end is the development of transferable analytical tools rather than an alternative content.
8. The effectiveness of Media Education can be evaluated by just two criteria:
     (a) the ability of students to apply their critical thinking to new situations, and
     (b) the amount of commitment and motivation displayed by students.
9. Ideally, evaluation in Media Education means student self-evaluation, both formative and summative.
10. Indeed, Media Education attempts to change the relationship between teacher and taught, by offering both objects for reflection and dialogue.
11. Media Education carries out its investigations via dialogue rather than just discussion.
12. Media Education is essentially active and participatory, fostering the development of more open and democratic pedagogies. It encourages students to take more responsibility for and control over their own learning, to engage in joint planning of the syllabus, and to take longer-term perspectives on their own learning.

13. Media Education is much more about new ways of working in the classroom than it is about the introduction of a new subject area.
14. Media Education involves collaborative learning. It is group-focused. It assumes that individual learning is enhanced not through competition but through access to the insights and resources of the whole group.
15. Media Education consists of both practical criticism and critical practice. It affirms the primacy of cultural criticism over cultural reproduction.
16. Media Education is a holistic process. Ideally it means forging relationships with parents, media professionals, and teacher-colleagues.
17. Media Education is committed to the principle of continuous change. It must develop in tandem with a continuously changing reality.
18. Underlying Media Education is a distinctive epistemology: Existing knowledge is not simply transmitted by teachers or "discovered" by students. It is not an end, but a beginning. It is the subject of critical investigations and dialogue out of which new knowledge is actively created by students and teachers.

Source: Masterman (1989)

Other definitions have come from various global organizations such as the European Commission and UNESCO. The European Commission's definition of media literacy, articulated in its communication on a European approach to media literacy in the digital environment, states:

> Media literacy is generally defined as the ability to access the media, to understand and to critically evaluate different aspects of the media and media contents and to create communications in a variety of contexts. (European Commission, 2009)

The UNESCO's Media and Information Literacy Curriculum for Teachers outlines the components of Media Literacy as follows:

- Understand the role and functions of media
- Understand the conditions under which media fulfill their functions
- Critically analyze and evaluate media content
- Use of media for democratic participation, intercultural dialogue, and learning
- Produce user-generated content
- ICT and other media skills (UNESCO, 2011)

From these definitions it is easy to see that the media literacy movement has very much had an international bent, from the United Kingdom, Canada, Australia, Spain, and more. Some of the "forefathers" in the area of media literacy are people such as Marshall McLuhan, David Buckingham, Len Masterman, and others who have provided us with some fundamental perspectives used around the world. Historically, the work done internationally has long set the precedent for what is working and used in schools and curriculum, whether in North America, Asia, or Australia:

> In Australia, media literacy is actively promoted within the primary and secondary curriculum in all states. In some states it is dealt with under the guise of English and, in others, it is offered within an Arts framework. In the later years of high school in some states, Media Studies is offered as a stand-alone option. However, the primary focus still appears to be on broadcast media, rather the newer digital media. (Penman & Turnbull, 2007)

European Association for Viewer's Interests (EAVI) is an independent, not-for-profit international civil society organization registered in Brussels. EAVI was created to facilitate the "unifying process of all those who support citizens' and consumers' interests in the fields of media" (EAVI, 2005). This organization focuses on the digital citizen and represents media literacy as follows:

> Media literate citizens are those who are aware of the content they use, how they found it, who is constructing and providing it. Furthermore they are wise, ethical and effective in media use. Literate citizens are able to fully participate in public life and interact with other people, benefiting from services and using the media as a resource in a safe way. They are open to learn, explore and have fun with the media. They will also be informed consumers when shopping and locate reliable sources of information. They are not passengers, but are in the driving seat deciding where to go. They are AWARE. (EAVI, 2005)

Diverging from the global community, the United States has been looked upon as being latent and even regressive in the integration of media literacy into the classroom curriculum (Tyner, 1998). Although in countries such as Canada, England, and Australia media literacy has become a defined area of study, in the United States it continues to be a work in progress, despite many additions to school curricular and reform movements. Despite these facts, the Center for Media Literacy has established a set of key concepts and key questions to focus the learning and understanding of media literacy education in the United States. They are:

- Who created this message?
  o All media messages are constructed.

- What creative techniques are used to attract my attention?
  o Media messages are constructed using a creative language with its own rules.
- How might different people understand this message differently?
  o Different people experience the same media message differently.
- What values, lifestyles, and points of view are represented in, or omitted from, this message?
  o Media have embedded values and points of view.
- Why is this message being sent?
  o Most media messages are organized to gain profit and/or power. (Center for Media Literacy, 2002)

Marshall McLuhan, a Canadian academic who during the 1960s wrote *Understanding Media*, was credited as a founding father in the study of media literacy for his comment, "The medium is the message." McLuhan (1964) had predicted that technology and media were growing at a rapid pace, and that schools needed to adapt techniques for students to learn and process the information they were receiving, by, at that time, only television and radio. As a university professor, he could easily see that his students were consumed by the media, but that he had not kept up. In many ways, this observation changed his life and his belief that the media were to change all our lives (Tyner, 1998).

Addressing some of these issues related to change within schools in the United States is the Partnership for 21st Century Skills, which is both a guide to curriculum and standards for information and media literacy, and a group of individuals from the private and public sector. This cohort gathered together to address concerns related to what they believed a 21st-century student should look like and what schools should be doing in order to accomplish the goal of educating him or her. In their first report, presented in 2002, they indicated that we have a growing community of learners who use technology on a regular basis, but our schools, although attempting it, are unable, or in some cases unwilling, to reinforce the skills learned (Partnership for 21st Century Skills, 2006). We know that students understand social networking such as Snapchat and Instagram, comprehend how to blog, text each other on a regular basis, play intricate and detailed video games, and so much more (Lenhart, 2015). Yet, if we were to ask a classroom teacher, and even a library media specialist, to demonstrate the same knowledge, the numbers are not there (Kist, 2005). Instead, our focus has been on the regular classroom instruction, which has not kept up with the new waves of technology in use. Due to the slow change in education, a gap has been created. Moreover, educators are reluctant to move into the discussion or a lesson on the use of digital media literacy, because it would take away the time devoted to the curriculum they must teach due to mandated state testing and the new teacher evaluation system. In essence, the curriculum has placed a strangle hold on the adoption, growth, and implementation of media literacy education that is much needed for today's digital youth.

There is no question that the world is moving at a very fast pace, and the classroom of tomorrow must be ready to do the same. This conclusion is shared by educators involved with UNESCO, the Partnership for 21st Century Skills and various media literacy interest groups globally. Their charge has been to find curricular connections that would bring students closer to a place where they can work and live in a community where the media, technology, and other multimedia platforms are a part of their daily lives. The question paramount to educators within these groups and throughout the communities of learning is, how can public education better prepare students for the 21st century? The best definition of what 21st-century skills look like is described by the Partnership for 21st Century Skills:

> Teaching through the use of relevant real-world examples, applications and settings to frame academic content for students, enabling them to see the connection between their studies and the world in which they live. (Partnership for 21st Century Skills, 2006)

This definition defines exactly what media literacy does in the classroom and why it is considered a 21st-century learning skill. Media literacy should be fully incorporated into the classroom and used in a variety of ways alongside curricular topics, as questions regarding media arise throughout the academic school year. The point is that media literacy in the curriculum is about sharing an experience while teaching and learning how it affects the recipient of the message.

In some communities of learning, media literacy is sometimes looked at as a separate subject area, but it is a tool best used in combination within the school curriculum. As Elizabeth Thoman (1997), the founder of the Center for Media Literacy, states, "Media Literacy is not a new subject to teach, but a new way to teach all subjects." The media permeate all content areas. Over time, the ideas of media literacy education have shifted and changed with the wave of new technologies and the influences that have come with the new mediums. Here is a contextual formulation of what media literacy education should be for today's digital age, based upon my own experiences working with teachers, policymakers, parents, and most importantly students (De Abreu, 2014).

Media literacy education...

...engages the teacher and the learner simultaneously so that a give and take relationship can exist within the framework of the classroom, thereby becoming an equalizer of shared information.

...necessitates a place in the core curriculum because it has become an instrumental avenue for the growth of knowledge within those traditional areas of learning.

...extends an opportunity for outreach when dealing with issues of safety and security in today's cybersociety.

...serves the wider community by being instrumental in teaching parents, law officers, and other interested parties who are invested in our school communities to access, analyze, evaluate, and produce media messages.

...creates a conscious understanding of the importance of text and images as they transcend the spaces that they are shelved within be it television, the internet, social networking sites, or video games. (De Abreu, 2014)

It is very hard to believe that schools have been able to keep from teaching about the media and popular culture, especially when you consider that the media have long been dominating the educational infrastructure. But, that is exactly what has happened. The topics shaped by the media seem to breed fear in teachers, because they are afraid to deal with the questions that may arise from the discussion. There is also a worry that they would not know what their students are talking about on a given topic. This fear, more than any other, has deterred teachers from implementing this type of instruction in the classroom. In part, this is because the role of the teacher has long been as the leader of the classroom. Venturing into media and popular culture could upset the tenuous balance of power that exists in the educational structure.

Media Literacy education is...

...the ability to teach and think critically about various media platforms.

...an acknowledgment of the pleasure of the media to the user which is also extended to those critical conversations in the class which ask the teacher at times to extend beyond their comfort level.

...about processing the changes in our digital age while listening to the student users and their knowledgeable capacity of these new realms of learning.

...a voice for all students, but especially to those who do not get to speak up on how their media—their likes and dislikes, impact them personally. (De Abreu, 2014)

Media literacy provides for a wide spectrum of ideas to be exchanged, in which a student is sometimes the leader or guide and the teacher takes a step back and allows the student to take a step forward. While this concept may seem natural for some teachers, for others it is most difficult. However, being exposed to media does not necessarily mean that the student is media savvy, which is where media literacy has the greatest potential impact. With media literacy education, the teacher becomes more of a guide, one who may pose the question that needs to be discussed, but also the one who will redirect the conversation in order to open different avenues of thinking. This way of teaching is not always comfortable, nor is it easy. The best way to know that the material covered in the classroom is reaching students is to see how motivated they are to be in charge of their learning, especially on topics that are of most interest to them. As a colleague of mine noted to me recently, when he taught a lesson on musical artists in the science classroom (his lesson was on truth vs. fiction of scientific data, as suggested by movies and television shows), the students approached him at the end of the school year and told him that they were thrilled to have a modern-day topic used for discussion. They thought it was "cool" that he had broached the subject using popular culture texts.

Media literacy education is...

...a navigation tool for educators to discuss, challenge, critique, and understand how media, both traditional and new, has impact on students' beliefs, thoughts, behaviors, etc.

...a way to help students become empathetic to another person's difficulties, struggles, or concerns as it requires the participant to consider both sides of every issue.

...the opposite of censorship because it instead seeks to address head on the concerns and issues which arise from technology which makes many adults fearful.

AND,

...a platform for ultimately creating a digital citizen that can reach beyond the scope of their medium of choice i.e. computer or cell phone, to be a part of the global community that is seemingly within the grasp of each individual. (De Abreu, 2014)

These concepts are not singular, but encompass a wide range of themes that are under consideration in education circles. Programs in media literacy education typically cover such topics as the global community; curriculum using the variety of key concepts and questions from various countries and standpoints; and production using various tools such as video recorders, digital cameras, and iPods. Teachers who participate in these courses tend to come from a variety of cultures and diverse backgrounds, which creates rich discussions whether the classes are taught online or in person. The instructors in media literacy also come from various backgrounds, but many of them have been teaching media literacy education either nationally or internationally, therefore their experiences in the classroom are current and their perspective wide (Considine, 2004).

Critical components of media literacy education include, "being able to judge the credibility and accuracy of information presented in different formats, evaluating the author's intent and meaning, appreciating the techniques used to persuade and convey emotion, and being able to communicate through various media formats" (Scheibe, 2004, p. 60). Overall, the point of media literacy is to create critical awareness of messages that are transmitted on a daily basis. Media texts such as television, newspapers, radio, magazines, the Internet, etc., are constructions representing particular points of view. Part of the media literacy educator's job is to help students comprehend and deconstruct the design and development of these texts in order to be critical of their messages (Schwartz, 2001). This is quite similar to critical literacy and is only a new concept in its extension of critical literacy to the consumption of media. While teachers may understand that their students are captivated by these various media environments, their working knowledge of media is not always sufficient (Buckingham, 2003). Moreover, those who have an expanded knowledge of the media are not always able to draw on the students' interests and to foster higher-order thinking.

It is critical to understand the teacher's perceptions of the instruction of media literacy because this form of learning differs from traditional instruction. This form of learning asks the teacher often to give up the role of "teacher knows best" and transfers that role to the student, because students may be more knowledgeable about current popular media (Ferguson, 2001). Ferguson states that "the teacher knows best approach, when softened and disguised as education becomes patronizing" (p. 37). Students are often able to see this clearly and may tune out the teacher, especially when their media-saturated world is involved. At the same time, it is important to note that "knowing" the media is not the same as being critically discerning. Students need assistance in deconstructing media messages, gaining critical awareness, and understanding much of what they consume, which is where the value of teaching media literacy education can best be highlighted. The role of the learner becomes extended for students, and the teacher as a facilitator helps students to ask the key media literacy questions.

In many media literacy classrooms, students are put in the role of mentor and leader. They also become the more dominant figures in the dialogue because media literacy requires deconstructing text for oneself and because students are savvier than teachers. They have the power, and they are asked to bring their knowledge to the classroom and explain it, and then share with their classmates and teacher (Buckingham, 2003). For some teachers, this role may seem unacceptable, but in order to be a teacher of media literacy, one must accept this change in the classroom dynamics.

Another way that power plays into the ideas of media literacy is through the media themselves. Media involve representations of pleasure and power. Representation is explained by looking at symbols, meanings, and the construction behind the messages found in advertisements, news, and all other forms of media (Baird, 1998). Pleasure is often what individuals take from their relationship with the media The power of the media can be found in how audiences are defined—White or Black, rich or poor—and how media texts are constructed to make such audiences believe that they understand and see ideas and thoughts differently from everyone else (Buckingham, 2003b; Potter, 2013).

Carmen Luke states that "a recombination of these fields into a next generation of teacher education courses can give students the theoretical frameworks and practical applications for critical and analytic principles of media-cultural studies in teaching with, and about, new information technologies" (Luke, 2000). Therefore, looking at schools with teachers who use the media as texts for comprehension or production is a base point for teaching and learning.

References

Baird, S. (1998, September 18). If schools want to teach values, they have to talk media. *National Catholic Reporter*, 10–15.

Buckingham, D. (2003). *Media education literacy, learning and contemporary culture*. Malden, MA: Blackwell Publishing.

——. (2003b). Media education and the end of the critical consumer. *Harvard Educational Review*, *73*(3), 309–23.

Center for Media Literacy. (2002). *CML framework*. Retrieved from http://www.medialit.org/cml-framework

Considine, D. (September 2004). If you build it, they will come. *American Behavioral Scientist*, *48*(1), 97–107.

De Abreu, B. (2014). Grasping the complexities of U.S. educational policy and the classroom: How to move media literacy education forward. In B. De Abreu and P. Mihailidis, *Media literacy in action: Theoretical and pedagogical perspectives*. London, UK: Routledge.

Duncan, B. (1989). Eight key concepts of media literacy. *Media Literacy Resource Guide*. Toronto, ON, Canada: Ontario Ministry of Education.

European Association for Viewers' Interests (EAVI). (2005). *EAVI's mission & background*. Brussels. Retrieved from http://www.eavi.eu/joomla/about-us/mission

European Commission. (2009). *Study on the current trends and approaches to media literacy in Europe*. Retrieved from http://ec.europa.eu/culture/library/studies/literacy-trends-report_en.pdf

Ferguson, R. (2001). Media education and the development of critical solidarity. *Media Education Journal*, *30*, 37–43.

Halliday, A., & Blackburn, D. (2003). *Media literacy for global citizenship*. Mississauga, ON, Canada: World Vision Canada, Global Education. Retrieved from http://ourworldclass.tigweb.org/upload/medialiteracy.pdf

Kist, W. (2005). *New literacies in action: Teaching and learning in multiple media*. New York, NY: Teachers College Press.

Lenhart, A. (2015, April 9). *Teens, social media & technology overview 2015*. Washington, DC: Pew Research Center.

Luke, C. (February 2000). New literacies in teacher education. *Journal of Adolescent and Adult Literacy*, *43*(2), 424–35.

Masterman, L. (1989). *Teaching the media.* New York, NY: Routledge.

McLuhan, M. (1964). *Understanding media: The extensions of man.* New York, NY: McGraw-Hill.

Partnership for 21st Century Skills. (December 2006). *Results that matter: 21st century skills and high school reform.* Retrieved from http://www.21stcenturyskills.org/index.php?Itemid=114&id=204&option=com_content&task=view

Penman, R., & Turnbull, S. (July 2007). Media literacy: Concepts, research, and regulatory issues. *Australian Communications and Media Authority.* Melbourne, Australia. Retrieved from http://www.acma.gov.au/webwr/_assets/main/lib310665/media_literacy_report.pdf

Potter, W. J. (2013). *Media literacy* (7th ed.). Los Angeles, CA: Sage.

Scheibe, C. (September 2004). A deeper sense of literacy. *American Behavioral Scientist, 48*(1), 60–68.

Schwartz, G. (Spring 2001). Literacy expanded: The role of media literacy in teacher education. *Teacher Education Quarterly,* 111–19.

Thoman, E. (1997). *Skills and strategies for media education.* Los Angeles, CA: Center for Media Literacy.

Tyner, K. (1998). *Literacy in a digital world: Teaching and learning in the age of information.* Mahwah, NJ: Lawrence Erlbaum Associates.

UNESCO. (2011). *MIL curriculum for teacher education.* Paris, France: UNESCO.

2. World Literacy and ICTs: Educational Technologies

BELINHA S. DE ABREU

"It is part of the educator's responsibility to see equally to two things: First, that the problem grows out of the conditions of the experience being had in the present, and that it is within the range of capacity of students; and, secondly, that it is such that it arouses in the learner an active quest for information and for production of new ideas. The new facts and new ideas thus obtained become the ground for further experiences in which new problems are presented. The process is a continuous spiral."

—John Dewey, 1938

Technologies have influenced a great change in society and in education. As the number of hours that citizens connect with technology has increased, so has the need for educating students and the general public about the tools as well as the platforms that carry information. Information and communication technologies (ICTs) affect "working, accessing knowledge, socializing, communication, collaborating—and succeeding—in all areas of the professional, social, and personal life" (European Commission, 2013). This statement is true whether in Europe, the United States, or other parts of the world: our youth are directly impacted by the mass saturation provided by the digital world.

In the United States the online lives of users have grown exponentially, and young people in particular have become the most frequent users of the Internet through a variety of platforms from tablets and laptops to cell phones (Lenhart, 2015). Around the world, technology is used as a vehicle of communication by more and more people. Consider these statistics:

- The rate of Internet usage in Latin America/the Caribbean went up 660% between 2000 and 2008 (Internet World Stats, 2014).

- The rate of Internet usage in the Middle East went up 1,176% between 2000 and 2008 (Internet World Stats, 2014).
- The Asia Pacific market continues to see a significant increase in mobile subscriptions, with 1.4 billion net additions by the end of 2019 (Ericsson Mobility Report, 2014).
- At the end of 2014, the forecast was for 635 million mobile subscriptions in sub-Saharan Africa, with a prediction to rise to 930 million by late 2019, when it is estimated that three in four mobile subscriptions will be Internet-inclusive (Perry, 2014).
- 92.5% of the population in Sweden are Internet users (International Telecommunication Union, 2014).
- Cell phones are nearly universal in emerging and developing countries, but smartphones are less commonplace (Poushter, 2015).

As stated by the European Commission,

> Information and communication technologies (ICT) are rapidly changing global production, work and business methods and trade and consumption patterns in and between enterprises and consumers. ICT enables a radical change in structures of organisations and means of learning, researching, developing, producing, marketing, distributing and servicing digital and traditional goods and services. It also has a great potential to enhance the quality of life (European Commission, 2013).

The growing changes in technology have become a part of the educational dialogue and increasingly an area of concern, in which educators, policymakers, and others with a vested interest in education are examining the formation of thinking, learning, and perception that has arisen by the use of these tools. Since the early part of the 21st century, a transformation has taken place in the ways in which people are communicating via online and specifically social media. No longer are people using their stand-alone computers or laptops; instead their computing has shifted to the mobile device, whether it is in the form of a tablet, an iPhone, or some new innovative tool—thus allowing them to engage in their social networks faster and more readily. Communication, which was sometimes delayed and compromised, has become wider and greater, while the mode of exchange has become smaller and faster. As a tool for education, mobile technologies and e-learning are in a place of transition and growth.

These shifting changes have opened a dialogue, derived in part from educational researchers and educators, about the value of educational technologies. Many questions are being asked and considered in education circles, reflecting on the tools as well as the expectations of learning and teaching for both students and teachers. Some of these questions have to do with mobile technologies and their influence in the mainstream of current educational practices, but more are about how we can use these tools for altering the classroom. Questions under consideration include:

- Is mobile learning transformational?
- How do we value personalized learning, and how is that managed within the context of the traditional school?
- Can students become collaborative learners on online platforms?
- Through the use of new technologies, whether in a mobile setting or a traditional, computerized classroom, how do students demonstrate their learning to the teacher?
- How does the technology open up the dialogue of global citizenry?
- What types of professional development services are offered to teachers in order to bring about their own personal understanding of how these new technologies can truly impact classroom learning?

Reflecting on these questions articulates that schooling today can no longer be a one-size-fits-all in any classroom around the world. With the wide range of mobile technologies as well as other innovations taking place, teaching and learning must continue to transform in order for knowledge to be gained. New approaches and strategies must be used as the technologies influencing learners' lives are continuously evolving.

While the evolution of technology is growing, so must the consideration for how and why students are using technology. Technology for its own sake is not useful, nor does it guarantee a knowledge base for the user, especially when we are considering our youngest users. Much conversation, especially in third world countries, has been devoted to issues of access to the tools of technology. In the more advanced parts of the world, access to technology is less of an issue, but that has not made the user smarter. In many educational settings, computers are used as a resource for locating information or for the basics of word processing. Rarely are computers or other technology resources used as an opportunity for intellectual engagement in the elementary, middle, or high school setting. One value of ICTs and any kind of standardization of educational technology is as a point of evaluating and critically analyzing the messages that are carried via these platforms. The young are at an advantage in using the tools, and are able to maneuver through most platforms; the greater learning is in the depth in which they consider the media messages provided by accessing the Internet and other web resources. Helping them to differentiate between a good resource and one that is biased and factually flawed is where the work of education must be directed. Access to the tools will always be an issue in economies that are struggling and impoverished; but even when the tools are available most policymakers will consider it enough, and the work of critical thinking, understanding bias, and considering fact from fiction will be left behind.

Technology has always moved faster than education. This is evident to any person who walks into schools globally. Many places still teach with the chalkboard, whether it is in the United States, Europe, or the Middle East, while others are feeling the gravitational pull to e-learning, because it provides opportunities to step outside of the community. New forms of communicating are introduced regularly, and certainly more quickly than ever before. This fact is apparent from how our written and oral language has changed significantly in the last several years. Information and communication technologies (ICT) have become a part of the global discussion, especially as these technologies have been widely considered in the business industries. There is a realization that the development of the world and even a more efficient education system is dependent on knowledge dissemination. Further, the newest technologies now provide for an all-in-one depository that mixes traditional media such as radio and books with the latest method of delivery, whether in the shape of a tablet or an iPad. As stated in the ICTs and the education Millennium Development Goals (MDGs) guide:

> The swiftness of ICT developments, their increasing spread and availability, the nature of their content and their declining prices are having major implications for learning. They may tend to increase disparities, weaken social bonds and threaten cultural cohesion. Governments will therefore need to establish clearer policies in regard to science and technology, and undertake critical assessments of ICT experiences and options. These should include their resource implications in relation to the provision of basic education, emphasizing choices that bridge the "digital divide," increase access and quality, and reduce inequity. (InfoDev, 2015)

While the digital divide is real and exists even in the most affluent parts of the world, it is the interconnections of technology that are of most interest when discussing ICTs.

A term coined by Marshall McLuhan (1962) refers to a world in which communication technology unites people in remote parts of the world—"a global village." The television was thought to do this early on, as the pace of communication information and world news was increasing throughout the world. The Internet has superseded that idea with its ability to share culture instantaneously, even if it is not well understood by the communicator.

With the growth of the variety of technologies, educators must consider how these student content-creators and networkers can exist in the classroom.

This requires a reinforcement of understanding and knowledge from the lead educators in many schools. Educators who discount the value of social networking tend to fall into two categories: those who are not sure how to do it, and those who have chosen not to use it themselves. For many teachers, their concern is that they do not actually know how to use social network sites, or find mobile technologies, primarily cell phones, to be a bit precarious for use in the educational classroom, especially without any kind of formalized training. Several educators were asked their perspectives on this very idea:

> As for guidelines of having the mobile tools accessible in the school/classroom, I think that it would be vital for all teachers to have numerous training experiences with the materials prior to implementing them into the classroom. I think that the teachers should be provided with proper instruction and with numerous opportunities of how to incorporate these tools into the classroom. Without the knowledge of the advantages offered from the material, the tools wouldn't be utilized to the maximum capacity. (High School Educator)

> I do think there should be guidelines to using these types of technologies in the classroom because it can cause a lot of distractions. In the case of things like iPhones or iPods, there should be some kind of setting in place which disables things like Facebook or other distracting apps. As a teacher, I would want to make sure my students were not sitting and socializing with their friends or texting and doing things unrelated to school. There would definitely be my own rules/guidelines and settings in place on the mobile technology if I chose to use them with my students. (Elementary School Educator)

> I think to effectively incorporate the usage of mobile technology, the cell phones need to be available for all students to use, whether it is their personal device or (school) district-issue. I think there would also need to be a way to monitor the use of the cell phone, but how can a teacher have access to a child's personal cell phone, that would seem to be an invasion of privacy. Though it is likely not economically feasible in many schools, I believe the safest and most effective way to incorporate cell phones would be a standard district-issued device to all the students with age and classroom appropriate content readily available. If a district can manage to work out a corporate partnership, I think that would be the ideal scenario. I think that the use of cell phones in class can lead to an exciting chapter in education and virtually expand the classroom even more, but like several other platforms, it remains a tricky technology to effectively integrate. (Middle School Educator)

As is evident from these comments, educators are trying to find ways to negotiate having personal digital devices in the classroom as well as the evolution of new technology tools. Besides trying to understand and incorporate the new applications or "apps" into their classrooms, teachers are trying to find the boundaries for which the use of this tool makes sense. This seeming unbalance has created an atmosphere in schools where either the cell phone is banned completely or full reign is given to students, resulting in an uneasy relationship between students and teachers. In a study published in *American Secondary Education*, teachers had grave concerns and "obviously did not want to be complicit in activities that are illegal, unethical, or unfair to others" (Charles, 2012).

Furthermore, educators continue to struggle with the idea of connecting the cell phone to their already full curriculums. They understand that their students use, enjoy, and spend a great deal of time involved in it; but they haven't found insight into this part of their students' lives. This is really where the work in education circles worldwide has to begin, as the increase of knowledge would also help breed confidence in working in these areas that are dominated by youth (Buckingham, 2007). This paradigm shift is precisely where there needs to be more explorations, as "newer 'Smartphones' with multiple capabilities and similar handheld mobile devices are now being used deliberately in some places as a less-costly alternative to laptops in programs encouraging students to engage in academic pursuits" (Charles, 2012).

The reinforcement of ICTs to bridge the learning context with the larger business and world context must begin in the schools. As the language of ICTs has become a part of the dialogue of world culture, a certain amount of fluidity needs to be in place in order for connections to be made that consider the learning and teaching that is generated with new pedagogical changes, which have been initiated by various governments throughout the world. The paradigm of the singular educator in the enclosed classroom has been altered with the consideration of a global case for digitally supported students in digitally supported schools.

The growth of mobile technologies does offer a newfound flexibility within the confines of the classroom. ICTs' standards consider this very point. This flexibility also exists in the form of communication between teacher and students, students and teacher, and students and students. As part of this consideration, researchers are looking at the potential of learning processes, whether informal or formal, that are taking place through online chat or instant messaging. The line between classic written language and the syntax of text language is crossing over into the classroom. Yet, the potential for learning exists, and tapping into that area opens teachers to new teaching possibilities. The most current research shows that texting does not erode literacy skills. Wood, Kemp, and Waldron (2014), for instance, have noted that "as children learn, they go through a period during which they play around with language, figuring out alternate, creative ways of saying things. Researchers have noted kids doing this for years, in notes and letters—way before texting even existed."

A major paradigm shift is occurring in educational practices globally. ICTs have provided an umbrella for learning environments. In the United States, the International Society for Technology Education (ISTE) has also made provisions for ICTs in their standards, which have been developed for students, teachers, administrators, coaches, and computer science educators. More information for these standards can be found directly on their listed websites:

- ISTE Standards for Students
    - o http://www.iste.org/standards/standards-for-students
- ISTE Standards for Teachers
    - o http://www.iste.org/standards/standards-for-teachers
- ISTE Standards for Administrators
    - o http://www.iste.org/standards/standards-for-administrators
- ISTE Standards for Coaches
    - o http://www.iste.org/standards/standards-for-coaches
- ISTE Standards for Computer Science Educators
    - o http://www.iste.org/standards/standards-for-computer-science-educators

Measuring the knowledge obtained from ICTs in education and even education technology standards has been a part of the global dialogue for assessing learning. The Educational Testing Service (ETS) has developed an Information, Communication, and Technology Literacy Assessment that it calls the "iSkills Test," which measures student performance. This one-hour exam requires students to use a variety of technologies to perform a number of tasks, including acquiring and assessing information online, searching databases for specific data, creating a graph that supports a point of view, and developing a PowerPoint presentation presenting the information that has been researched (Wagner, 2014). The "iSkills" assessment is an "outcome-based assessment that measures the ability to think critically in a range of real-world tasks (ETS, 2015). As explained on the Educational Testing site, this one-hour exam:

- Features **real-time, scenario-based tasks** that measure an individual's ability to navigate, understand and critically evaluate the variety of information available through digital technology;
- Tasks mirror the way individuals use information in academic, business and personal contexts;
- Test content is balanced among the humanities, social sciences, natural sciences, practical affairs and popular culture;

- Meets information literacy and digital fluency requirements for accreditation and accountability initiatives and performance funding. (ETS, 2015).

This test is not used in the United States for assessment because it is more expensive to administer versus current testing methods. However, other methods can be used, which will be discussed in later chapters.

Young people need skills for working within social networks, for pooling knowledge within a collective intelligence, for negotiating across cultural differences that shape the governing assumptions in different communities, and for reconciling conflicting bits of data to form a coherent picture of the world around them (Jenkins, 2009). Social networks provide a glimpse of a society that exists somewhere, but is usually not matched by the hometowns of student users. The Internet has made global communications both a possibility and a necessity. More importantly, it has made the ease of connecting real and ever-present. The end result is that this generation of students is the first to be fully integrated into Information Communication Technology (ICT) since birth—a conclusive fact that needs to be considered, and which cannot continue to be ignored by schools, administrators, teachers, or parents (Considine, Horton, & Moorman, 2009).

Meaningful use of educational and information technology is what mobile and new technologies can offer to our technologically invested students. Students of this generation are motivated to look at the available tools differently. Fitting into these trends of new technologies are the social network tools that allow active engagement with the participatory culture, and creative connection that is described by Jenkins (2009) in his work *Confronting the Challenges of Participatory Culture in the 21st Century.* He states that 64% of teenagers have produced digital work, and they have done it through the use of mobile technology and social networking sites (Jenkins, 2009). These are the skills that he considers most essential for students in the new media landscape:

> *Play:* The capacity to experiment with the surroundings as a form of problem solving.
> *Performance:* The ability to adopt alternative identities for the purpose of improvisation and discovery.
> *Simulation:* The ability to interpret and construct dynamic models of real world processes.
> *Appropriation:* The ability to meaningfully sample and remix media content.
> *Multitasking:* The ability to scan the environment and shift focus onto salient details.

Distributed Cognition: The ability to interact meaningfully with tools that expand mental capacities.

Collective Intelligence: The ability to pool knowledge and compare notes with others toward a common goal.

Judgment: The ability to evaluate the reliability and credibility of different information sources.

Transmedia Navigation: The ability to follow the flow of stories and information across multiple modalities.

Networking: The ability to search for, synthesize, and disseminate information.

Negotiation: The ability to travel across diverse communities, discerning and respecting multiple perspectives, and grasping and following alternative norms. (Jenkins, 2009)

Moreover, the new media literacies shift the focus of skills that need to be learned, as the modalities of online developments have a foundation in community-building and the development of social skills through collaboration and networking. The technological vehicle changes the passive classroom into one in which the lessons and learning are very active. It allows for the propagation of the message that learning is a two-way street, and sometimes even multidimensional. Furthermore, it brings the world closer together through the global connections that can be made through the use of any of these tools.

As cell phones have become more advanced with the smartphone, and the applications or "apps" become more innovative and fitting, there are candid conversations going on in educational circles as to how these tools can be repurposed for the classroom. They already attract students and encourage the text language development, but could also be much more. The fact that they are available anytime and anywhere also makes the use of mobiles a strong potential enhancement for instructional development. There are several learning activities that can be done with the idea of "anytime, anywhere," from podcasting and other oral recordings, to mobile geotagging and geocaching, digital storybooks, photo projects, research and information gathering, and even a classroom response system (Kolb, 2011).

The idea of using mobile phones in learning has been widespread in countries all around the world. Uganda, Afghanistan, and certain South American countries have been using mobile phones as opportunities for collaboration and growth, especially because regular Internet connections are poor (Morrison, 2012).

With all the technology already available, it is hard to believe that newer technology could still be ahead. The combination of mobility, social media, and numerous wireless access points creates conditions in which customized learning opportunities are bound to happen. Certainly, we are stepping into a time of accessorized, wearable technologies such as the Gear watch by Samsung, the Apple iWatch, and Google Glasses. Beyond the technologies is the rise of discussions that personalized learning is the wave of the future, and instrumental, given the increase of online learning and the availability of products such as smart tablets.

Our language and understanding of technology has also been growing exponentially. Massive Open Online Course (MOOC), big data, cybersecurity, meme, selfie, trolling, hashtag, avatar, etc., are among some of the new words introduced into our global society (Chatfield, 2013). While the actual officiating of a word entering the dictionary takes much longer, it has been recently noted that the growth of words related to technology has risen dramatically. The language of technology also plays into the learning of technology, which is why it has become of greater importance for education to keep up with the moving trends, as they are not going away, but just increasing with the flow of information.

The New Media Consortium released a report detailing 10 trends in Iberoamerican education technology: the whenever/wherever learning component; the easy accessibility to resources, thus challenging educators to consider how students aggregate information; reviewing the way teacher training programs currently exist and considering how new technologies will fundamentally change teaching strategies; social and civic responsibility and empowerment, which now comes from easy accessibility to mobile technologies and social networks globally; student-oriented learning; the implementation of the hybrid model of learning where students can be either in class or online; movement to the cloud and how that will impact current information technologists and departments; the self-interests of the students and their own adoption of technologies that better suit their own education needs; broadband availability, which allows for a decentralization of storage components; and lastly, the idea of the flipped classroom, where the student is as much instructor as learner, and where class time is freed up for projects (Durall, Gros, Maina, Johnson, & Adams Becker, 2012).

The civic component of mobile technologies, in particular, is a focal point for continued research, and for educational consideration as we look at the idea of engaged citizenship. Mihailidis (2014) comments on this very point:

> Today digital media platforms and mobile technologies have integrated seamlessly into the daily routines of citizens around the world, to the point that young citizens no longer organize their lives around information, but instead organize information around their lives. The results of this shift point to a new civic culture that is dependent on media for daily functions, knowledge about issues, and communication with friends, family, and acquaintances. (p. 18)

These types of conversations are evolving and will continue to increase as more educators, policymakers, and individuals internationally begin to consider the possibilities of a connected classroom on a worldwide scale.

Comparing what is happening in the classroom in the United States to what is happening in the classroom in Turkey, and vice versa, has given voice to the power of technology made possible by the mobility of new technologies. Furthermore, on a worldwide scale, a shared vision of where collaboration and growth can happen in the area of educational technology will be a continued discussion in educational circles worldwide, including ideas about what kinds of learning can be done through the cloud.

Adding to the conversation is the work being done by the United Nations Educational, Scientific and Cultural Organization (UNESCO), which is a specialized agency of the United Nations. As stated in the UN charter, the purpose is to "contribute to peace and security by promoting international collaboration through education, science, and culture in order to further universal respect for justice, the rule of law, and human rights along with fundamental freedom" (UNESCO, 1945). As part of this global initiative, a focus was placed on media literacy education. Instead of looking at the media as the enemy, this organization took the stance that the media were part of the public discourse, a part of participatory democracy, and that their role should be to create informed citizenry.

The idea that media were a part of the culture of society was an accepted principle. Education in the understanding, evaluation, and provision of a media source was a necessary extension, which was missing at all teaching levels: primary, secondary, higher, adult, and lifelong education. As David Buckingham (2001) states, "The media have increasingly penetrated all areas of social life: it is now impossible to understand the operations of the political process or of the economy, or to address questions about cultural and personal identity—or indeed about education—without taking account of the role of the media. Among the most significant changes are technological developments, economic developments, social developments, [and] globalisation" (p. 3). Effective education was the ultimate goal that lead to the Grunwald Declaration, which states:

> We therefore call upon the competent authorities to:
>
> 1. initiate and support comprehensive media education programs—from pre-school to university level, and in adult education—the purpose of which is to develop the knowledge, skills and attitudes which will encourage the growth of critical awareness and, consequently, of greater competence among the users of electronic and print media. Ideally, such programs should include the analysis

of media products, the use of media as means of creative expression, and effective use of and participation in available media channels;

2. develop training courses for teachers and intermediaries both to increase their knowledge and understanding of the media and train them in appropriate teaching methods, which would take into account the already considerable but fragmented acquaintance with media already possessed by many students;

3. stimulate research and development activities for the benefit of media education, from such domains as psychology, sociology, and communication science;

4. support and strengthen the actions undertaken or envisaged by UNESCO and which aim at encouraging international co-operation in media education (UNESCO, 1982).

Since 1982, UNESCO has grown and shifted with the dialogue of media literacy and media education, and that continued growth has shaped a curriculum and a study of this field at various universities around the world. Current universities include the Autonomous University of Barcelona, Spain; the University of Cairo, Egypt; Tsinghua University, Beijing, China; Temple University, Philadelphia, USA; the University of Sao Paulo, Brazil; Queensland University of Technology, Australia; University of the West Indies, Kingston, Jamaica; and Mohamed Ben Abdellah University, Fez, Morocco (Horton & Keiser, 2008).

In 2008, UNESCO launched a teacher education enrichment project. In the creation of this project, there was a merging of two curriculums: media literacy and information literacy. This tied in with the growing Information and Communication Technologies (ICTs) discussion that was also developing in education reform across the world.

As part of the ongoing initiatives by UNESCO and the development of the Media and Information Literacy and Intercultural Dialogue (MILID), a collaboration was created—the Alliance for Civilizations. The specified goals are:

- Act as a Observatory for critically analyzing: the role of Media and Information Literacy ("MIL") as a catalyst for civic participation, democracy and development; for the promotion of free, independent and pluralistic media; as well as MIL's contribution to the prevention and resolution of conflicts and intercultural tensions and polarizations.
- Enhance intercultural and cooperative research on MIL and the exchanges between universities and mass media, encouraging MIL's initiatives towards respecting human rights and dignity and cultural diversity.

- Develop within the participant universities educational and media production practices that contribute to dissolving prejudice and intercultural barriers and favour global dialogue and cooperation among citizens as well as social and political institutions around the world. In addition to the international dimension, these practices will be reflected at the local level in the 8 cities or neighbourhoods in which the partner universities are located.
- Promote global actions relating to MIL (including adaptation of the UNESCO MIL Curriculum for Teacher Education and other relevant tools, publications, congresses, seminars, teaching resources, and faculty and students' exchanges) that could contribute towards stimulating dialogue and understanding among people of and within different cultures and societies.
- Create a virtual centre to research on, and study and develop MIL initiatives aimed at the creation of projects and publications linking universities and research centres.
- Promote and support other global media initiatives that could reinforce civic participation through open, free and independent media and information systems that favour intercultural dialogue and cooperation.
- Encourage and support citizen participation as well as educational and cultural institutions whose initiatives promote media and information literacy, cooperation and intercultural dialogue. (UNESCO, 2014)

This continued work has fostered the growth of workshops, programs, the development of national and international media and information literacy policies, as well as Training-the-Trainers workshops, which provide a cyclical base of learning, with the idea that participants will return to their own countries building on the knowledge gained and passing the information on, in order to increase the ideas and outgrowth fundamentally developed after the Grunwald Declaration.

The goal of creating learning partnerships that are strong and binding, in order to provide a well-conceived knowledge base, has continued with the work that UNESCO has proposed. Curriculum and evaluation methods have been developed that consider the various countries and representatives of the UN and the world beyond. Stakeholders from countries are brought to Paris regularly to meet on a yearly basis, to open up discussions and dialogue that continue to bring into focus the value and importance of media and information literacy. These representative groups of individuals are vital to the development of any type of global or world media literacy. As Bennett and Bennett (2004) suggest:

If we cannot bring our own cultural contest into perspective, then we cannot take the perspective of culturally-different others. And when we cannot take the perspective of others, we cannot imagine their reality, we cannot be competent in the intercultural communication demanded by multicultural societies and global intentionalities. (p. 23)

The focal point of world literacy through ICTs and the work of UNESCO have provided a continued opportunity and a growing base for educational prospects, with discourse carrying a global context.

References

Bennett, J. M., & Bennett, M. J. (2004). Developing intercultural sensitivity: An integrative approach to global and domestic diversity. In D. Landis, J. Bennett, & M. Bennett (Eds.), *Handbook of intercultural training* (3rd ed.) (pp. 147–65). Thousand Oaks, CA: Sage.

Buckingham, D. (2001). *Media education: A global strategy for development.* UNESCO, Sector of Communication and Information, Institute of Education, University of London, England.

Buckingham, D. (2007). *Beyond technology: Children's learning in the age of digital culture.* Cambridge, UK: Polity Press.

Charles, A. S. (2012). Cell phone: Rule-setting, rule-breaking, and relationships in the classroom. *American Secondary Education, 40*(3), 4–16.

Chatfield, T. (2013, April 17). The 10 best words the Internet has given English. *The Guardian.* Retrieved from http://www.theguardian.com/books/2013/apr/17/tom-chatfield-top-10-internet-neologisms

Considine, D., Horton, J., & Moorman, G. (March 2009). Teaching and reading the Millennial generation through media literacy. *Journal of Adolescent & Adult Literacy, 52*(6), 471–81.

Dewey, J. (1938). *Experience and education.* New York, NY: Touchstone.

Durall, E., Gros, B., Maina, M., Johnson, L., & Adams Becker, S. (2012). *Technology outlook: Iberomerican tertiary education 2012–2017.* Austin, TX: New Media Consortium.

Educational Testing Service (ETS). (2015). *The iSkills Assessment.* Princeton, NJ: Educational Testing Service. Retrieved from https://www.ets.org/iskills/about

Ericsson. (June 2014). *Ericsson mobility report.* Stockholm, Sweden. Retrieved from http://www.ericsson.com/res/docs/2014/ericsson-mobility-report-june-2014.pdf

European Commission. (2013, February 5). *ICT policy in brief.* Retrieved from http://ec.europa.eu/enterprise/sectors/ict/competitiveness/ict-brief/index_en.htm

——. (February 2013). *Survey of schools: ICT in education.* Retrieved from http://www.eun.org/c/document_library/get_file?uuid=9be81a75-c868-4558-a777-862ec-c8162a4&groupId=43887

Horton, F. W., & Keiser, B. E. (November/December 2008). Encouraging global information literacy. *Computers in Libraries*, 8–11.

InfoDev. (2015). Harness new information and communication technologies to help achieve EFA goals. *Quick guide: ICTs and the education Millennium Development Goals (MDGs)* (pp. 69–72). Retrieved from http://www.infodev.org/articles/quick-guide-icts-and-education-millennium-development-goals-mdgs

International Telecommunication Union. (2014). World telecommunication/ICT indicators database 2014. Retrieved from http://www.itu.int/en/ITU-D/Statistics/Pages/publications/wtid.aspx

Internet World Stats. (2014). *Internet users in the world.* Miniwatts Marketing Group. Retrieved from http://www.internetworldstats.com/stats.htm

ISTE. (2011). *ISTE standards for administrators.* International Society for Technology in Education.

Jenkins, H. (October 2009). *Confronting the challenges of participatory culture: Media education for the 21st century.* Cambridge, MA: MIT Press.

Kolb, L. (February 2011). Adventures with cell phones. *Educational Leadership*, 39–43.

Lenhart, A. (2015, April 9). *Teens, social media & technology overview 2015.* Washington, DC: Pew Research Center.

McLuhan, M. (1962). *The Gutenberg galaxy: The making of typographic man.* Toronto, Canada: University of Toronto Press.

Mihailidis, P. (2014). *Media literacy and the emerging citizen: Youth engagement and participation in digital culture.* New York, NY: Peter Lang.

Morrison, N. (2012, November 9). The role of technology in global learning. *The Guardian.* Retrieved from http://www.guardian.co.uk/teacher-network/teacher-blog/2012/nov/06/technology-global-learning-teaching

Perry, S. (2014, January). Bridging Africa's digital divide. *African Trader.* Retrieved from http://www.africantrader.co/wp-content/uploads/magazines/MagazineArchive/Dec2014Jan2015.pdf

Poushter, J. (2015). *Key takeaways on technology use in emerging and developing nations.* Pew Research Center. Retrieved from http://www.pewresearch.org/fact-tank/2015/03/19/key-takeaways-technology-emerging-developing-nations/

Rainie, L. (2015). *Internet, broadband, and cell phone statistics.* Pew Research Center. Retrieved from http://www.pewinternet.org/2010/01/05/internet-broadband-and-cell-phone-statistics/

UNESCO. (1945). *UNESCO constitution.* Retrieved from http://portal.unesco.org.

UNESCO. (1982). *Grunwald declaration on media education.* International Symposium on Media Education at Grunwald, Germany. Retrieved from http://www.unesco.org/education/pdf/MEDIA_E.PDF

UNESCO. (2014). *UNESCO-UNAOC UNITWIN on media and information literacy and intercultural dialogue.* Retrieved from http://www.unaoc.org/communities/academia/unesco-unaoc-milid/

Wagner, T. (2014). *The global achievement gap*. New York, NY: Basic Books.

Wood, C., Kemp, N., & Waldron, S. (2014). Exploring the longitudinal relationships between the use of grammar in text messaging and performance on grammatical tasks. *British Journal of Developmental Psychology, 32,* 415–29.

3. *Global Media Events and Moments*

BELINHA S. DE ABREU

"It might come as a surprise to you that some of history's greatest American journalists are working right now, exceptional minds with years of experience and an unshakeable devotion to reporting the news. But these voices are a small minority now and they don't stand a chance against the circus when the circus comes to town. They're overmatched. I'm quitting the circus and switching teams. I'm going with the guys who are getting creamed. I'm moved that they still think they can win and I hope they can teach me a thing or two. From this moment on, we'll be deciding what goes on our air and how it's presented to you based on the simple truth that nothing is more important to a democracy than a well-informed electorate. We'll endeavor to put information in a broader context because we know that very little news is born at the moment it comes across our wire. We'll be the champion of facts and the mortal enemy of innuendo, speculation, hyperbole, and nonsense. We're not waiters in a restaurant serving you the stories you asked for just the way you like them prepared. Nor are we computers dispensing only the facts because news is only useful in the context of humanity. I'll make no effort to subdue my personal opinions. I will make every effort to expose you to informed opinions that are different from my own."

—Will McAvoy, HBO's *The Newsroom*

While the "medium is the message" may have been the dictate under Marshall McLuhan, the fact remains that in the United States the news media have been marginalized by focusing on popular culture events that are not representative of global voices and events. Over time, the medium of television news has been limiting the inclusion of messages from around the world, because of a perceived lack of interest among United States citizens (Guthrie, 2010; Mihailidis, 2012). After the Cold War ended, the way in which news agencies invested in the dispensing of global news appeared to change. Foreign affairs offices were closed. News agencies began to cut back on their overseas bureaus, and the news became less about the world, and more internalized.

The lack of knowledge of global content became a joke for late-night comedians such as Jay Leno and David Letterman. Jay Leno, in particular, took this lack of knowledge to another level in his nightly segments entitled "Jaywalking," where Leno would ask people on the street simple trivia questions such as "How many Great Lakes are there?" or "What's the biggest country in South America?" The purpose of the segment was, of course, to create late night fodder; but at the same time it served to highlight the lack of knowledge among many people about current and world events (Jensen, 2014).

The lack of interest in world news was most noticeable before the events of September 11, 2001, as most of the news being reported had to do with popular culture events. In fact, ABC News had been promoting an exclusive with Mariah Carey, who at the time had been hospitalized after an apparent emotional meltdown that created speculation about her mental health (ABC News, 2001). After the events of September 11, the news world took on another shape. The coverage intensified on the global aspect of the media, as the question of "why" led to a review of conduct, information, and misinformation that was not being analyzed on the global front. In later reports from news anchors, discussion pointed to the fact that news agencies had been cutting back on their foreign affairs offices for years (Mihailidis, 2012; Utley, 1997). As Utley (1997) explains:

> According to the Tyndall Report [in 1997], total foreign coverage on network nightly news programs has declined precipitously, from 3,733 minutes in 1989 to 1,838 minutes in 1996 at ABC, the leader, and from 3,351 minutes to 1,175 minutes at third-place NBC. [...] The decline has pushed network news producers to the apparently logical, if journalistically undesirable, conclusion that foreign news is expendable unless it is of compelling interest to a mass audience. The new litmus test at network news programs is whether viewers (in the producers' opinion) will instinctively "relate" to the story. As in other industries, as choice increases, power shifts from the producer to the consumer. (Utley, 1997)

In a more recent Tyndall Report from 2013, there was glaring negative response to how news was covered yet again, especially in regards to ABC news coverage:

> 2013 marks the year when ABC World News finally rejected the mission of presenting a serious newscast. ABC covered all four of the major domestic policy stories least heavily: the Budget debate, the Healthcare rollout, Gun control, and National Security Agency surveillance. Same with foreign policy: ABC spent least time on the civil war in Syria and its chemical weapons disarmament, the military

coup in Egypt, and on Afghanistan. Instead, ABC stepped up its coverage of Sports and Show Business, and highlighted morning-style reporters Ginger Zee (weather) and Paula Faris (personal finance tips). Weather aside, the only major stories that ABC covered competitively were True—the George Zimmerman trial and Ariel Castro's Cleveland hell house—and Celebrity: London's baby prince. ABC's newscast is now certifiably Disneyfied. (Tyndall Report, 2013)

With infotainment taking over the majority of the news networks on a nightly basis, the greater issues facing the world were going unnoticed. More importantly, the United States government was also not focusing their priorities on the issues faced by Islamic countries. Much of the world had been unaware of the issues related to a growing unrest that was perpetuating problems that would lead into the occurrence of September 11. Even warnings and memos by chief counterterrorism expert Richard Clarke, which discussed a possible attack, had gone mostly ignored for lack of belief that the issues arising would in fact impact the United States. According to Leffler (2011):

> Before September 11, the Bush administration had focused its foreign policy attention on China and Russia; on determining whether a Middle East peace settlement was in the cards; on building a ballistic missile defense system; and on contemplating how to deal with "rogue" states such as Iran, Iraq, Libya, and North Korea. […] Top officials did not consider terrorism or radical Islamism a high priority. Richard Clarke, the chief counterterrorism expert on the National Security Council staff, might hector them relentlessly about the imminence of the threat, and CIA Director George Tenet might say the lights were blinking red. But Secretary of State Colin Powell, Secretary of Defense Donald Rumsfeld, and National Security Adviser Condoleezza Rice were not convinced. (Leffler, 2011)

The issues regarding the lack of coverage of foreign affairs news events were highlighted more negatively as discussions of the day's events continued, post-September 11. Countries and names that were considered far off and were not well-known became a part of the conversation among the general public. The worries grew of what we didn't know, and what we should have known. Was our lack of knowledge so evident because of the lack of perceived interest in foreign affairs and the global nature of society? In "All News is Local," Richard Stanton identifies this point as a major flaw in journalism coverage in the United States. Stanton (2007) states that journalists know citizens from the United States will not care about news unless it affects them on at least the local level, or presents itself as entertainment. The result is news outlets slanting stories away from the straight facts, toward distractions and local, but irrelevant, connections (Stanton, 2007). This can be seen in the way major tragedies are handled, as the first comment made by news anchors is often whether or not there is a local connection to the town or even the United States in general.

Thomas Jefferson encapsulated much of this sentiment about media coverage in his writings about the media in his lifetime: "Indeed the abuses of the freedom of the press here have been carried to a length never before known or borne by any civilized nation" (quoted in Conant, 1962). His statement stands today—over 100 years later. The decisions that are made in how and what is trusted to the general public are done at the editorial level. Already, those decisions have made viewers less informed and less knowledgeable about world events. This point is emphasized by Mihailidis (2012), when he discusses the changing news landscape:

> Traditional models for newspapers have eroded to their core, foreign bureaus have disappeared at alarmingly fast speeds, and journalists find their resources diminished and their ability to investigate a story at odds with the immediacy of the Internet. Television news, meanwhile, has become fertile ground for polarizing banter, editorial glamour, and self-serving sound bites. On the Internet, news outlets have found few sustainable models for news production and dissemination as they struggle to compete with a vast world of civic entrepreneurs. As communication industries across the board continue to deregulate, the news world has become a survival of the fittest, where ratings, markets, and profits trump content, depth, and diversity. (Mihailidis, 2012)

Indeed, the changing news landscape is also in a state of flux. News happens every day, and the method of delivery is also changing with new innovations. Therefore, keeping up with the flow of information has shifted with the new mediums and avenues provided by technologies.

The World Wide Web opened another avenue by which people could gather information. Initially, the aim for the individual user was for him or her to be able to find the information. Increasingly, information was being made available through various websites. Some were created by individual users, and others by the major networks that most people know such as ABC News, CNN, and Fox. CNN, in particular, had grown in value for audiences in countries where the news media were censored or controlled. The Internet provided people with a means for obtaining information, but it also created dichotomy among global citizens who struggle with the ideals of freedom of the press (National Intelligence Council, 2008). The World Wide Web has provided an access point to information that was not obtainable before its inception.

> Through communication technologies like the World Wide Web, people also have access to increasing amounts of information about what is happening in their own and other countries. This is especially important in countries where

media are government controlled. For example, people in Pakistan and Afghanistan learn more about military actions in their countries by accessing CNN.com than through their local newspapers. In some ways, the Internet has democratized information, in that more people control and disseminate information than ever before. For example, there are some 32,000 Internet police in China, who frequently find and arrest people for criticizing the government online. They block search engine sites, close Internet cafés, and block e-mails; they can even [...] reroute Web site traffic to alternate sites maintained by 23 routers in Shanghai and Beijing. In spite of this and other governments' attempts to limit their citizens' access to computer-mediated communication (CMC), the Internet is providing information, world news, and possibilities for interpersonal communication that were not available previously. (Martin & Nakayama, 2010)

The Internet provided for grassroots news efforts that have taken off with social networks such as Twitter and Facebook. The Arab Spring, a popular uprising that began in December 2010, was most noted for taking to Twitter, to move forward the issues the citizenry was facing during key periods of the 2011 Tunisian and Egyptian uprisings. The agenda was propagated by news reporters who realized that these types of social networks were reaching a wider audience and influencing change faster than the regular news media. Formats provided by social networks were considered non-elite points of entry for news content. The receivers of the content were the general public, but eventually included the more elite news agencies. New agencies such as ABC News, CNN, and FOX News went to Twitter for information from sources that were on the ground as military strikes were occurring. News reporters became the brokers for news sources who were intent on getting the message out to the world on what was happening in their countries. In an interview with *The Guardian*, Andy Carvin, from National Public Radio, who is credited with bringing to the forefront the value of Twitter as a news source especially during times of crisis, voiced some of the positives and negatives related to using this format for communicating news. Carvin states:

> The reality is that many of my sources would not be alive today if they weren't working under pseudonyms. They are working under difficult circumstances to get information out. Though it's questionable quite how secure these networks are, users will leave if they don't feel in control. The reality of any internet service is that it's a service you don't have full control of. These are businesses with their own goals and agendas and interests, and there's no way to avoid that, but users will go to communities and tools that suit their own needs as well, so we see a lot of dissidents using these tools because they feel they have certain amount of control. (Kiss, 2011)

The ideas that Carvin discusses represent the discussion on perspective and perception as related to the distribution and curation of news. Each day news reports are communicated and filtered. At the forefront is the sender of the information, and following is the receiver or whoever is judged to be the receiver. In Stanton's (2007) writings, he examines the idea of whether the media should be leading or following. The shift in conversation has occurred with the changes presented by the transition of new media and new media tools for conveying information such as Twitter and Facebook. In the case of social media, it is the group dynamics of these networks that places information in the public view. However, the more elite news media run in another direction. As the media seek out stories, they also create the pace and the place for what is transmitted out to the public. In effect, they select material that exemplifies a consensus view, but oftentimes neglects a variety of events that fall outside of the established mold. It is perhaps for these reasons, and also the immediacy of the transference of information, that Twitter has become such a popular new media tool.

In some ways, social networks have become the public ombudsmen for the news media, by posting corrections, providing news, and reminding news agencies that there is a public to whom they are accountable. The issues related to Brian Williams, former news anchor of NBC News, are a reflection of the powerful role the public can have in checking the news media. The story of Brian Williams's news demise came from his embellishment of his helicopter journey in Iraq, where he stated that it was shot down by a rocket-propelled grenade (Steel & Somaiya, 2015). While the military magazine *Stars and Stripes* was given credit for tipping off the inaccurate account of what had transpired, it was later revealed that soldiers on the ground had tried to go to NBC directly to relay that the report was false. Military soldiers and veterans, in their outrage about the reporting, took to Twitter and Facebook to make sure that the story was being highlighted for the public. *Stars and Stripes* was tipped off to the problem with Brian Williams's story, and sought to right the incident. When interviewed, Williams admitted that his reporting of the story was inaccurate (Tritten, 2015). He had, in fact, been in another helicopter that had no such encounter. In order to counteract the campaign that had already begun on Twitter to remove him from the air, and the negative comments posted on his own Facebook page, Williams posted his own apology on Facebook to the servicemen:

> To Joseph, Lance, Jonathan, Pate, Michael and all those who have posted: You are absolutely right and I was wrong. In fact, I spent much of the weekend thinking I'd gone crazy. I feel terrible about making this mistake, especially since I found my OWN WRITING about the incident from back in '08, and I was indeed on the Chinook behind the bird that took the RPG in the tail housing just above the ramp. Because I have no desire to fictionalize my experience (we all

saw it happened the first time) and no need to dramatize events as they actually happened, I think the constant viewing of the video showing us inspecting the impact area—and the fog of memory over 12 years—made me conflate the two, and I apologize. (Gold & Byers, 2015)

Following this statement, Williams did go on the air and apologize, but this was not enough for a public that had placed their trust in a person who was considered one of the most well-respected and trusted anchors. He was put on a six-month suspension, which in broadcasting life can be considered a death sentence.

The need for an ombudsman is ever more apparent in a socialized news media environment, and it existed in news media for years before the race to be first became more important than the story itself. Ken Auletta, writer of *The New Yorker's* Annals of Communications column and author of several books on the media and technology, was interviewed for the *Frontline* series *News Wars*, and stated: "So the press has a mixed record like every institution has a mixed record. And we do better if we admit our mistakes. That is why it's a healthy thing to see ombudsmen or public editors or correction boxes, or to see press critics online, who hold us to account" (PBS Frontline, 2013). Accountability is the key factor in what happens in how news is represented in any mass media format. With the presence of new technologies that supersede the delivery of mass media, this piece becomes a bigger part of the puzzle; but it also comes with its own difficulties, as information moves fast. The scale of pace is felt worldwide, and while global news agencies tend to spend more time on the key, influential stories, they too have been met with criticism for not reporting accurate information. As this issue continues to be a cause of concern for reporters, editors, and media owners, the economic impact on the industry will either serve to marginalize the voices of the public, or the industry will be pushed out of the way, as those voices take a stronger foothold through social media threads and hashtags.

When graduate students in a class on establishing worldwide technologies were asked about news agencies and the variations on how news is reported, their responses were thought-provoking and enlightening, while at the same time indicative of the changing world in which mediated messages are filtered out to the public. Specifically, these students were asked to respond to the following questions:

- How does the impact of media coverage affect our lives daily?
- As Americans (United States) are we less informed than our global counterparts?

- Is it important for us to have a global perspective when looking at the news here at home or abroad?
- Lastly, at what point does the media's obligation to report news become less about the event and more about the ratings game in your opinion?

Each of the students reviewed three pieces of material before answering this question: Richard Stanton's book *All News Is Local: The Failure of the Media to Reflect World Events in a Globalized Age*; a National Public Radio (NPR) audio clip about the Israeli-Palestinian conflict; and an article written by Matti Friedman entitled, "An Insider's Guide to the Most Important Story on Earth."

Emily, a second-year graduate student, admits in her response to being swayed by media coverage in her point of view on world events:

> I do think that media coverage impacts my daily life particularly in how I view other countries. In Stanton's book *All News Is Local*, he writes about the framing of news. He specifies: "When organizations, governments, and individuals frame an issue or event, they do so with different stakeholders in mind" (p. 23). Interestingly Robert Entman (a political communications scholar) added to this definition of framing by suggesting that, in Stanton's words, "frames focus our attention on some aspects of reality while blurring or avoiding others, [thus] they have the potential to provide different stakeholders with diffuse reactions" (p. 23). I do think that western media coverage often has a specified frame as determined by the journalist and editor with a particular stakeholder in mind (new media, general public, community groups, etc.). This was particularly evident for me in the NPR audio clip about the Israeli-Palestinian conflict, which addressed Matti Friedman's article "An Insider's Guide to the Most Important Story on Earth" that criticized western coverage of the conflict. Friedman speaks about the effect of framing on the story. He mentions understanding the conflict in context with the scenario akin to a volcano, with the lava being radical Islam. I really enjoyed listening to both journalists (Bronner from *The New York Times* and Friedman from The Associated Press) describe how the tension has been reported. Friedman argues that western media covers the actions of the Israeli government very critically and that it ignores Hamas's culpability. It turns a blind eye to Hamas and does not take local people and their ideologies seriously enough. The West sticks to the story of a possible two state solution, with Israel being the strong power often making the wrong moral choice. Bronner argues that reporters do not actively try to frame the conflict as "Israeli aggression against citizens," but that it is just very hard to find evidence, pictures, or data of Hamas military actions. (Emily, Graduate Student)

For Christine, another graduate student, her perceptions indicate uncertainty of what the public knows, when it comes to world news in general:

When it comes to Americans being less informed, I'm not sure. I do think our news stories are focused in on what is happening within our own country and those stories that affect us, and have less concern for what is happening in the world outside these issues and events; however, I think that this is also a result of our country being a bit more isolated. We share our borders with very few countries, and have been taught to value self-sufficiency. We are taught to view ourselves as the most important and greatest country in the world; while we have freedom of speech, we are taught and, in a sense, conditioned to uphold "American" principles. I think many of our global counterparts are exposed to more stories simply from being more directly affected by what is going on, and may be more informed because of this. In today's world, I think it's becoming more and more important to have a global perspective. (Christine, Graduate Student)

Christine goes on to discuss her beliefs regarding the role of the media, especially the way in which our society has become globalized by the influences of technology. She also makes the connection that, in the media, stories are sometimes duplicated to fill air time, without necessarily having any substance:

In my opinion, the role of the media is to report news and to share stories and events as objectively as possible; however, I also feel that the media is ultimately a business in which the ratings and the finances factor heavily. I found Stanton's section on "herding" interesting in this regard because, let's face it, how different is the news on each of the different channels on TV or in different newspapers? The major stories are pretty much identical, with the exception of a few details. There is also a rush to be the first to report on something, which sometimes leads to the circulation of false details. The coverage of the Sandy Hook shooting illustrated this for me so clearly as the news media began to report the shooting, we had multiple shooters; Mrs. Lanza was a teacher and then a substitute in the school; and other such information that later proved to be false, yet fed the media frenzy of the tragedy. Each news source had to be the first to report and was in competition with the others, which is something that probably happens more than we realize. (Christine, Graduate Student)

This need to be first hinders responsible journalism, the motive for which should be accuracy, rather than immediacy. This struggle is felt by news agencies worldwide and is exemplified every time a world tragedy occurs that becomes an international event. One recent story regarding Germanwings Flight 9525, which headlined the news for weeks, provided hour-by-hour reports with much speculation (including terrorist attacks and other mysterious and unexplained occurrences) for why this airplane ended up crashing in the French Alps. As the days progressed, the story began to change, with reports that the pilot was depressed and, in fact, the cause. Reporters theorized that the pilot had intentionally made the plane rapidly descend into the mountains in order to destroy it. In the midst of the news reports and speculation, it was noted that the parents of the airplane pilot had heard this news through reporters, and not from investigators. The need to be first superseded the need to inform the pilot's parents of this dreadful result, as the media frenzy grew.

Ultimately, the role of media is at a difficult junction, where media conglomerates will need to make decisions regarding what news agencies should be covering, what needs to be reported, while analyzing the value of what they do and how it will impact generations to come. As the character Will McAvoy from the HBO program *The Newsroom* states in his late night appeal to audiences to understand the role of television news:

> We stood up for what was right. We fought for moral reasons, we passed laws, struck down laws for moral reasons. We waged wars on poverty, not poor people. We sacrificed, we cared about our neighbors, we put our money where our mouths were, and we never beat our chest. We built great big things, made ungodly technological advances, explored the universe, cured diseases, and we cultivated the world's greatest artists and the world's greatest economy. We reached for the stars, acted like men. We aspired to intelligence; we didn't belittle it; it didn't make us feel inferior. We didn't identify ourselves by who we voted for in the last election, and we didn't scare so easy. We were able to be all these things and do all these things because we were informed. (Sorkin & Mottola, 2012)

Is not the critical goal for us to have an informed global public? We aspire to foster users and viewers that do not jump on false bandwagons in order to create and consume more news with little value, which leads to further misinformation and a public that is kept perpetually ignorant.

References

ABC News. (2001). Mariah Carey says "breakdown" overblown. *Good Morning America*. Retrieved from http://abcnews.go.com/GMA/story?id=125557

Conant, J. B. (1962). *Thomas Jefferson and the development of American public education.* Berkeley: University of California Press.

Friedman, M. (2014, August 26). An insider's guide to the most important story on earth. *Tablet.* Retrieved from http://www.tabletmag.com/jewish-news-and-politics/183033/israel-insider-guide

Gold, H., & Byers, D. (2015, February 4). Brian Williams apologizes for false Iraq story. *Politico.* Retrieved from http://www.politico.com/blogs/media/2015/02/brian-williams-apologizes-for-false-iraq-story-202130.html

Guthrie, M. (2010). *Pew report shows traditional media in decline: Project for Excellence in Journalism study finds cable news faring better than broadcast, no sustainable online model.* Broadcasting & Cable. Retrieved from http://www.broadcastingcable.com

Jefferson, T., & Peterson, M. D. (Eds.). (1984). *Thomas Jefferson: Writings*. Des Moines, IA: Library of America.

Jensen, J. (2014). "The Tonight Show" without Jay Leno: Like the man said, it's time to go. *Entertainment Weekly*. Retrieved from http://www.ew.com/article/2014/02/07/tonight-show-without-jay-leno-essay

Kiss, J. (2011, September). Andy Carvin: The man who tweets revolutions. *The Guardian*. Retrieved from http://www.theguardian.com/media/2011/sep/04/andy-carvin-tweets-revolutions

Leffler, M. (2011, September/October). September 11 in retrospect. *Foreign Affairs*. Retrieved from http://www.foreignaffairs.com/articles/68201/melvyn-p-leffler/september-11-in-retrospect

Martin, J. N., & Nakayama, T. K. (2010). *Intercultural communication in contexts*. New York, NY: McGraw-Hill. Retrieved from http://www.rasaneh.org/Images/News/AtachFile/15-8-1390/FILE634561743619907963.pdf

Mihailidis, P. (2012). *News literacy*. New York, NY: Peter Lang.

National Intelligence Council. (2008, November). *Global trends 2025: A transformed world*. Retrieved from http://www.aicpa.org/research/cpahorizons2025/global-forces/downloadabledocuments/globaltrends.pdf

NPR. (2014, October 10). Two journalists debate coverage of Israel-Palestine. *On the Media*. Retrieved from http://www.onthemedia.org/story/two-journalists-debate-coverage-israel-palestine/

PBS Frontline. (2013). Interview with Ken Auletta. *News War*. Retrieved from http://www.pbs.org/wgbh/pages/frontline/newswar/interviews/auletta.html

Sorkin, A (Writer), & Mottola, G. (Director). (2012, June 24). We just decided to (Season 1, Episode 1). In A. Poul (Producer). *The newsroom*. Los Angeles, CA: Home Box Office.

Stanton, R. C. (2007). *All news is local: The failure of the media to reflect world events in a globalized age* (Chapters 1 and 3). New York, NY: McFarland & Company.

Steel, E., & Somaiya, R. (2015, February 10). Brian Williams suspended from NBC for 6 months without pay. *The New York Times*. Retrieved from http://www.nytimes.com/2015/02/11/business/media/brian-williams-suspended-by-nbc-news-for-six-months.html?_r=0

Tritten, T. (2015, February 9). In his words: Brian Williams's interview with *Stars and Stripes*. *Stars and Stripes*. Retrieved from http://www.stripes.com/news/us/in-his-words-brian-williams-interview-with-stars-and-stripes-1.328590

Tyndall Report. (2013). *2013 year in review*. Retrieved from http://tyndallreport.com/yearinreview2013/

Utley, G. (1997, March/April). The shrinking of foreign news: From broadcast to narrowcast. *Foreign Affairs*. Retrieved from http://www.foreignaffairs.com/articles/52854/garrick-utley/the-shrinking-of-foreign-news-from-broadcast-to-narrowcast

Part 2
Curating Global Voices:
Contributing Authors

4. Creating a Global Community of News Literacy Practice

RICHARD HORNIK
MASATO KAJIMOTO
JENNIFER FLEMING

Introduction

The ability to sort reliable from unreliable information is becoming an increasingly important life skill in the digital age, as more and more people around the world live large parts of their lives online, thanks to the widespread proliferation of Internet-enabled digital technologies. One needs look no further than the staggering prediction that by 2020 approximately 80% of the world's adult population will own a smartphone, the fastest-selling and most ubiquitous gadget in history (*The Economist*, 2015). Understandably, interest in media literacy education—that is, education programs designed to develop the ability to access, evaluate, and analyze mediated messages—is rising on a global scale. As a result, media literacy is diversifying in terms of the nationalities and disciplines of educators and researchers represented in the field (Hobbs, 2010; Mihailidis, 2012; Potter, 2010).

News literacy instruction is considered a specialized approach to media literacy education, in the sense that it shares many of the same analytic goals of media literacy education, such as teaching students how to access, analyze, and evaluate media messages. However, lessons and activities in news literacy classrooms focus exclusively on news texts and images—how to identify them, how to analyze them, and how to deconstruct them. Much like media literacy education, there is no one way to define or teach news literacy. Even so, a dominant news literacy instructional paradigm has emerged in the United States—a paradigm RobbGrieco and Hobbs (2013) refer to as the "journalism school" approach to news literacy. They call it this because former or practicing journalists typically created pedagogies in the category, and thereby journalism school variants of news literacy instruction tend to reflect Western press system views on information and democracy (p. 22).

There are two primary sources of the journalism school approach to news literacy: Alan Miller of the News Literacy Project and Howard Schneider, founding dean of the School of Journalism at Stony Brook University in New York. Miller, a former investigative reporter with the *Los Angeles Times*, founded the News Literacy Project in early 2008. The organization develops and delivers innovative curricula designed to teach middle and high school students in the United States how to sort fact from fiction and to give them an appreciation for the role of a free press in a democracy.[1] Schneider, the former editor of *Newsday*, began experimenting in 2006 with ways to teach non-journalism students in his classes at Stony Brook how to identify and analyze news texts, because he feared students were becoming overwhelmed by the fast-moving and convoluted digital information environment.

Working with a team of journalists-turned-college-educators at Stony Brook, Schneider created a freshman-level news literacy class and defined news literacy as an ability to judge the reliability and credibility of news reports. For Schneider (2007), the aim of news literacy instruction is to teach students how to stop and think critically about the torrents of information available to them, as if the words and images are on a printed page instead of quickly flashing across a computer, television, or smartphone screen. More than $3 million was raised from a variety of foundations to support the development, instruction, and expansion of the Stony Brook conceptualization of news literacy to other universities and ultimately into high schools across the United States.

The Stony Brook Center for News Literacy's Overseas Partnership Program (OPP) was created in 2012, thanks to an anonymous donor who believed that young people in transitional countries—those moving from autocratic to more open ruling systems, and/or those moving from rural to more advanced economies—might particularly benefit from learning how to judge the authenticity of information. The program developed through formal and informal outreach to international educators, who found out about the curriculum online or through their personal teaching networks. Educators from more than 10 countries have subsequently participated in OPP-sponsored workshops and training sessions, where they began the process of adapting and adopting the curriculum to suit the unique needs of their students and to reflect the geopolitical and media system realities of their home nations.

The purpose of this chapter is to gain insight into how this global network of news literacy practitioners came about; how educators in Hong Kong, Vietnam, and Poland adapted and adopted the Stony Brook curriculum; and how news literacy advocates in Asia and Eastern Europe plan to continue outreach and education efforts started by the OPP, through the creation of regional news literacy instructional training centers.

Theoretical Orientations

Unlike other types of media content such as movies, novels, TV dramas, and comic books, news stories are supposed to be representing "real" people in "real" situations. In many democratic societies around the world, the conventional understanding is that journalists are obliged to include only facts of what "really" happened in their news reports. If a reporter or a news organization crosses this sanctified line between news (reality) and fiction (imagination) by making up fictitious details, they would be publicly condemned for the breach of social trust. Although such scandals are unearthed regularly (perhaps more often than they should be) in many countries, at the fundamental level, it is perhaps safe to say that ordinary media audiences expect news stories to reflect at least some aspects of "reality," with no made-up details.

Altschull (1990) describes journalists as "dedicated empiricists; it is the facts that they are after" (p. 2). The Commission on Freedom of the Press (1947) builds on this fact finding philosophy in its recommendations on how American news media can better serve democracy: "It is no longer enough to report *the fact* truthfully. It is now necessary to report *the truth about the fact*" (p. 22) [emphasis in original text]. On the possibilities, imperfections, and powers of the press in society, German philosopher and political theorist Hannah Arendt (1968) concludes: "The telling of factual truth comprehends much more than the daily information supplied by journalists, though without them we should never find our bearing in an ever-changing world and, in the most literal sense, would never know where we are" (p. 261).

Of course, it would be naïve to develop a discussion of journalism with the notion that the public believes everything it sees or reads on TV news or in newspapers; but this general belief about the "realness" of news stories nonetheless indicates the nature of news as perceived in many societies. Schudson (2003) writes of this magnitude of news in modern society by stating that news "has become—where it was not three centuries ago or even two centuries ago—a dominant force in the public construction of common experience and a popular sense of what is real and important" (p. 13). The understanding that news producers organize and circulate the knowledge and information about the "real" world is significant. It indicates that the news audience's experience with "reality" is, in fact, not a direct individual experience but a mediated encounter with media content and messages (see Entman, 2004; Lippmann, 1922/2007; McQuail, 2005).

In addition, it could be argued that routine consumption of news stories is, in fact, something very primitive and fundamental in human society. In any known civilization, news sharing—from exchanging family tidings and other information (for hunting, farming, and so forth), to making announcements, and even to gossiping—has been unquestionably part of human life since ancient days. Kovach and Rosenstiel (2007) categorize this desire to know the news in order to make sense of the social "reality" as a "basic human impulse" (p. 1). They argue that our social relationships and "character judgments" are partly formed by observing the ways people react to knowledge and information. In other words, the consumption of news is an essential part of human socialization, which influences how individuals perceive the world they live in.

To put it another way, the mass media, as the name aptly suggests, work as coordinators between individuals and social groups by providing information, knowledge, and pseudo-experience in the language commonly shared among the groups. Because "news" media are supposed to show "facts," news stories are at the forefront of providing shared experience of the "reality" among the public. To borrow Schudson's (2003) words, "we can speculate, without much in the way of proof, that news builds expectations of a common, shared world" (p. 8). For these reasons, media literacy educators from around the world have often included instruction on how to analyze news texts critically in their programs (see Buckingham, 1999; Considine, 1995; Flanagin & Metzger, 2000; Hobbs, 1998, 2007; Hobbs & Frost, 2003; Kubey, 2004; McBrien, 2005; Mihailidis, 2009; Mihailidis & Hiebert, 2005; Moeller, 2009; Potter, 2008).

Media literacy tends to be a catch-all term to describe pedagogies designed to teach students how to access, evaluate, and analyze all types of media and content genres (Aufderheide, 1993). Hobbs (2010) defines media literacy as a "constellation of life skills that are necessary for full participation in our media-saturated, information-rich society" (p. vii). Silverblatt and Enright Elicieri (1997) describe it as "a critical-thinking skill that enables audiences to decipher the information that they receive through channels of mass communications and empowers them to develop independent judgments about media content" (p. 48). The normative premise of the media literacy movement is that schools should neither ignore nor blindly accept the curriculum that media are already teaching students outside of the classroom. The United States lags behind comparable countries such as Canada, Australia, and Great Britain in the widespread development and adoption of instructional strategies that teach students how to analyze media thoughtfully (Kubey & Baker, 1999).

Silverblatt (2001) suggests that media education programs must be designed to reflect the fact that media messages are produced with different techniques and for different purposes. Zettl (1998) adds to this proposition with a theoretical model that breaks down the analysis of media into steps that guide the examination of media texts from different aesthetic points of view. Buckingham et al. (2005) argue that media literacy needs to reflect better the unique purposes of educators: "Different social groups may also develop and require different forces of media literacy in line with their motivations and preferences in media use. As such, we need to beware of adopting a reductive or mechanistic approach to assessing levels of media literacy" (p. 4). Therefore, the purpose of media *and* news literacy education programs can vary depending on the theoretical and disciplinary orientations of their creators.

For example, those responsible for the journalism school approach to news literacy primarily base their instructional theories and practices on journalistic methods and mindsets (Fleming, 2014). In fact, news literacy instruction as practiced by Stony Brook journalism educators is the antithesis of all-encompassing approaches to media literacy education. Stony Brook news literacy architects and instructors, the majority of them practicing or former journalists, are unapologetic for differentiating journalistic texts from other kinds of media messages, and the analytic lenses and deconstruction lessons they teach are drawn heavily from specialized journalistic methods of gathering information and evaluating sources (Klurfeld & Schneider, 2014; Loth, 2012).

Ashley, Maksl, and Craft (2013) take a different theoretical approach to news literacy, in the development of a news media literacy, or NML, scale. The research team turns to ideas gleaned from critical media literacy in the design of the NML scale they created and tested with surveys completed by undergraduates. Inspired by Marxist ideas of superstructure and Gramsci's theories of cultural hegemony, arguments for critical media literacy rely on the premise that media play significant roles in creating, maintaining, and propagating unequal and oppressive power relationships in society. Theorists and educators who support and experiment with critical media literacy, which for all intents and purposes is another specialized variant of media literacy education, are most concerned with the "crucial dimensions" of race, gender, class, and sexuality in media (Kellner & Share, 2007, p. 62).

Mihailidis has also experimented with conceptualizations of news literacy from predominantly academic and more traditional media literacy vantage points, such as frameworks developed by the U.S.-based National Association for Media Literacy Education (2007), instead of strictly journalistic perspectives seen in the Stony Brook curriculum (Mihailidis, 2009; Mihailidis & Hiebert, 2005). For example, in the edited book *News Literacy: Global Perspectives for the Newsroom and the Classroom*, Mihailidis (2012) and his contributing authors explore intersections between media literacy and news literacy in education spaces around the world. In addition, he argues that with every shift in technology comes a transition in information—how it is gathered, processed, and distributed. For Mihailidis, the shift in digital news gathering, production, and distribution brings new civic voices to democratic discourses once predominantly controlled by journalist gatekeepers and agenda-setters; therefore, he argues that news literacy pedagogies, no matter their disciplinary origins, need to reflect the collaborative realities of digital news production and consumption.

The Stony Brook News Literacy Curriculum

The 14-unit news literacy curriculum developed in the School of Journalism at Stony Brook University is designed to help students develop critical thinking skills in order to judge the reliability and credibility of information, whether it comes via print, television, or the Internet. The primary authors of the freshman-level course, Howard Schneider and James Klurfeld, were both reporters and then editors of *Newsday*, often ranked as one of the United States' top 10 newspapers, before joining academe. Subsequent collaborators Dean Miller and Richard Hornik also had been successful print journalists. Since 2011, the course has increasingly shifted its reliance on examples from print media to online and social media, as it became increasingly clear that 21st-century students are consuming news and information far differently from their predecessors.

Instructors adhering to the Stony Brook news literacy model use heavily illustrated lectures and fresh, ripped-from-the headlines examples, followed by hands-on exercises, to help students identify and assess news texts, understand how journalism works, and explore why information is such a powerful force for good and ill in modern societies (Fleming, 2014; Klurfeld & Schneider, 2014; Loth, 2012). The ultimate outcome of news literacy instruction at Stony Brook is for students to build critical thinking skills about news by learning how to:

1. Recognize the difference between journalism and other kinds of information and between journalists and other information purveyors;

2. In the context of journalism, recognize the difference between news and opinion;
3. In the context of news stories, analyze the difference between assertion and verification and between evidence and inference;
4. Evaluate and deconstruct news reports based on the quality of evidence presented and the reliability of sources; understand and apply these principles across all news media platforms;
5. Distinguish between news media bias and audience bias.

Underlying these skills, news literacy instructors present and reinforce four key concepts:

1. Appreciation of the power of reliable information and the importance of a free flow of information in a democratic society;
2. Understanding why news matters and why becoming a more discerning news consumer can change individual lives and the life of the country;
3. Understanding how journalists work and make decisions and why they make mistakes;
4. Understanding how the digital revolution and the structural changes in the news media can affect news consumers; understanding new civic responsibilities as publishers as well as consumers.

With a $1.7 million grant from the Knight Foundation awarded in 2006, the Stony Brook Center for News Literacy (CNL) was established to develop, catalog, and spread the curriculum to other universities and into high schools across the United States (Finder, 2007). As of spring 2015, over 10,000 undergraduates have taken the news literacy course at Stony Brook, and more than 50 universities in the United States have adopted or adapted all or part of the course. The CNL also hosts summer workshops for high school teachers, so the teachers can integrate news literacy lessons into their classes.

The Robert R. McCormick Foundation and the John D. and Catherine T. MacArthur Foundation subsequently funded the creation of a Stony Brook CNL Digital Resource Center (DRC), which is a searchable database drawing on the terabytes of materials. The DRC debuted in spring 2015. It offers lecture slides, lesson plans, videos, and other resources developed by the CNL staff and their academic partners, to educators interested in integrating news literacy teaching and learning principles into their lessons.[2]

The Stony Brook Center for News Literacy's Overseas Partnership Program

In 2012, an anonymous donor offered the Stony Brook Center for News Literacy a grant of $250,000 over three years to try to spread the news literacy curriculum to educators from vastly different media cultures, with a particular focus on East Asia and on transitional societies, ones in which the media environment had relaxed over the past decade. For example, in places like Poland and other parts of the former Soviet Union, the demise of the Communist Party on the surface means that control over news media has been ceded to the marketplace. However, evidence suggests new, supposedly more democratic regimes often use economic and legal pressures to influence coverage (Gross, 2002). In Asia, over the past 20 years government entities have loosened their control over news media in places such as China, Myanmar, and Vietnam, yet the state still imposes either post facto censorship or guidance on sensitive stories without dictating every element of coverage (Abbott, 2011; Reporters Without Borders, 2014; The Hong Kong Journalists Association, 2014). Thus, the result in many countries is a strange hybrid of what looks like Western news coverage in many cases, but in reality is often heavily influenced by political regimes (see De Beer, 2009; Hachten & Scotton, 2012; Simon, 2014).

This has created challenges for news audiences who do not know which stories adhere to Western journalistic principles of independence, verification, and accountability, and which are the products of political or corporate propaganda—challenges the donor hoped news literacy instruction and training would help alleviate. The Stony Brook Center for News Literacy's Overseas Partnership Program (OPP) was officially formed in 2012 shortly after its founding director, Richard Hornik, who is lead author of this chapter, experimented with localizing American news literacy lessons in Hong Kong. The initial anonymous grant was subsequently matched by the Simons Foundation in 2014, bringing the total amount of funds dedicated to creating a global news literacy community through OPP outreach efforts to $500,000.

Hong Kong: Planting the Multinational Instructional Seeds

In February 2012, Stony Brook School of Journalism Dean Howard Schneider sought out Professor Ying Chan, founding director of the University of Hong Kong's Journalism and Media Studies Centre (JMSC) and herself a former reporter for the *New York Daily News,* to explore how to teach news literacy overseas. They decided that the first test to see if news literacy pedagogy developed for American students could be taught outside of the United States would happen at the University of Hong Kong (HKU). The task of adapting the course into the JMSC's "Principles of Journalism" course, mandatory for all journalism majors and minors, was offered to Hornik, who had taught news literacy at Stony Brook as a lecturer for five years and who had spent over seven years in Beijing and Hong Kong during his career as an editor and reporter at TIME magazine.

After spending many hours in July and August trying to adapt the course to an Asian audience, Hornik discovered that meant stripping out as many of the American references and examples as possible, by no means a simple task given that the course was created and had evolved in an American academic setting. Lessons about the First Amendment and the role of the press in the United States had to go, as did most of the illustrative current events examples assembled since the course was created in 2006.

In order to make room for the experiential elements of the original JMSC course and still cover in the depth the essential elements of Stony Brook curriculum, Hornik identified what he believed were the most salient news literacy principles that could easily transcend borders and social systems. These include:

1. The Power of Information—Why students should care about being able to determine the reliability of the information they receive
2. What Is News?—An analytical framework to sort out the difference between information that has been verified by an independent and accountable source and that which merely entertains, promotes, or avoids filters
3. Truth and Verification—How journalists (and other reliable providers) ensure the accuracy of the information they publish
4. Balance, Fairness, and Bias—Looking out not only for the prejudices of information providers, but also those we carry within ourselves.
5. New Challenges for Consumers—How to navigate new media, particularly social media, and the importance of taking responsibility for the information we pass along to others.

Restructuring the HKU course and editing the existing lectures turned out to be the easy part for Hornik. Far more challenging was coming up each week with 10–15 local examples to illustrate the often-abstract concepts used in the course. Some weeks entailed 20 hours or more of research, and not just for the lectures. The course relies heavily on classroom and homework exercises that force the student to apply the principles of the course as soon as they are introduced in class, and those activities require local material.

The classroom response more than made up for the work involved. Hornik found that the HKU students were more interested and engaged in news and current events than their American counterparts. Part of that stemmed from the political debate that had been raging in Hong Kong at the time, over imposition in local schools of a "National Education" curriculum designed to inculcate in young people a greater sense of Hong Kong's post-1997 place as a part of the People's Republic of China.

According to Hornik, the students from the mainland were just as engaged as their Hong Kong classmates and became a reliable source for new, non-American examples for the course. In fact, one complaint about the course was that there were too many Chinese examples. For example, the students pointed to Chinese netizens' use of indigenous versions of Twitter and Facebook to force China's government-controlled news media to alter coverage of events, such as an anti-Japanese demonstration that erupted in Chengdu, Sichuan in 2012. Xinhua, the official news agency of the People's Republic of China, first reported that only 250 people participated, but wound up revising the story to reflect more accurate accounts, after ordinary citizens posted photographs showing thousands of people at the demonstration. The students from Hong Kong and Mainland China alike also forced Hornik to devote far more attention than had been the case in Stony Brook classrooms to the role of social media in gathering and disseminating news and information.

The success of the initial HKU news literacy experiment encouraged Hornik to tackle the daunting prospect of attempting to spread the newly "de-Americanized" news literacy curriculum to other Asian universities, particularly in China (see Hornik & Kajimoto, 2014). Having spent over a decade covering authoritarian regimes in Europe and Asia as a reporter and editor for TIME, Hornik doubted that even reform-minded officials and educators in China and Vietnam would allow the teaching of a course that encouraged their people to be skeptical about the reliability of information. To his surprise, he found genuine interest.

Hornik attributes this initial interest, in part, to news literacy's focus on critical thinking skills, a growing imperative for academics and educators around the world as social media channels, enabled by highly personalized digital media devices, become the primary methods of information distribution and consumption worldwide (see Pew Research Center, 2014, 2015). In addition, it is important to remember that the rise of social media has changed the power of information equation, even in authoritarian regimes. Governments now understand that their citizens have access to a flow of unfiltered information that includes both rumor and fact. News literacy is viewed as one potential instructional strategy to deal with that challenge.

The first Stony Brook–associated news literacy training sessions outside of the United States took place in December 2012 in Phnom Penh, Cambodia and Hong Kong. Two dozen academics from mainland China, Vietnam, Myanmar, and Cambodia attended the workshops. The training sessions in Asia have evolved since then, during which time more than 40 academics from 12 countries have received instruction in the basic elements of the Stony Brook approach to news literacy during summer institutes hosted by the Asia-Pacific Digital Citizens Project at the University of Hong Kong and led by Hornik and Masato Kajimoto, an assistant professor at HKU and a co-author of this chapter. The one constant has been a requirement that all participants be both fluent in English and conversant in the fields of journalism and communications. In addition, it was important to Kajimoto and Hornik to do everything possible to help participants translate or interpret the course to fit the unique socio-cultural, political, and media environments of another country.

At the end of all workshops, participants are asked to present their ideas of how they might use news literacy's key elements. Some participants present their plans for teaching the whole course at the university level, but many have more limited goals, such as to teach the principles of journalism to student journalists, to enliven the teaching of English as a second language, to aid in the teaching of digital literacy in elementary school, or to teach critical thinking in high school. To provide further insight into how the Stony Brook approach has worked in international contexts, it is instructive to look at two of the most disparate examples— Vietnam and Poland.

Vietnam: Becoming "Smart" News Readers

Huyen Nguyen, a lecturer in journalism at the University of Social Sciences and Humanities (USSH) in Ho Chi Minh City, heard about the first news literacy workshop Hornik planned to conduct in East Asia through an email invitation Hornik had sent to her department. In order to increase the appeal of the workshop to be held in Phnom Penh, OPP offered to cover not only accommodations and fees for participants, but also travel expenses for those from Vietnam and Myanmar. Nguyen led the USSH delegation of four junior instructors. In order to maximize their benefit, the group videotaped the two days of presentation. Nguyen recalled:

> It was the first time I realized how varied information could be. Living in Vietnam, we were taught, and we were teaching students, as if propaganda was the

core of journalism. The stunning moment was not that we realized propaganda was different from journalism, but that I realized we had never been courageous enough to differentiate these two things. (H. Nguyen, personal communication, May 3, 2015)

Nguyen said that participation in the December 2012 workshop also allowed her to become familiar with issues of self-censorship, and that she felt "sad" when she realized that she had been controlled by communist ideology. She added that she was somewhat fearful at the beginning of the workshop, because she imagined the cultural police would charge her with crimes against the Party if she taught the course the same way it was done in the United States. But she said her concerns were abated when Hornik encouraged participants to modify the course to suit their own instructional needs and social systems.

In 2013, Nguyen and her colleagues believed so much in the potential of news literacy education in Vietnam, they developed a proposal for a program to run two-day news literacy workshops for undergraduates at universities in six southern Vietnamese cities. The proposal included the following objectives:

1. To raise awareness among college students about the growing confusion between news and other kinds of information in the Internet era.
2. To assist them with critical thinking skills to (a) distinguish between news and other kinds of media; (b) have sound judgments of the credibility and reliability of news; and (c) become smarter news/media consumers.
3. To encourage them to get more involved in social debates hosted by the press by posting and sharing only the truth over the Internet.
4. To encourage college teachers and local journalists to help students and young people sort out fact from fiction and news from entertainment, in both traditional and new media, and in doing so, be more responsible for their own work.

The Bureau of Educational and Cultural Affairs' Office of Alumni Affairs at the U.S. Consulate in Ho Chi Minh City awarded $19,000 to the program. By way of preparation, Nguyen attended the first News Literacy Summer Institute hosted by Hornik and Kajimoto at the University of Hong Kong in July 2013. She also invited Hornik to Ho Chi Minh City to address the 30 academics and journalists she had recruited for the training projects. Over the next nine months, she and her colleagues not only laid the groundwork for workshops in six cities, but also developed a 100-page printed manual titled,

"Manual for Smart Readers," to summarize what they believed should be essential news literacy lessons and activities in Vietnamese classrooms.

Nguyen's team subsequently held workshops at four institutions: USSH, Nha Trang University, An Giang University, and Yersin University in Da Lat City. In total, 277 undergraduates completed the two-day course. Nguyen, who is currently studying for her PhD in communications at Ohio University, continues to advocate for news literacy in Vietnam. She said she has been lobbying administrators to establish a news literacy course at her university, and she wants students across Vietnam to learn how to become "smart" news readers. To do so, she has selected five young "charismatic" speakers who participated in the workshops she organized to take the lead and help spread the word about news literacy on social media: "They have a fan base on Facebook, and they are well-known among the Vietnamese journalism community. Thanks to them, 'smart readers' became a brand name, a social trend. Recently, I was very happy when the mainstream media started using my words" (H. Nguyen, personal communication, May 3, 2015).

Poland: Bringing News Literacy to Eastern Europe, the Caucasus, and Central Asia

The impetus for the Overseas Partnership Program initiatives in Poland came through a chance encounter at a Washington, DC, Tripartite Young Leaders Conference in 2013. Between sessions, Hornik laid out the basics of news literacy to Rafal Wisniewski, at the time a PhD candidate in international security studies in the Faculty of Political Science and Journalism at Adam Mickiewicz University (AMU) in Poznan, Poland, about three hours by car west of Warsaw. Wisniewski, who is now a lecturer at AMU, and his colleagues at *R/evolutions: Global Trends & Regional Issues*, a newly formed, online academic journal, applied for a grant from the Poznan municipal government to invite Hornik to AMU for university and public lectures on the importance of news literacy.

Shortly after that trip in April 2014, Wisniewski and two of his university colleagues, Eliza Kania and Agnieszka Filipiak, attended a one-week News Literacy Summer Institute at Stony Brook. Their university paid for their travel expenses, while the OPP covered accommodations, meals, and tuition. In an email interview in spring 2015, Wisniewski said the summer institute provided an opportunity for foreign educators to exchange ideas and "know-how" between experienced and prospective news literacy teachers. He added that he learned a lot and quickly realized that the key to teaching news literacy would be the identification and integration of examples from local Polish news sources: "As we were required to search for examples and media cases from our own country, we were able to better grasp the main ideas of the course. That also proved to be a starting point for our Polish curriculum" (R. Wisniewski, personal communication, May 1, 2015).

In the fall 2014 semester, Wisniewski, Kania, and Filipiak taught a news literacy course in Poland for the first time. Using innovative marketing techniques, including a lively video developed during the summer institute at Stony Brook, the course attracted more students than could be accommodated. In a report reflecting on their experiences, the educators wrote that the localization efforts included discussions of "peculiar" Polish regulations that restrict speech, such as laws against speaking offensively about religion or laws against insulting the president. The educators also stated in the report that the emphasis on current affairs and the multitude of activities designed to give students opportunities to understand, apply, and practice news literacy principles and skills were strong points of the pedagogy. Wisniewski, Kania, and Filipiak are currently working to make news literacy a mandatory course for all AMU journalism majors and minors. The dean of their program, Tadeusz Wallas, agreed in March 2015 to become the head of the first Center for News Literacy in Europe and the second outside the United States. The other is the Asia-Pacific Digital Citizens Project at the University of Hong Kong, which is led by Kajimoto.

The European news literacy center will serve as a clearinghouse for materials and knowledge, as well as organize instructional institutes on news literacy for educators from Eastern Europe, the Caucasus, and Central Asia. The first institute was held in July 2015. The Stony Brook Center for News Literacy Overseas Partnership Program provided financial support, as well as one senior instructor; the AMU faculty was responsible for the curriculum, logistics, and recruiting and selection of participants. In addition to OPP support, five of the participants were funded by the European Union's Erasmus Mundus program that focuses on faculty and students from non-EU countries in those regions. Educators from Bulgaria, Kyrgyzstan, Kazakhstan, Georgia, Tajikistan, Ukraine, Belarus, Serbia, Armenia, Pakistan, Latvia, Uzbekistan, and Romania were selected to participate in the summer 2015 institute.

Even with more than 140 applications, Wisniewski said that enrollment in the first institute was limited to 15 participants, so as to allow for one-on-one tutorials with experienced news literacy educators, as well as to help facilitate small group discussions about which American news literacy lessons are appropriate for Eastern Europe, the Caucasus, and Central Asia classrooms and which ones should be excluded or significantly altered to reflect the diverse and complex social-cultural contexts and geopolitical realities of the countries in the region. He added that the strategy of turning to local news media for real-life, fresh examples was central to the training.

Discussion and Future Directions for Global "Making Sense of News" Programs

News literacy instructors at Stony Brook are driven by a passion for the public interest that is inspired and informed by their previous careers as journalists (Fleming, 2014). The heart of news literacy instruction at Stony Brook rests on the assumption that the key to civic culture in the digital age is not a more virtuous press, but rather a more virtuous news consumer who demands verified information provided by independent and accountable news outlets and appreciates high-quality, investigative, watchdog journalism (Schneider, 2007). Fittingly, news literacy education is positioned in the United States as a pedagogical pathway to an informed and engaged citizenry.

But as the Stony Brook approach to news literacy instruction spreads abroad and into transitioning societies, or even into countries without democratic traditions or freedom-of-expression and freedom-of-the-press legal protections, the lofty democratic desires of the civic-inspired pedagogy fall to the wayside and its commitment to the development of critical media analysis skills becomes essential. In other words, educators in these countries are motivated almost exclusively by the information-processing skill-potential of news literacy instruction, as opposed to its civic empowerment aspirations. This is evidenced by experiences in Vietnam where educators experimenting with news literacy lessons dismiss references to democracy and freedom of expression that are highlighted in American classrooms in favor of "smart" news-reading frameworks aimed at teaching students how to sift through mountains of information to figure out the most relevant facts needed to make judgments, reach conclusions, or take actions.

The outlook is similar in Hong Kong with key distinctions, understandably, given the drastically different cultural, historic, economic, and geopolitical realities between Hong Kong and Vietnam. While Vietnam is ruled by one party and is classified by The World Bank (2014) as a "lower middle-income country" with a per capita income of just over $2,000, Hong Kong represents a technologically and economically advanced society with deep liberal democratic and free press traditions that have clashed recently with the often "invisible hand" of Chinese power and censorship under the "one country, two systems" doctrine (The Hong Kong Journalists Association, 2014). Regardless, news literacy instruction in Hong Kong is not viewed as a way to push for democratic reforms, but rather to help students "make sense" of news and information flashing across traditional news and social media channels delivered through increasingly sophisticated and ubiquitous digital technologies such as smartphones.

This philosophy is seen in the title of Kajimoto's Massive Open Online Course, or MOOC, that was informed by Stony Brook news literacy lessons and activities. The six-week course offered through edX, a leading MOOC provider and platform that offers courses to worldwide audiences, often at no charge, is called "Making Sense of News." The outcomes of the "Making Sense of News" MOOC include distinguishing news from opinion, media bias from audience bias, and assertion from verification; applying critical thinking skills to examine the validity of information; contextualizing the knowledge gained from news reports; keeping up with and responding quickly to daily news events; and making informed decisions. More than 7,000 people from 146 different countries registered for the first "Making Sense of News" MOOC in summer 2015.[3]

Kajimoto, who visited news literacy educators at Adam Mickiewicz University in Poland, said he believes that it might be easier for news literacy to spread in Europe, compared with his experiences in Asia. According to Kajimoto, there seem to be more funding opportunities in Europe, because countries there are often far better off economically than many Asian countries; there seem to be more understanding and support for media and news literacy education in Europe, because the field is more established there (see Masterman, 1985, 1998); and language does not seem to be as big a barrier in Europe as it is in Asia, where he finds it is difficult to find like-minded colleagues who are fluent in English and who can afford to travel in order to network and share research and instructional ideas.

Looking ahead, the Center for News Literacy's Overseas Partnership Program at Stony Brook will shift its efforts toward building the resources and capabilities of its regional partners. In particular, the Center for News Literacy at Adam Mickiewicz University in Poland and the Asia-Pacific Digital Citizens Project at the University of Hong Kong will take over not only spreading the curriculum and managing the educator training programs, but also tracking the activities of past workshop participants. In both cases, and as the new centers develop, the CNL will provide support in terms of funding and access to the latest teaching materials.

Ultimately, the story of the Stony Brook Center for News Literacy's Overseas Partnership Program told in this chapter demonstrates the interconnected, interdisciplinary, and international nature of media literacy education in the 21st century. By including examples and voices from Hong Kong, Vietnam, and Poland, a dynamic, diverse, and multinational picture of a growing global community of news literacy educators, committed to teaching young people how make sense of news and find reliable information, is revealed. These understandings, in turn, can help inform and perhaps inspire educators from around the world to experiment with news literacy and/or media literacy techniques, at a time when calls for reform in education at all levels grow louder, to address the needs of increasingly globalized, technology-dependent societies.

Notes

1. For more information on the News Literacy Project, visit: http://www.thenewsliteracyproject.org
2. For more information about the CNL and/or to access materials in its Digital Resource Center, go to: http://www.centerfornewsliteracy.org
3. For more information on the "Making Sense of News" MOOC, visit: https://www.edx.org/course/making-sense-news-hkux-hku04x

References

Abbott, J. P. (2011). Electoral authoritarianism and the print media in Malaysia: Measuring Political Bias and Analyzing Its Cause. *Asian Affairs: An American Review, 38*(1), 1–38. doi: 10.1080/00927678.2010.520575

Altschull, H. J. (1990). *From Milton to McLuhan: The ideas behind American journalism.* White Plains, NY: Longman.

Arendt, H. (1968). *Between past and future: Eight exercises in political thought.* New York, NY: Viking Press.

Ashley, S., Maksl, A., & Craft, S. (2013). Developing a news media literacy scale. *Journalism & Mass Communication Educator, 68*(1), 7–21. doi: 10.1177/1077695812469802

Aufderheide, P. (1993). Aspen Institute report of the national leadership conference on media literacy. Aspen, CO: Aspen Institute.

Buckingham, D. (1999). Young people, politics and news media: Beyond political socialisation. *Oxford Review of Education, 25*(1–2), 171–84. doi: 10.1080/030549899104198

Buckingham, D., Banaji, S., Burn, A., Carr, D., Crammer, S., & Willett, R. (2005). *The media literacy of children and young people: A review of the research literature on behalf of Ofcom.* London, UK: Centre for the Study of Children.

Commission on Freedom of the Press. (1947). *A free and responsible press: A general report on mass communications—newspapers, radio, motion pictures, magazines, and books.* Chicago, IL: University of Chicago Press.

Considine, D. (1995). Are we there yet? An update on the media literacy movement. *Educational Technology, 35*(4), 32–43.

De Beer, A. S. (Ed.). (2009). *Global journalism: Topical issues and media systems* (5th ed.). Boston, MA: Pearson Education.

Entman, R. M. (2004). *Projections of power: Framing news, public opinion, and U.S. foreign policy.* Chicago, IL: University of Chicago Press.

Finder, A. (2007, May 9). Telling bogus from true: A class in reading the news. *New York Times,* p. 8.

Flanagin, A. J., & Metzger, M. J. (2000). Perceptions of Internet information credibility. *Journalism & Mass Communication Quarterly, 77*(3), 515–40. doi: 10.1177/107769900007700304

Fleming, J. (2014). Media literacy, news literacy, or news appreciation? A case study of the news literacy program at Stony Brook University. *Journalism & Mass Communication Educator, 69*(2), 146–65. doi: 10.1177/1077695813517885

Gross, P. (2002). *Entangled evolutions: Media and democratization in Eastern Europe.* Baltimore, MD: Johns Hopkins University Press.

Hachten, W. A., & Scotton, J. F. (2012). *The world news prism: Challenges of digital communication* (8th ed.). Malden, MA: Blackwell Publishing.

Hobbs, R. (1998). Building citizenship skills through media literacy education. In M. Salvador & P. M. Sias (Eds.), *The Public Voice in a Democracy at Risk* (pp. 57–76). Westport, CT: Greenwood.

——. (2007). *Reading the media: Media literacy in high school.* New York, NY: Teachers College Press.

——. (2010). *Digital and media literacy: A plan of action.* Washington, DC: The Aspen Institute.

Hobbs, R., & Frost, R. (2003). Measuring the acquisition of media-literacy skills. *Reading Research Quarterly, 38*(3), 330–55. doi: 10.1598/rrq.38.3.2

Hornik, R., & Kajimoto, M. (2014). "De-Americanizing" news literacy: Using local media examples to teach critical thinking to students in different socio-cultural environments. *Asia Pacific Media Educator, 24*(2), 175–85.

Kellner, D., & Share, J. (2007). Critical media literacy is not an option. *Learning Inquiry, 1*(1), 59–69. doi: 10.1007/s11519-007-0004-2

Klurfeld, J., & Schneider, H. (2014). *News literacy: Teaching the Internet generation to make reliable information choices.* Washington, DC: Center for Effective Public Management at Brookings.

Kovach, B., & Rosenstiel, T. (2007). *The elements of journalism: What newspeople should know and the public should expect.* New York, NY: Three Rivers Press.

Kubey, R. (2004). Media literacy and the teaching of civics and social studies at the dawn of the 21st century. *American Behavioral Scientist, 48*(1), 69–77. doi: 10.1177/0002764204267252

Kubey, R., & Baker, F. (1999). Has media literacy found a curricular foothold? *Education Week, 19,* 56.

Lippmann, W. (1922/2007). *Public opinion.* Sioux Falls, SD: NuVision Publications.

Loth, R. (2012). What's black and white and retweeted all over? Teaching news literacy in the digital age. *Joan Shorenstein Center on the Press, Politics and Public Policy Discussion Paper Series.* Boston, MA: Harvard College.

Masterman, L. (1985). *Teaching the media.* London, UK: Routledge.

——. (1998). Foreword: The media education revolution. In A. Hart (Ed.), *Teaching the Media: International Perspectives* (pp. vii–xi). Mahwah, NJ: Lawrence Erlbaum.

McBrien, L. J. (2005). Uninformed in the information age: Why media necessitate critical thinking education. In G. Schwarz & P. U. Brown (Eds.), *Media Literacy: Transforming Curriculum and Teaching* (pp. 18–34). Malden, MA: Blackwell Publishing.

McQuail, D. (2005). *McQuail's mass communication theory.* Los Angeles, CA: Sage.

Mihailidis, P. (2009). Beyond cynicism: Media education and civic learning outcomes in the university. *International Journal of Learning and Media, 1*(3), 19–31.

——. (Ed.). (2012). *News literacy: Global perspectives for the newsroom and the classroom.* New York, NY: Peter Lang.

Mihailidis, P., & Hiebert, R. (2005). Media literacy in journalism education curriculum. *Academic Exchange Quarterly, 9*(3), 162–66.

Moeller, S. D. (2009). *Media literacy: Understanding the news.* Washington, DC: Center for International Media Assistance.

National Association for Media Literacy Education. (2007). *Core principles of media literacy education in the United States.* Retrieved from http://namle.net/wp-content/uploads/2009/09/NAMLE-CPMLE-w-questions2.pdf

Pew Research Center. (2014). Emerging nations embrace Internet, mobile technology. Retrieved from http://www.pewglobal.org/files/2014/02/Pew-Research-Center-Global-Attitudes-Project-Technology-Report-FINAL-February-13-20146.pdf

——. (2015). *The smartphone difference.* Retrieved from http://www.pewinternet.org/files/2015/03/PI_Smartphones_0401151.pdf

Potter, W. J. (2008). *Media literacy* (4th ed.). Los Angeles, CA: Sage.

——. (2010). The state of media literacy. *Journal of Broadcasting & Electronic Media, 54,* 675–96.

Reporters Without Borders. (2014). *World Press Freedom Index 2014.* Retrieved from http://rsf.org/index2014/en-index2014.php

RobbGrieco, M., & Hobbs, R. (2013). *A field guide to media literacy education in the United States* (working paper). Retrieved from http://mediaeducationlab.com/sites/mediaeducationlab.com/files/Field%20Guide%20to%20Media%20Literacy%20.pdf

Schneider, H. (2007). It's the audience, stupid! *Nieman Reports, 61*(3), 65–68.

Schudson, M. (2003). *The sociology of news.* New York, NY: W. W. Norton & Company.

Silverblatt, A. (2001). *Media literacy: Keys to interpreting media messages.* Westport, CT: Praeger.

Silverblatt, A., & Enright Eliceiri, E. M. (1997). *Dictionary of media literacy.* Westport, CT: Greenwood Press.

Simon, J. (2014). *The new censorship: Inside the battle for global media freedom.* New York, NY: Columbia University Press.

The Economist. (2015, February 28). *Planet of the phones: The smartphone is ubiquitous, addictive and transformative.* Retrieved from http://www.economist.com/news/ leaders/21645180-smartphone-ubiquitous-addictive-and-transformative-plan et-phones

The Hong Kong Journalists Association. (2014). *Press freedom under siege: Grave threats to freedom of expression in Hong Kong.* Retrieved from http://www.hkja.org.hk/site/ Host/hkja/UserFiles/file/annual_report_2014_Final.pdf

The World Bank. (2014). *Vietnam overview.* Retrieved from http://www.worldbank.org/ en/country/vietnam/overview

Zettl, H. (1998). Contextual media aesthetics as the basis for media literacy. *Journal of Communication, 48*(1), 81–95. doi: 10.1111/j.1460-2466.1998.tb02739.x

5. Digital Remix for Global Media Literacy

MICHAEL ROBBGRIECO

Broadcast media students edit video clips together from English, Qatari, and American news networks and insert text commentary to create messages about global hunger issues. A troop of 10-year-old girls explores how using different songs as soundtracks for a Girl Scouts recruitment ad changes its meanings and appeal. High school media arts students create DVD commentaries, defending their creative work in making mashup videos from found video clips, as transformative uses of cultural artifacts. What skills and knowledge are these young people learning through making and discussing digital remix? How do these activities relate to their participation in digital and global culture? How do we deal with the ethical and legal issues of using others' work? Why spend valuable learning time remixing, rather than creating new work? What should educators think about when designing remix activities for media literacy development? This chapter addresses these questions by discussing case studies around the vignettes above, in relation to scholarship in remix studies and media literacy education.

Digital remix, the practice of selecting, manipulating, and combining existing digital media texts to produce new work, holds great promise for developing global media literacy. While some teachers perceive remix negatively, as derivative or unethical in terms of piracy and plagiarism, other educators have embraced digital remix practices in classrooms and youth media programs to pursue a wide range of learning goals, from culture-jamming civic engagement to developing video editing and composition skills. In this chapter, I will discuss several potential benefits (+) of engaging learners in digital remix, including:

+1) opening possibilities for using diverse cultural resources and personally meaningful texts;

+2) negotiating various identity discourses across cultural and national
boundaries;

+3) integrating analysis, production, and critical reflection through collaborative learning;

+4) practicing skills of juxtaposition, sequencing, and multimodal composition;

+5) exploring the nature of creativity and authorship;

+6) engaging in ethical and legal debates around copyrights, fair use, and
plagiarism; and

+7) taking political and civic action by exposing and transforming dubious media messages.

With these opportunities, several challenges (–) must be overcome to optimize learning, including the following common concerns about remix:

–1) celebrating conspicuous consumption and ephemeral pop culture;

–2) focusing on narrow cultural interests and niche digital communities;

–3) promoting shallow engagement with content and mere spectacle
without critical thinking;

–4) emphasizing technical minutiae of editing and copy/paste shortcuts;

–5) encouraging derivative production, devaluing originality, and sacrificing personal voice;

–6) confusing or ignoring ethical and legal issues of intellectual property; and

–7) reproducing oppressive messages of mass media ideology.

After reviewing the scholarship on remix studies that has articulated the
potential benefits and challenges for teaching and learning outlined above,
I will illustrate how particular instructional strategies may address concerns
while optimizing the benefits for supporting global media literacy development. To do so, I draw on action research from my own experiences teaching university students and Girl Scouts through remix activities, as well as
my participant observation research in a high school media arts class, where
students studied remix culture and made video remixes. Three case studies
show how designing activities to support global media literacy development
through digital remix depends upon the following instructional strategies:
choosing remix tools in relation to learners' technical skills and experience;
providing content access and/or requirements for source texts; fostering

peer collaboration for technical support and creative teamwork; facilitating critical dialogue about phases of source text selection and analysis, production process, and product assessment; supporting participation in remix culture in and beyond the classroom; and balancing curricular learning goals with student voice through student choice over form and content.

The Rise of Remix Culture

Digital remix involves selection, manipulation, and recombination of elements from source texts to create new media texts, or to produce altered and repurposed versions of the source texts. Remix culture involves global information flows, global memes, and cross-cultural transformations of meaning, as artists play with media artifacts, identities, and representations from all over the world. Many scholars trace the current use of the term remix back to the practice of music recording artists in the 1970s, who produced extended versions of songs for dance halls or manipulated elements of individually recorded tracks to create new versions of previously released songs (Navas, Gallagher, & Burrough, 2015). Remixing and sampling of prior recordings became common across the globe in the hip-hop and reggae music of the 1980s and 1990s, as well as in the electronic dance music of the 1990s (Hebdige, 1987; McLeod, 2015). With the widespread use of digital authoring tools and networked computers enabling the manipulation and sharing of digital media texts in the late 1990s and the new millennium, the term remix came to apply broadly to recombinant creativity across different media forms. After founding the Creative Commons in 2001, an online repository for digital media texts for free use under particular licensing stipulations, legal scholar Lawrence Lessig popularized the notion of a rising global "remix culture" (Navas, Gallagher, & Burrough, 2015), which he described as embracing practices of "read/write" and "copy/paste/share," as opposed to the "read only" culture of 20th-century media, made for consumption rather than reuse (Lessig, 2008). Lessig has argued for developing intellectual property law to favor users rights, by showing how remix practices have been part of basic human creativity in modes of speech, music, and writing throughout history:[1]

> Remix with "media" is just the same sort of stuff we've always done with words.... We all expect we can quote, or incorporate, other people's words into what we write or say. And so we do quote or incorporate, or remix what others have said. The same with "media." [...] Like a great essay or a funny joke, a remix draws upon the work of others to do new work. It is creativity supported by new technology. (p. 82)

Lessig's arguments for freer culture incorporate ideas of other scholars who describe digital remix practices as affording greater cultural and democratic participation.

As everyone from mashup artists to Facebook users employs basic digital authoring software applications and networked communications platforms to select, manipulate, and combine existing media texts to create and share new works in new contexts, digital remix has been heralded as emblematic of the rise of participatory culture and the convergence of media consumers and producers in the 21st century. Cultural studies media scholar Henry Jenkins (2006) describes participatory culture, wherein "consumers are invited to actively participate in the creation and circulation of new content" (p. 290). Using elements of the popular culture products they adore, fans write their own stories, make their own videos, and remix and make their own versions of songs, to celebrate and extend the pleasure they derive from engaging with pop culture products. Jenkins describes these celebratory remix practices as a new sort of folk art, where traditions and composition skills are shared and developed voluntarily in communities of common interest. Economics scholar Yochai Benkler (2006) claims that the resources of production skills and creativity in remix practices more evenly distribute democratic power through the networked information economy:

> There is something normatively attractive, from the perspective of "democracy" as a liberal value, about the fact that anyone, using widely available equipment, can take from the existing cultural universe more or less whatever they want, cut it, paste it, and make it their own—equally well expressing their adoration as their disgust, their embrace of certain things as their rejection of them. (p. 276)

Benkler's argument does not imagine a utopian ideal, with the Internet enabling total democratic participation and symbolic production for all. Instead, he compares the emerging networked information economy to the industrial information economy model of the 20th century. Compared to the centralized power of dominant entertainment, news, and political public relations mass media industries in the last century, the emerging networked information economy offers much more individual autonomy for voicing opinions and getting them heard by many people. Several case studies in the work of both Jenkins (2006) and Benkler (2006) show how remix practices may make significant contributions to political opinions and movements. Examples range from the crass and superficial, such as blending presidential candidate John Kerry's face with the comic, undead television character Herman Munster, to the more sophisticated, such as editing video of Donald Trump trying to fire George W. Bush to make the point that he cannot, but voters can. As Jenkins (2006) explains:

> I would suggest that crystallizing one's political perspectives into a photomontage that is intended for broader circulation is no less an act of citizenship than writing a letter to a local newspaper [...and] passing such images to a friend is no more and no less a political act than handing them a campaign brochure or a bumper sticker. (p. 222)

Beyond participation, scholars have discussed how remix practices offer opportunities to resist dominant cultural ideologies and negotiate identities, since before the proliferation of networked digital media.

Remix practices can be important for historically oppressed sub-cultural groups making space for negotiating identities within a dominant culture. In *Cut 'n' Mix* (1987), critical cultural studies scholar Dick Hebdige describes how the remix practices of Caribbean musicians created space for identity expression that negotiated a history of slavery, religious oppression, and economic exclusion for people of African descent under White European imperial governments in Jamaica, Trinidad, and other island nations. Beginning in the 1960s, dub reggae musicians used consumer products—records, tape decks, and sound systems—to build new music by "talking over" popular dance records. As DJ musicians slowed down, sped up, mixed, and added their own vocals to different popular records, they created new versions of songs that connected with the dance community in new ways. Hebdige shows how this remix practice of "versioning" allowed artists to incorporate, innovate, and proliferate a variety of identity options within the sub-culture. For example, Jamaican musicians reworked the stereotype of the "rude boy," the rebel individual fighting the oppressive system that dominated early popular reggae records, by adding images of religious Rastamen, an image in turn transformed from a lazy marijuana smoker to a political activist—all through creating new versions of existing work. The new versions evolved into new genres of reggae, and created a sense of shared history and identity possibilities, both within the Black Jamaican communities and in the popular culture. Hebdige draws parallels between this evolution of identity work through remix in Caribbean music and the evolution of hip-hop music in the United States. In a contemporary response to Hebdige's sub-cultural studies, Caribbean media and youth cultures scholar Rupa Huq (2006) recommends a theoretical perspective on identity work that moves beyond sub-cultural resistance of dominant culture to account for more fluid, multi-ethnic, global youth taste cultures that pick and choose between a variety of global popular media to appropriate and transform meanings into both local and digitally networked contexts where individual and community identities play out. As demonstrated in the preceding sentence, Huq claims that youth identity work is very complex and difficult to describe. What is less complex and less difficult to recognize is the continued and increasing importance of remix practices for identity work among youth cultures:

> For young people in multi-ethnic modernity, pop music is a form of social practice to be created as well as a cultural text to be consumed. In both cases, youth are adept at constructing their own meanings in keeping with the reflexive biography notion of individualization. (p. 166)

This concept of reflexive biography situates young people as co-writers of their own identities, involving a negotiation between choices in media consumption and in media production, and inherited characteristics of race, gender, and class. Remix practices afford an explicit means of exploring, transforming, and communicating these negotiations.

Remix in Education: Theory and Research

In 2006, Henry Jenkins wrote, "More and more literacy experts are recognizing that enacting, reciting and appropriating elements from preexisting stories is a valuable and organic part of the process by which children develop cultural literacy" (p. 182). Many examples from the subsequent years support this claim, as remix practices and remix culture have become focal points for teachers and scholars of composition and educational technology, including: *The Remix: Revisit, Rethink, Revise, Renew* theme of the 2010 Conference on College Composition and Communication, the largest U.S. professional association for college composition teachers and scholars; the reorganization of Florida State University's graduate program in rhetoric and composition around the concept of remix (Yancey, 2009); and the emergence of textbooks showcasing remix practice, like English professor Catherine Latterell's *Remix: Reading and Composing Culture* (2010). Influential in this increasing focus on remix in education is the work of multi-literacies researchers who shift the discussion of literacy from a focus on a centralized set of skills and formal knowledge to an emphasis on the diverse social contexts of a plurality of literacies practices (Cope & Kalantzis, 2000).

Drawing on case studies of youth engaging in online remix activities (e.g., photoshopping, soundtracking videos, machinima, fan fiction, etc.),[2] Lankshear and Knobel (2011) position remixing among "new literacies" that youth learn from peers in their own communities of practice in digital media, recommending the inclusion of remix in educational settings to help students participate in digital cultures and formal academics more fully. Similarly, the foundational white paper for the digital media and learning strand of media education, *Confronting the Challenges of Participatory Culture: Media Education for the 21st Century* (Jenkins, Clinton, Purushotma, Robinson, & Weigel, 2006), includes remix among eleven new media literacies, calling it "appropriation—the ability to meaningfully sample and remix content" (p. 3), and claiming that the practice of digital remix "makes visible the degree to which all cultural expression builds on what has come before [...,] a process by which students learn by taking culture apart and putting it back together" (p. 32). However, the scholars also noted reluctance and resistance among educators to incorporate digital remix, due to concerns over originality and legality:

> School arts and creative writing programs remain hostile to overt signs of repurposed content, emphasizing the ideal of the autonomous artist. Yet, in doing so, they sacrifice the opportunity to help youth think more deeply about the ethical and legal implications of repurposing existing media content, and they often fail to provide the conceptual tools students need to analyze and interpret works produced in this appropriative process. (Jenkins et al., p. 33)

Thus, in addition to continuing to argue for expanded notions of authorship and creativity, proponents of bringing digital remix to education must overcome copyright confusion.

Realizing that teachers are unlikely to engage learners in remix practices if they think that they are illegal, regardless of whether or not such activities might support deeper critical thinking about ethical and legal issues, a group of U.S. researchers and lawyers led a coalition of educators to articulate *The Code of Best Practices in Fair Use for Media Literacy Educators* (American University Center for Media & Social Impact, 2010). Culled from focus group and survey research with educators throughout the United States, the code outlines typical contexts and situations for making transformative use of copyrighted material in communities of media literacy education practice, which includes examples of remix practices, like creating a sequence of video clips to illustrate a concept. In U.S. law, courts rule on the fair use of copyrighted materials on a case-by-case basis, judging whether or not a challenged work makes transformative use of the copyrighted work in terms of four factors: purpose (commercial, educational, etc.); nature (journalism, fiction, etc.); amount and substantiality (of the portion used in relation to the whole source work); and effect (on potential markets for the source work) (U.S. Copyright Act of 1976, section 107). Although copyright law is national and applied based on the laws of the nation where the work was created, users' rights in U.S. law have strong global influence:[3]

The U.S. fair use provision is often the default exception internationally for business, since it is widely assumed that if work is seen as fair use in the U.S., it will not be contested elsewhere. Fair use also exists in the Philippines and Israel, and has been regarded in copyright reform discussion elsewhere. (Aufderheide, 2015, p. 271)

Citing examples from educator testimonies gathered through research to produce the *Code of Best Practices in Fair Use*, media literacy scholar Renee Hobbs observed: "With the rise of digital media, transformativeness is becoming a valuable concept" (Hobbs, 2010, p. 9). Her book *Copyright Clarity: How Fair Use Supports Digital Learning* (2010), and the related free curricular materials available online from the Media Education Lab, provide many reasoning exercises, activities, and case studies to help educators and teen through adult learners to understand and exercise users' rights, which are essential for integrating remix practice in the classroom. Indeed, most research on digital remix in educational settings involves discussion of the tensions between users' rights and owners' copyrights—and the case studies below are no exception.

The potential for digital remix to involve identity work and critical resistance to oppressive media messages, as shown in cultural studies of remix culture, has not been lost on education scholars. In his theoretical framework for the edited volume of research on informal literacies of youth around the world, *New Media Literacies and Participatory Popular Culture across Borders*, Williams (2012) observes, "People involved in reading and writing transnational popular culture make connections—and often consciously seek contact—across cultures that broaden their sense of culture and identity" (p. 25). Williams relates remix practices, as a global new media literacy, to Kraidy's theory of cultural hybridity (2005), which posits that local communities negotiate meanings from mass media through their identities and effect the global flow of ideas and information, albeit through uneven and unequal power dynamics. Case studies of youth new media literacies in informal settings show that identity work in global communication through digital remix is not an easy or smooth process: "Just as there are connections made and conversations negotiated across cultures in online affinity spaces, there are also moments of miscomprehension, cultural stereotyping, and insult and anger" (Williams, 2012, p. 28). Ethnographer of youth media cultures Mizuko Ito has commented that there is a hidden digital divide between youth who participate in digital culture as more sophisticated producers of remix media (kids who "geek out"), with greater capacity to affect change in online communities and shape identities in digital culture, and a majority of youth who participate by "hanging out" or "messing around," primarily consuming and sharing popular culture (Ito,

2009). To develop more sophisticated participation in popular culture, some educators point to the potential of political remix for teaching youth to critically consume and respond to mass media messages (Burwell, 2013; Dubisar & Palmeri, 2010; Long, 2015). Analyzing and producing remixes that offer critical commentary on popular culture is seen as a way to assert personal and local cultural identities that may conflict with stereotypical popular culture representations, and possibly affect wider discourse.

Research on how remix practice works (or fails) in educational settings and pedagogy is far less common than theoretical discussions and case studies of informal youth media practices, arguing for the potential educational affordances of digital remix. A few recent studies have discussed how digital remix practice in the classroom supports core media literacy development and can connect to a wide range of other learning goals across the curriculum, including the study of literature (Jenkins & Kelley, 2013), multimodal composition (Vasudevan, 2010; Williams, 2014), civic engagement (Barron, Gomez, Pinkard, & Martin, 2014), and news (Mihailidis, 2011). My discussion of the following cases adds to this emerging literature describing the pedagogy of digital remix in relation to media literacy development—with special attention to cross-cultural and global learning.

Case 1: College Students Remix Global News Clips[4]

In the spring of 2009, I engaged 20 media studies and production majors enrolled in a required communication theory course at a large, urban U.S. university in making and discussing digital remixes, as a way to synthesize theoretical ideas in creative media production and to demonstrate their new knowledge of course content. To deepen learning about mass media effects theories of second-level agenda setting, I asked students to use the (now defunct) *Know the News* remix tool at the *Link TV* website, to edit together clips of television news stories from several media sources from around the world.[5] According to McCombs and Shaw (1972, 2013), journalists frame stories in ways that influence how the public understands the news. News frames make some aspects of a story more salient than others. The typical assignment is to have students write an essay analyzing TV news segments for evidence of how sequence, production choices, and editing create salience through framing certain details. However, I was interested in balancing analysis and production as a best practice for media education (Buckingham, 2003; Hobbs, Felini, & Cappello, 2011), which I thought would be particularly beneficial for my production-focused students, many of whom loathed the prospect of a theory course.

The remix tool allowed users to sample from news segments on current events curated by topic, to insert title screen clips at any point with their own text comments, and to share their own remixed video sequences. My assignment read as follows:

> At the *Know the News* website, go to the "Global Pulse remixer" and remix clips to create your own two-minute news package about: 1) world food crisis (groups A & B); 2) economic crisis (group C); or 3) Rising oil/fuel prices (group D). Be prepared to share notes about what aspects of the issue you chose to frame as most salient and how you emphasized the importance of those aspects in your remix.

The next day, students shared their two-minute remixes in small groups on laptops and discussed what they learned, liked, and disliked about the remix texts and process. I listened, taking notes as I drifted between groups, before convening a large group debrief around two student remixes.

In the large group, the first clip that we discussed opened with a White, male, BBC World newscaster with a British accent in front of a collage of images of world agriculture, saying, "Now, you may have experienced severe price shock at that once-a-week trip to the supermarket, but for millions of others around the world, finding enough to eat and affording it is a daily struggle." Cut to title logo "Global Pulse" with a generic "Dum, dum-dum" sound tag, followed by a talk bubble with the text (inserted by the student), "The world is going hungry...." Cut to an Al Jazeera montage (identified by the corporate logo) of people of color carrying food on their heads and a woman with a baby in arms pounding grain in a bowl, with a female British accent voiceover, "Feeding the hungry, the United Nations says the dramatic rise in food prices has become a challenge of global proportions." Another title screen flashes, followed by the (student-inserted) text, "Even in this 21st century when we surround ourselves with technology and intelligence, there are still people all over the world who are without food." A series of five 10-second clips from various global news sources offers newscasters recounting instances of panic buying, protests over food prices, long lines and fights in stores, and "rocketing" rice and wheat prices in Vietnam, Indonesia, Egypt, and Peru—each clip appearing as a self-contained fact flowing into a single coherent news story about world food crisis. A title screen flashes with another (student) text comment, "So many people around the world are without food, and America is doing...?" A male, Arab-accented, English voice cites statistics of America burning grain to produce fuel over a montage of agriculture and fuel production ending with a shot of the pundit claiming, "This is a crime against humanity." A final title screen shows the comment,

"A crime against humanity, that's how America is viewed…I bet your Big Mac is tasting fantastic right now."

For discussion, I required remix creators to listen to others' comments before discussing their intentions. One student responded to the use of all non-U.S. media reporters: "The clips make it seem like a story about problems in other places." Another added: "It sets up a *we*, or *us*, and a *them* through framing." Students also noted effects of the text comments inserted into the story: "The things she wrote make it seem like a crime against the world. And then she ends by blaming America." The student who produced the remix explained her purpose in terms of her sense of national identity, social justice, and a desire to provoke activism: "I just felt angry seeing the clips and thought about how fat we are in the U.S. So, I wanted make it [world hunger] our problem with my remix. Like, I guess I wanted people to feel guilty so maybe they'd do something." Deliberate use of sequence and juxtaposition as composition techniques were integral to her process: "I tried to set up the idea of people at home all comfy with the first clip, then show all the problems, and finish with how the U.S. doesn't care but should." She described the importance of constructing her argument as a remix rather than producing her own report on the issue: "Using the real news makes it seem credible," which resounded with most students in discussing their feelings about producing their remixes. This example was representative of the style that most students used to produce their remixes, presenting personally meaningful arguments on global issues as coherent news stories consisting of clips that resonated with their views while maintaining the pacing and style of the mainstream news sources from which they sampled—thus reproducing the aura of credibility from traditional news ethics and production values, as well as the ideological viewpoints of many of the source clips.

I chose the second remix for large group discussion because its style contrasted sharply with the first, subverting dominant news style to create oppositional messages. The second remix opened with a title screen reading, "As the global hunger crisis strengthens, food sources continue to weaken. Research analysts speculate that the growth in biofuels is to blame." A White, male, British, BBC World newscaster talking head reports, "The price of food has moved relentlessly higher, up 50% in five years." The image then jumps through a noticeable, glitchy cut to the same shot of the newscaster (from later in the source clip), saying, "The world's capacity to respond to famine is failing." The sequence abruptly cuts to an American newscaster talking head mid sentence, "…partly because of the use of corn-based ethanol in gasoline." An image of fuel production appears with the Arab-accented pundit's voiceover about burning grain for biofuels as a "crime against humanity" (as above in the first remix). In this style, a series of two-to-five second clips, some jumping within the same sampled news report, juxtaposes alternating voices of American national newscasters from Al Jazeera and BBC sources, with sound bites and visuals establishing statistics and images of global hunger, food shortages, and fuel production in rapid, repeating sequence. After 90 seconds, another (student-inserted) title screen reads: "If high oil prices increase the demand for biofuel, and biofuel consumes a resource used to feed a starving population, who can say it's not to blame?" Images of grain and fuel production, with the British-accented voiceover, "By next year, nearly a third of the corn crop in the U.S. will be destined for fuel," cut to a showroom of new trucks with an enthusiastic American-accented voiceover, "And all of it, just in time for the flex-fuel cars Detroit is easing onto showrooms now." About half of the students laughed out loud at this ending.

In discussion, students noted the transformative uses of source clips in terms of how the purpose and meanings changed: "This one has something to say. It's like, it's not just showing us the story, or even the story with comments." Some suggested that the techniques were deceptive: "It's twisting the stories to send a message about biofuels." Several students saw this "twisting" of the source clip meanings as humorous: "It's funny. [How so?] I don't know, the end is like a punch line." The editing style also garnered strong responses: "The quick edits make you notice the way it's put together, so you think about how it's trying to make you think something. But it's cool how all the lines flow with each other." This comment supports the notion that remixes call attention to the constructedness of media texts (Jenkins & Kelley, 2013), a core concept of media literacy. The creator of this remix described his intentions in terms of his critical response to the source clips: "I thought it was ridiculous how they kept blaming biofuels for world hunger, so I wanted to make fun of that." He also discussed his approach as satirical, admitting that he exaggerated what he saw as a flawed argument to appear more absurd: "I don't know. I guess I wanted it to be…ironic, I guess. I was playing around with how much I could distort the story." However, only half of the students saw the satire as directed at the absurdity, while others thought the message was earnest. I used this as a teachable moment to call attention to how different people understand media messages differently, another key media literacy concept. I asked whether or not this seemed like a successful remix given the variety of responses, and student opinion was split. The creator said that he was fine with the mixed response: "Humor's like that. Some people get it, and those are the ones I care about for this kind of thing." His comment implied particular beliefs about remix, including the notion that his message would identify niche audiences of people who share his views.

On an open-ended survey item asking for feedback about what they learned from this remix assignment, students reported deepening their understanding of the target concept. One student said, for instance: "I learned that the news stations many times frame issues in certain ways to appeal to their audience, and I became more familiar with the tools of the remixer through this assignment." Many responses expressed a sense of agency in framing news: "[I learned] that you can take any piece of information and use it in different ways." Several students echoed a theme of frustration with being limited by the tool in choosing source clips, for example: "We were given predetermined news clips, with few subjects to choose from. If the media establishes what we think about, I think the remixer showed us how positioning can create a point of view about certain topics, but not so much the ability to present the topics of choice." Others connected the ease of the process afforded by the tool with the possible effects of remix practice on public perception: "I learned how easy it is to agenda set and possibly affect the way the public views a situation, whether intentionally or not."

The remix activity was effective for learning about framing in news.[6] All remixes showed thoughtful attention to sequencing and employment of juxtaposition for specific goals. Class discussion allowed the authors to see how their choices communicated their purposes to their classmates. Students took advantage of the opportunity to transform their roles as news consumers into news producers, by remixing to express their own ideas and feelings. Despite the website's focus on journalistic norms addressing objectivity, fairness, and balance, my students did not all adhere nor aspire to these norms. The two example cases represent how some students used the news clips to establish credibility and present stories as straight news, sometimes injecting additional commentary, while others played with editing to call attention to message construction and a particular framing message. The activity engaged students in practicing media literacy skills, as they analyzed their own responses to news stories to choose a purpose for their new version. They evaluated clips according to their own framing purposes, which they communicated multimodally through sound bites, selected images, and text screens. In addition to the choices of their own remix processes, viewing and discussing other students' remixes gave students a sense of the variety of possible frames and purposes that can be communicated from the same narrative and semiotic material.

Although I had not anticipated much in the way of negotiating cultural identity from this exercise, some students seized the opportunity to assert their cultural position within the issue discourse. Many students commented on appreciating the opportunity to analyze different global news sources, and a few invoked their own ethnic or national heritage in discussion ("Being Jewish, it was interesting to see Al Jazeera's take on..."; "As a Russian American..."; etc.). Of the two remixes discussed above, one sought to create oppositional meanings about issue simplification through ironic use of editing, while the other seized on a theme of global class struggle to express guilt and responsibility for others' welfare. That said, the limited selection of source texts constrained the meaningful connections and cultural identity negotiations with which students could create. Many complained about the limitations of the content selection and the tool (no ability to alter soundtrack, add music, use visual transitions or graphics, etc.). However, I believe these limitations allowed the assignment to be manageable; more freedom of content access would have demanded more time, as would a more complex tool with a steeper learning curve. While these options may allow greater meaningfulness in students' connections to source texts and more sophisticated multimodal expression, they also require greater attention to media languages and technical skill, which were beyond the scope of this lesson. On the other hand, the assignment design obviates ethical issues around remix practice. By using a tool self-contained in a website that owns rights to all of its content, this remix lesson skirts issues of copyright, fair use, and even plagiarism (all clips are labeled "for educational use" and carry source logos and graphics as citations). This does not make these issues unimportant. In fact, without follow-up activities to address these issues, a remix assignment like this may introduce some to the world of remix without any legal or ethical orientation, and further the confusion about such issues for others. Details of the following case show how addressing questions of users' rights as part of instructional design for learning through digital remix supports global media literacy learning.

Case 2: Grade 9–10 Media Arts Students Make Mashups and Argue Fair Use[7]

In the spring of 2011 in a large U.S. East Coast city, I observed and supported instruction in a public high school media arts class of 22 students, led by a veteran media production and art teacher who designed a unit where students collaborated to learn about remix culture and to produce mashup videos. The instructor, Lex (a pseudonym), introduced the notion of remix culture through viewing and discussing the film *Rip: A Remix Manifesto* (2009).[8] He assigned a vocabulary term from the film, for each student to research and share in a presentation of its meaning and history with class, using multimedia examples of the following concepts: turntablism, mc, break, funk, mashup, sample, fair use, copyright versus copyleft, rip, open source, crate digging, manifesto, culture jamming, sequencer, peer-to-peer, sampler, transformative versus derivative, creative commons, and hip hop. After this introduction, Lex gave his students access to a folder of videos he curated, and asked them to sample two-second clips to make a 20–30 second remix video.[9] He described the curated videos as follows:

> One was like a news broadcast from 1979, we used a *Metropolis* clip, and a Japanese McDonald's commercial [...,] one music video about two people in a vehicle underwater and some monster was after them, a clip of Godzilla, like smashing things, and a clip of a bad TV movie about a big earthquake in San Francisco—all these things that I found that I thought were interesting, some news-related, some film-related, some commercials. And I said it [the student remix] could not be a music video. So, they could use the original soundtrack that was with the piece, or they could block out the sound and add their own, [which] they had to make themselves in Garageband [music software]. (Lex, pseudonym, personal communication, April 10, 2010)

Without further instruction, students got to work—but many did not know what to do. When they asked for clarification, Lex just said, "Smash it together." He floated around the room, engaging students in discussion about their process. Later, he described the process to me as follows: "They always ask, 'What do you want me to do with it?' Just smash it together. Like, what looks interesting? How does this go together? Then, we started going frame by frame, and asking, 'What does that make you think about?'" The students that I observed were engaged in the process of playing with the clips, finding visual motifs through juxtaposition (e.g., series of faces expressing surprise, a sequence of explosions) and suggesting narrative (e.g., a chase scene, a romantic interlude). Lex was enthusiastic about the results: "I got some really interesting things. Lots of reversings and moving back and forth." He was pleased that students took time to analyze clips, thinking about how meaning and affective responses were constructed and how they might use them: "It's important, just making them aware of those emotions that they're getting from visual input, because they're quick to associate. I mean, we read media very very intuitively; it's sort of built into us now." I observed that many students felt like their work "didn't make sense." Lex was comfortable with their ambiguous feelings, saying, "I think that there's some students in my class who, even if they don't get it right away, they get their own version of it. They get they're manipulating something that was just kind of fixed." Students became much more invested in their work when Lex challenged them in the next part of the assignment to discuss their remixes in terms of fair use.

In pairs, students interviewed each other, asking questions about whether the remix creator had made transformative use of the source clips. After rehearsing their responses, they used a simple online application called Voice-Thread to create a voiceover for their remix, pausing on still images, to discuss fair use in the style of a "DVD extra," with which students were familiar—film directors discussing their intentions as bonus material on movie discs. Questions about transforming purpose and nature yielded complex responses, with some students adamant about creating new meanings in new contexts, for example: "Well, this [*Metropolis* clip] part was from like a sci-fi movie, but I am using it as a flashback for these other characters from an old commercial who I sampled to look romantic. I mean, that shot there, it looks just like the old one, like they're remembering. It's the opposite of futuristic." Others were less sure: "I don't really know how these scenes were used in the old movies and commercials. All that punching and stomping and stuff exploding over and over, backwards and stuff—that's funny to me. But maybe it was funny before too." While all were confident that their two-second samples were transformative in terms of amount, they had conflicting ideas about the effect on potential markets. Some talked about how the learning benefits to student artists were important and that they couldn't see how distribution of their work hurt the market for the source works. But others thought in terms of their identities as creators: "I don't know. I think if somebody else used my work like this, I might not like it. Like, if you saw this [remix] first, it might ruin it [the source film] for you." Many thought that permission and attribution were important for economic and ethical reasons: "We should have to give credit, so then people can go see where we got this stuff if they like it, and then the original artists might make money." Thus, students engaged with the complexity of users' rights and copyrights, as well as ethical issues around attribution and authorship. By the end, some felt that they had made something new, with artistic value for society (or at least their class and learning process), while others felt like the work was derivative, "just borrowing" and "not really like making something yourself." Lex embraced this range of outcomes, satisfied that the students had gained conceptual tools and vocabulary for thinking critically about the nature of creativity.

Lex's instructional design engaged students as participants in remix culture in an odd way. With the introductory film and vocabulary assignment, students gained a shared knowledge of remix culture and history, and used many of the terms and concepts in their discussions of their own remix production work. However, due to the school's restrictive policy on Internet use and various levels of home access to technology, students could not capture clips of their choice from the web; they had to work with the instructor's choices. While this limited their personal connections to the source clips, it also freed students to play with clips for their immediate, ahistorical aesthetic appeal. This simulated how Internet users often encounter new information on the web, by chance, while forcing students to engage the clips as material for their own expression—a practice of experienced remix artists. This approach was much different from the aims of more commonly described exercises in literature on remix in education: political remix to counter dubious mass media messages, remix for learning course content, or remixing as a fan of particular media to become a more active cultural participant. By distancing students from the media they like and know best, this approach may have allowed students to be more critical of the clips and of their own uses, as media education students are often reluctant to be critical of the media they love and may be disempowered by critical thinking disturbing their pleasures (Buckingham, 2003; Turnbull, 1998). However, without follow-up exercises to apply the critical aesthetic, ethical, and legal reasoning in more personally meaningful contexts, students may be unlikely to transfer their new skills and knowledge to their uses of the popular culture that matters most to them. The final case discusses how remix in education offers opportunities to integrate pleasures productively, in personally meaningful media and critical thinking.

Case 3: Girl Scouts Soundtrack a Recruitment Ad and Discuss Meaning Making [10]

In the fall of 2008, I co-taught a workshop called *Mix & Match* for over 100 Girl Scouts, ages 10–12, in which participants soundtracked a Girl Scout promotional ad with new music choices and discussed their remixes using key questions of media literacy. The workshop was part of the *Your Life Online, On-Air, and On Screen* event at Temple University, hosted by the Media Education Lab. The event aimed to offer a fun experience in practicing media literacy skills of analysis and production. For each of our four, 45-minute sessions of 26 girls, pairs of learners shared desktop computers where a promotional ad for their organization appeared on each screen, beside several small media player icons for 10 different pop songs curated by my co-teacher, a connoisseur of pre-teen pop music. Before the remix activity, we introduced the notion of a theme song.

We asked each girl to write down what might be a good theme song for her life ("for you and your friends, for your family, or for an important memory"). We talked about the importance of being respectful about people's choices, since music is very powerful and personal, and introduced our two key media literacy ideas: music has embedded values and messages; and, different people feel and understand music differently. Then, each participant introduced herself to another girl that she did not yet know well by describing her personal theme song choice. After this icebreaker had activated knowledge about music and tastes, we briefly discussed the different reasons for their choices (lyrics, music, feelings, connections to life events, etc.), connecting to our two key concepts. We then told the group that we were going to have fun trying out different ideas for a theme song for the Girl Scouts. They viewed the original ad on the large screen. Then, they viewed a version with "a different song that my wife (the author's) would have chosen back in her day as a scout." With the lyrics to "Girls Just Wanna Have Fun" by Cyndi Lauper on screen, we asked: "Why do you think she liked it? What messages are in the song? Do the messages fit the scouts? How is the video different with this song?" These questions prompted learners to think about the intentions of the creators of both the remix and the ad in relation to the other key media literacy concepts we had introduced. The preliminary discussion also let us reinforce the ethic of respectful sharing, as we reframed comments like, "Maybe she just liked bad music," with suggestions like, "Could that hurt her feelings if she were here? How could we say that with respect? For instance, 'maybe she liked different music from me and my friends; we like heavier beats…'." After this large group activity, pairs of girls played the ad on computers (with its original sound muted), trying each of the pre-loaded songs to choose "the best theme song to go with this video to represent you and your friends as scouts." With the two or three scout leaders and parents who attended each session, we engaged the pairs of learners in discussion and troubleshot any technical issues. As they made their choices, we polled them to find the most popular theme song, which we then projected on the big screen to discuss as a whole group. Different pairs of girls identified different values represented in the new theme song, and pointed to how the lyrics and music supported the visual messages of the ad, and to how the remix represented their experience in Girl Scouts.

In our debriefing discussion afterward, the co-instructors and the scout leaders agreed that the activity was successful in engaging all the girls in having fun with remix and media literacy discussion. We all had the impression that most girls engaged in practicing critical thinking using our target concepts through analysis of the source clips and through playing with soundtracking with the different songs, starting at different points to sync the video and sound, and considering the different effects on meanings. Scout leaders emphasized how the production element was the key to the fun, and that it gave them ideas for addressing their parental concerns about their kids consuming media uncritically. We agreed that the remix activity allowed the students to use their informal popular culture knowledge to communicate and negotiate their identities from different social contexts as friends, family members, and Girl Scouts. It also made the girls consider how their organization represented them, and how they would choose to represent themselves as Girl Scouts to others through music and images. The media literacy discussion brought a formal academic dimension to their informal literacies and vice versa. We noted how many of the girls wanted to try another favorite song as the theme for the ad, and that some planned to do so at home. Thus, the activity afforded opportunities for girls to negotiate identities by connecting their personal tastes with social identities and cultural representation in mass media, and also encouraged some to participate further in remix culture.

Discussion

In each of the cases above, instructional design involved total teacher control over the source works that learners used for digital remix. This choice allowed teachers in the first two cases to ensure that students went beyond their usual discourse communities and taste cultures in using cultural resources for new recombinant productions. It also allowed teachers to focus practice on texts they deemed worthy of student engagement and to address common concerns about source material being within the bounds of appropriateness for their learning institutions. However, by sacrificing student choice over source material, the lessons in digital remix likely missed opportunities to engage students in negotiating aspects of their identities, tastes, and opinions that were most meaningful to them. Still, the common concerns over appropriateness and legality that compel teachers to limit students' access to cultural resources are well founded; as shown in other research on remix practice in the classroom, even when educators have limited students to videos licensed for educational use, they have run into complex issues:

> Any time we introduce a truly networked media resource into the classroom, students are, in a sense, "entering" popular culture, with all its chaos, disruptions, and distractions. As the class explored the ccMixter site, many students gravitated toward sexually explicit and verbally graphic content; they listened to, and in one case transcribed, content that would not normally be encountered in schools. For NML researchers, the ccMixter site came to represent the competing values of defining a more expansive, expressive, and participatory learning community, on the one hand, and protecting children from the (real and perceived) dangers of unregulated communities, on the other. (Kelley, Jenkins, Clinton, & McWilliams, 2013, p. 35)

Thus, design strategies for digital remix in education must negotiate historical tensions between protectionism and empowerment paradigms of global media education. Just as remix practice offers opportunities to learn by nego-tiating identities and values across cultures, so it challenges instructors to negotiate the differing global flows of appropriateness in digital media for their local contexts.

Several factors impacted the choice of technology tool in each case. The traditional use of remix practice in vocational media production is to train stu-dents to edit video according to preferred professional principles and meth-ods (Blanchard & Christ, 1993; Buckingham, 2003), which involves a tool focus and an unquestioned mass media ideology that historically has led many critical media literacy educators to focus on media analysis rather than pro-duction (RobbGrieco, 2014). In the cases above, learners engaged in remix with minimal focus on tool training, and with the freedom to negotiate their own aesthetic and ethical perspectives with those that they encountered in the source clips. The instructor's choice of tools that students could use intu-itively, or of tools with which they had prior experience, facilitated a focus on the communication process.

Each case shows instructors engaging learners in critical dialogue about key concepts of media education: production, media languages, representa-tions, and audiences (Buckingham, 2003). Although some research suggests that participation in remix culture can help learners develop competencies in using such concepts spontaneously through practice and affinity (Jenkins et al., 2006), Buckingham (2003) and Hobbs (2004) warn that use of core media literacy concepts does not always occur implicitly; educators must prompt students to reflect on the consequences of their choices before, during, and after production, in order to develop reflective and reflexive habits of mind for media production practice. These cases illustrate how instructional design can integrate critical reflection at each stage of the remix process, while also negotiating the historical tension between production and analysis in media literacy pedagogy.

Finally, the instructional design partially determined the sorts of eth-ical and legal challenges that learners addressed in digital remix practice. The case of remixing global news inspired students to create messages that both subverted and reproduced the mass media messages while engaging them in critical dialogue about the political implications of remix. The case involving media arts high school students did not engage political issues in the production phase, but connected to ethical issues around the nature of creativity and authorship by engaging legal reasoning with fair use con-cepts in the meta-production activity of recording a commentary track. The Girl Scouts case celebrated personal pleasures and identifications with music while making space to assert personal and social tastes through wider cultural representation.

Concluding Thoughts

Optimizing global media literacy learning through digital remix hinges on strategic choices in instructional design, including the following:

- providing content access and/or requirements for source texts;
- balancing curricular learning goals with student voice through student choice over form/content.
- fostering peer collaboration for technical support and creative teamwork;
- choosing remix tools in relation to learners' technical skills/experience;
- supporting participation in remix culture in and beyond the classroom; and
- facilitating critical dialogue about phases of source text selection/ analysis, production process, and product assessment.

The balance of teacher and student control over source texts partially determines the range of cultural resources and identities that learners may use in remix practice. Without requiring learners to do so, many may choose not to engage with media texts from other cultures around the globe, or from beyond their own tastes. Requiring learners to demonstrate particular knowledge, reasoning, skills, or participation (valued by the teacher or educational institution) will be more meaningful if balanced with opportunities for students to control choices over what they say and how they say it through remix. Likewise, the choice of tool can affect how much focus on technological minutiae will be required in relation to other learning goals. Fostering peer collaboration can support experimentation with production techniques while making learners consider multiple perspectives on meaning making throughout the production process. The degree to which learners are allowed to engage with remix cultures and audiences affects the prospects of using their new knowledge beyond the educational setting. Sharing work publicly, or with other groups of learners through digital networks, can be risky, but the practice introduces authentic opportunities to negotiate cultural exchanges and confront ethical and legal issues in digital remix. Finally, by prompting students to reflect on the consequences of their creative choices in selecting, composing, and sharing remixes, learners engage in inquiry around key concepts of media literacy and develop reflective habits for media production practice and cross-cultural communication.

Notes

1. Other scholars argue that studies of remix culture should consider the materiality of media texts and the ability to use fragments or copies of media texts as elements of composition (Borschke, 2015), without extending the metaphor of remix to include all sorts of creative uses of language, sound, and visuals valorized for their new contributions to culture through transformative uses, which may discount important non-transformative remix practices.

2. For a brief visual introduction to a range of remix practices, see the Center for Social Media's video, *Remix Culture*: http://www.cmsimpact.org/fair-use/videos/podcasts/remix-culture

3. To explore users' rights in law from nations around the world, consult the work of the Global Expert Network on Copyright Users' Rights online: infojustice.org/flexible-use.

4. Data collection for this account included my personal reflections of class work, artifacts of student work (blog entries about and screen captures of remix assignments), and anonymous surveys on learning outcomes. For each case discussed in this chapter, data analysis sought themes in evidence of student learning in field notes, and in student production choices exhibited in artifacts of student work. Details reported here have been selected anecdotally to illustrate potential benefits and concerns of remix practice for media literacy learning as synthesized from prior scholarship.

5. Although this tool is no longer available, user-friendly online video editing tools are freely available, like Mozilla's *Popcorn Maker*, which encourages remixing content from any source online, inserting text commentary, and sharing remixes—albeit without any centralized collection of media texts nor overt educational objectives as in the *Know the News* tool. However, there are self-contained remix tools available online for educational purposes, like the LAMP's *Mediabreaker*, which encourages critical responses to mainstream media through remixing of user-uploaded video, and allows sharing after the administrators make a fair use determination.

6. On a survey item, most students rated the remix assignment "very effective" for learning about agenda setting (4 on a 5 point scale), including students who did not complete the homework assignment. No student rated it below a 3 for "somewhat" effective.

7. Data for this case were collected through field notes from participant observation, which included recorded conversations with the instructor reflecting on the unit and detailed notes on student remix productions for the assignments.

8. *Rip: A Remix Manifesto* by Brett Gaylor is available at the website http://ripremix.com/

9. Students used video and sound editing software on desktop computers. They all had training and practice in class in using the software prior to this assignment.

10. Data for this report were limited to artifacts of planning sessions and notes from the debriefing session with co-instructors and Girl Scouts troop leaders.

References

American University Center for Media & Social Impact, Media Education Lab at Temple University, & Program on Information Justice and Intellectual Property at the Washington College of Law. (2010). *Code of best practices in fair use for media literacy education.* Washington, DC: American University. Retrieved January 25, 2009 from http://www.centerforsocialmedia.org/resources/publications/code_for_media_literacy_education

Aufderheide, P. (2015). Copyright and fair use in remix: From altruism to action. In E. Navas, O. Gallagher, & X. Burrough (Eds.), *The Routledge companion to remix studies* (pp. 270–82). New York, NY: Routledge.

Barron, B., Gomez, K., Pinkard, N., & Martin, C. (2014). *The digital youth network: Cultivating digital media citizenship in urban communities.* Cambridge, MA: MIT Press.

Benkler, Y. (2006). *The wealth of networks: How social production transforms markets and freedom.* New Haven, CT: Yale University Press.

Blanchard, R. O., & Christ, W. G. (1993). *Media Education & the liberal arts: A blueprint for the new professionalism.* Hillsdale, NJ: Lawrence Erlbaum.

Borschke, M. (2015). The extended remix: Rhetoric and history. In E. Navas, O. Gallagher, & X. Burrough (Eds.), *The Routledge companion to remix studies* (pp. 104–15). New York, NY: Routledge.

Buckingham, D. (2003). *Media education: Literacy, learning, and contemporary culture.* Malden, MA: Polity.

Burwell, C. (2013). The pedagogical potential of video remix: Critical conversations about culture, creativity, and copyright. *Journal of Adolescent and Adult Literacy, 57*(3), 205–13.

Cope, B., & Kalantzis, M. (Eds.). (2000). *Multiliteracies: Literacy learning and the design of social futures.* London, UK: Routledge.

Dubisar, A., & Palmeri, J. (2010). Palin/Pathos/Peter Griffin: Political video remix and composition pedagogy. *Computers & Composition, 27,* 77–93.

Hebdige, D. (1979). *Subculture, the meaning of style.* London, UK: Methuen.

——. (1987). *Cut 'n' mix: Culture, identity and Caribbean music.* London, UK: Comedia.

Hobbs, R. (2004). A review of school-based initiatives in media literacy education. *American Behavioral Scientist, 48*(1), 42–59.

——. (2010). *Copyright clarity: How fair use supports digital learning.* Thousand Oaks, CA: Corwin.

Hobbs, R., Felini, D., & Cappello, G. (2011). Reflections on global developments in media literacy education: Bridging theory and practice. *The Journal of Media Literacy Education, 3*(2), 66–73.

Huq, R. (2006). *Beyond subculture: Pop, youth, and identity in a postcolonial world.* New York, NY: Routledge.

Ito, M. (2009). *Hanging out, messing around, and geeking out.* Cambridge, MA: MIT Press.

Jenkins, H. (1992). *Textual poachers: Television fans & participatory culture.* New York, NY: Routledge.

——. (2006). *Convergence culture: Where old and new media collide.* New York: New York: University Press.

Jenkins, H., Clinton, K., Purushotma, R., Robinson, A. J., & Weigel, M. (2006). *Confronting the challenges of participatory culture: Media education for the 21st century.* Chicago, IL: MacArthur Foundation. Retrieved August 20, 2007 from http://www. digitallearning.macfound.org/

Jenkins, H., & Kelley, W. (2013). *Reading in a participatory culture: Remixing* Moby Dick *in the English classroom.* New York, NY: Teachers College Press.

Kelley, W., Jenkins, H., Clinton, K., & McWilliams, J. (2013). From theory to practice: Building a "community of readers" in your classroom. In H. Jenkins, W. Kelley, K. Clinton, J. McWilliams, & R. Pitts-Wiley (Eds.), *Reading in a participatory culture: Remixing* Moby Dick *in the English classroom* (pp. 25–39). New York, NY: Teachers College Press.

Kraidy, M. (2005). *Hybridity: The cultural logic of globalization.* Philadelphia, PA: Temple University Press.

Lankshear, C., & Knobel, M. (2011). *New literacies: Everyday practices and social learning* (3rd ed.). Maidenhead, UK: Open University Press and McGraw-Hill Education.

Latterell, C. G. (2010). *Remix: Reading and composing culture.* Boston, MA: Bedford/ St. Martin's.

Lenhardt, A., & Madden, M. (2005). *Teen content creators and consumers.* Washington, DC: Pew Internet & American Life Project. Retrieved August 20, 2007 from http:// www.pewInternet.org/PPF/r/166/report_display.asp

Lessig, L. (2004). *Free culture: The nature and future of creativity.* New York, NY: Penguin.

——. (2008). *Remix: Making art and commerce thrive in the hybrid economy.* New York, NY: Penguin.

Long, E. (2015). Mediabreaker: Remix tool to foster the next generation of John Stewarts. *BoingBoing* [Blog post, May 20, 2015]. Retrieved May 22, 2015, from http:// boingboing.net/2015/05/20/mediabreaker-remix-tool-to-fo.html

McCombs, M. E., & Shaw, D. L. (1972). The agenda-setting function of mass media. *Public Opinion Quarterly, 36*(2), 176–87.

McCombs, M. E., Shaw, D. L., & Weaver, D. H. (Eds.). (2013). *Communication and democracy: Exploring the intellectual frontiers in agenda-setting theory.* New York, NY: Routledge.

McLeod, K. (2015). An oral history of sampling: From turntables to mashup. In E. Navas, O. Gallagher, & X. Burrough (Eds.), *The Routledge companion to remix studies* (pp. 83–95). New York, NY: Routledge.

Mihailidis, P. (2011). (Re)mix, (Re)purpose, (Re)learn: Using participatory tools for media literacy learning outcomes in the classroom. *Action in Teacher Education, 33*(2), 172–83.

Navas, E., Gallagher, O., & Burrough, X. (2015). Introduction. In E. Navas, O. Gallagher, & X. Burrough (Eds.), *The Routledge companion to remix studies* (pp. 1–12). New York, NY: Routledge.

RobbGrieco, M. (2014). *Media for media literacy: Discourses of the media literacy education movement in Media & Values magazine*. [Doctoral dissertation, Temple University]. Proquest Dissertations and Theses, doi: 3671948.

Turnbull, S. (1998). Dealing with feeling: Why girl number twenty still doesn't answer. In D. Buckingham (Ed.), *Teaching popular culture: Beyond radical pedagogy* (pp. 88–106). London, UK: UCL Press.

Vasudevan, L. (2010). Literacies in a participatory, multimodal world: The arts and aesthetics of web 2.0. *Language Arts, 88*(1), 43–50.

Williams, B. (2012). The world on your screen: New media, remix, and the politics of cross-cultural contact. In B. Williams & A. Zenger (Eds.), *New media literacies and participatory popular culture across borders* (pp. 17–32). New York, NY: Routledge.

——. (2014). From screen to screen: Students' use of popular culture genres in multimodal writing assignments. *Computers & Composition, 34*, 110–21.

Yancey, K. B. (2009). Re-designing graduate education in composition and rhetoric: The use of remix as concept, material, and method. *Computers in Composition, 26*, 4–12.

6. *Fostering Global Competencies and 21st-Century Skills through Mobile Learning*

KRISTINE SCHARALDI

"One looks back with appreciation to the brilliant teachers, but with gratitude to those who touched our human feelings. The curriculum is so much necessary raw material, but warmth is a vital element for the growing plant and for the soul of the child."

—Carl Jung

Background and Rationale

In our highly digitized society, people are consuming information, communicating with others, capturing and posting images, and interacting with hyperlinked multimedia content through mobile technologies as normal and expected activities throughout the course of the day. Mobile digital devices are ever present and utilized in environments and contexts in new ways as applications and hardware become more customized and accessible. Mobile tools are depended on for dozens of tasks that involve connecting, producing, and sharing for work and play.

Access to mobile technologies for learning is a trend that is showing increasing momentum. Schools and districts are supplying mobile learning devices and wifi networks to support one student per device (1:1), bring your own device (BYOD), and other initiatives that include digital standardized test platforms and blended learning programs. Personal mobile device use is reaching new levels of access according to the latest Speak Up 2014 Research Project led by Project Tomorrow®, a nonprofit organization that seeks to collect and report data reflecting the use of technologies for learning. As reported in the findings in *Digital Learning 24/7: Understanding Technology—Enhanced Learning in the Lives of Today's Students*, 46% of students surveyed in grades 3–5, 68% of students surveyed in grades 6–8, and 82% of students surveyed in grades 9–12 are using smartphones (Project Tomorrow, 2015). Also communicated in the Speak Up 2014 National Research Project findings is that 75% of the youth respondents believe that mobile devices should be in the hands of each student during the school day, with 58% of survey takers already using a personal smartphone during class time. The students who voiced their learning preferences in the 2014 Speak Up survey led Project Tomorrow to conclude that

> today's students are incredibly interested in learning. While they may not always be interested in typical classroom instruction, they are very engaged when learning mirrors the holy trinity of the student vision for a 21st century educational experience: learning that is socially-based and collaborative, learning that is untethered from the traditional constraints or limitations of education institutions, and learning that is digitally rich in context and relevancy. (Project Tomorrow, 2015, p.15)

Along with the growing interest, availability, and usefulness of mobile digital tools in the hands of school-aged youth, there is also a rise in the ability for students to consume, create, and participate in media-rich online spaces. Mobile devices, and the applications that are usable on them, are advancing in terms of features and connectivity. As mobile technologies continue to evolve, it is more and more common for smartphones, tablets, and ebook readers to have built-in cameras that can capture images and video, and microphones that can record audio. Most mobile devices are capable of joining networks via cellular or wifi connectivity that is offered in locations including libraries, shopping centers, eateries, homes, and other places. Since the devices are connecting to the World Wide Web, various social networks are accessible for youth to interact with, such as text messaging, Twitter, Instagram, YouTube, and Vine. Whether it is reading or viewing information shared by others or producing and uploading messages with visuals and captions, students are engaging with media regularly from many sources. The need for parents and educators to address new skills and literacies is becoming more necessary.

How can educators help develop students' skills and mindsets to engage successfully in social networks and learning spaces both physical and digital, local and global? And ultimately, what is the aim of modern curriculum and the integration of technologies into school-based instruction and learning? It is clear that in these times of on-demand and instant access to a wealth of information in various forms, including text, visual, audio, and video, the methods of instruction, assessment, and delivery of content are shifting. Learning materials are plentiful, varied, and crowd-sourced. Connecting to people can now happen with a few finger taps on a screen. Teachers and books are no longer the predominant sources of knowledge. Educators, then, are challenged to design learning experiences that serve to go beyond students' building of knowledge to a realm of meaningful connections, skills, and understandings that are "lifeworthy" (Perkins, 2014).

A report by the World Economic Forum entitled "New Vision for Education: Unlocking the Potential of Technology" (2015) states:

> To thrive in a rapidly evolving, technology-mediated world, students must not only possess strong skills in areas such as language arts, mathematics and science, but they must also be adept at skills such as critical thinking, problem-solving, persistence, collaboration and curiosity.

The World Economic Forum has organized what are collectively referred to as 21st-century skills into three categories: *foundational literacies*, which comprise core content and literacies; *competencies*, such as creativity and collaboration; and *character qualities*, including cultural awareness, adaptability, and leadership. Social-emotional learning and character education are also being emphasized in modern curricula through anti-bullying, anti-discrimination, and other similar programs that are being mandated in some states (New Jersey Revised Statutes, 2013). Empathy is being recognized as a desirable skill in educational and business domains (Townsend, 2012), as is the importance of the "whole child" approach (ASCD, 2015).

In order to address the cognitive and affective skills of students while supporting standards-based learning objectives, several frameworks and models have been developed by organizations to assist educators in designing units and lesson activities. Universal Design for Learning (UDL), described in more detail in another chapter in this publication, is one such framework that outlines key considerations in applying understanding of brain networks to provide multiple means of engagement, representation, action, and expression (CAST, 2015).

Another model to help guide educators in modern learning design is the global competency model. Created as part of the Council of Chief State School Officers' EdSteps Project, in conjunction with the Asia Society Partnership for Global Learning, this model outlines four key dimensions of global competence: *investigating the world*, *recognizing* and *weighing perspectives*, *communicating ideas*, and *taking action* (Asia Society, 2010). The development of these competencies is concurrent with the building of content area knowledge and applying that knowledge to deepen understandings. Global education offers an excellent starting point for implementing project- and inquiry-based approaches that provide opportunities for students to have ownership in the learning process. By engaging students in interdisciplinary learning that offers rich experiences to explore, analyze, share, and act on ideas of real-world significance, educators can foster a sense of purpose in our young people so they do not just care about issues but feel empowered to take steps to make a difference.

Mobile Technologies that Support Global Competence and 21st-Century Skill Development

There are many technology tools and applications that can be utilized for educational activities that foster global competence and the development of 21st-century skills. In this section we will explore the potential of using web-based platforms, such as news and video sites, that can be accessed from Internet-connected mobile devices. Example projects and recommended strategies will also be shared.

News and Current Events as Entry Points

One web-based resource that provides access to news and stories from around the world is Newspapermap.com. The website home page is a world map with colored icons pinpointing the locations of digital newspapers. This screen is an excellent starting point for an exercise in which to have students participate to help them expand their global awareness. Teachers can pose questions such as "What do you notice?" The icons are color-coded by language. For example, a view of North America shows yellow icons saturating the middle of the continent that represent the newspapers that are published in English, red icons that represent Spanish newspapers mostly in the south of the continent, and white icons that represent French newspapers in some patches of northern areas. While not all newspapers in the world are indexed in this effort, it is useful for discovering patterns in geography and languages that are displayed. Having the map-view navigation allows interaction between locations and information and will likely introduce users to new places and their languages.

It is amazingly simple to access current editions of newspapers from worldwide locales by tapping on the icon and then the name of the newspaper. A translation tool immediately provides a version of the text in the chosen language. The screen of content that was once not understandable quickly becomes readable and accessible for the user. There is no download needed to interact with this website, and the translation tools and content can be accessed on any Internet-connected device for free.

There are ample learning opportunities available in conjunction with online applications like Newspapermap.com that foster the development of 21st-century skills and global competence. Students are able to read local news stories from different locations about various topics, from current events to sports, and may make comparisons between their own experiences and those that can now be accessed. Also, students can learn about perspectives published from people all over the world that can help inform and deepen understanding of issues and stories of concern. Students can predict and analyze which stories are newsworthy in different locations and why, thus developing understanding of the cultural, political, and other influences on published news. With an inquiry-based approach students are encouraged to drive the investigation of these topics, allowing them to tap into their curiosities and connect with content in meaningful ways. A site like this makes it easy to feel connected to the global community and a part of the larger society of world citizens whose struggles and accomplishments are brought closer, thus cultivating empathy and new possibilities for opening students' hearts and minds.

Another online provider of news articles and digital nonfiction stories is Newsela.com. This web-based platform offers daily news articles and access to the archives of published stories on broad topics such as war and peace, science, law, health, arts, and sports. Newsela has licensing agreements with content providers including the Associated Press and Scientific American. Every weekday there are three new articles posted on the Newsela home page that are added to the growing archive of over 1,000 stories. There are search options that allow users to find articles by key word, recommended grade level, and specific reading standard. Once an article is selected the user has the option of choosing to read it as originally published or tapping on a button to choose one of four additional versions that have been rewritten by Newsela journalists at different reading levels. The content of every article is available in five versions that range from approximately second grade reading level through adult, using Lexile measures of readability.

Newsela offers additional features for educators and students to use when engaging with the site. Some are free and others are offered only to paid subscribers to Newsela PRO. Two free features are Newsela Elementary and Text Sets. Newsela Elementary offers an entry point to articles that are appropriate for students in the younger grades, removing access to stories in the Newsela archives that have more sophisticated themes. Text Sets are collections of articles on selected topics and make it easier for readers to follow stories and issues over time. Text Sets are accessible right from the Newsela home page and include topics such as "Innovation and Problem Solving," "Slavery and

Human Trafficking," "A Healthier World," and "Making Cultural Ripples." There are also Text Sets for Literature that make connections from current news stories to over 99 literary works read by students such as *The Lightning Thief*, *Number the Stars*, *Walk Two Moons*, and *Things Fall Apart*. PRO features include the ability of teachers to assign particular articles to their students, have students demonstrate comprehension of texts through quizzes and writing prompts, and use annotations such as highlighting and commenting to interact and engage more deeply with the text. Teachers and school administrators can view and analyze student responses and data to better understand and support learners' progress and needs.

For teachers of students in grades 2–12, there are a number of great opportunities that a service like Newsela can provide. One main benefit is the ease with which all students can engage in reading the same article content at each individual's comfortable level. Since students bring in their own unique skills and experiences to the classroom due to a number of factors, there is typically a variation in not only the reading level but also the background knowledge that each learner will have on a particular topic. Newsela's articles that are rewritten for different reading levels take into account the vocabulary, sentence structure, and other demands on the reader and provide easy access to a simpler or more complex version of the text with one simple tap on the screen. It is challenging for teachers to find flexible, nonfiction content that can support cross-curricular and timely topics and also appeal to students for informational and self-selected reading. Newsela provides this all through one website.

From posts on the Newsela blog, it is apparent that students are not only consuming media but also taking action after reading about stories that have meaning for them. One example of this is described in the blog post about a fifth grade class in California that viewed an article about a law forcing migrant workers to relocate after the end of the growing season. The blog post (Newsela, 2015a) describes how the students were so interested in this topic that they chose to miss their holiday party so they were able to read and talk about the article. The students felt that the law caused difficulties for the migrant families, and as a result they composed a letter to the California State Department of Housing and Community Development describing their concerns. A follow up post on the Newsela Blog (2015b) shares an update on this story that includes a letter from a California state official who responds to the class and shares additional information. Another result is that the students themselves became the subject of news media by having articles written about their story (Austin, 2015). This illustrates the real-world experiences that young people are able not only to learn about and participate in, but also to initiate and produce, and therefore develop 21st-century literacies in authentic and meaningful contexts.

Both Newspapermap.com and Newsela.com offer increased opportunities for users to access and engage with contemporary global content. Expanded sources and customized tools such as translation and reading level adjustment remove some of the traditional barriers to incorporating printed media resources. It is now possible for educators to find relevant content and media to support rich learning experiences for students to not only learn about the world but also to ask questions, want answers, make discoveries, and become active and concerned global citizens.

Video Content, Creation, and Sharing

The popularity of using video to bolster learning is enabled by increased access to the tools to consume, create, access, and share multimedia content. While there are many websites that store and provide access to video content, the most well-known and accessed site is YouTube. YouTube is a global hub of media for entertainment and learning, with millions of videos freely shared through its channels. YouTube provides unprecedented opportunities to consume multimedia messages put out by a wide variety of sources, perspectives, and motivations, and to upload original media content to push out to anyone in a worldwide audience who chooses to watch.

For educational purposes there are very few online sites that are utilized as much as YouTube by learners. YouTube allows people to learn informally, on demand, and wherever they are with mobile devices. Many videos that are posted are by amateur experts and enthusiasts who enjoy sharing their passion and helping others. Schools, teachers, educational providers, and individuals are creating YouTube channels and sharing multimedia content with students, parents, community members, and interested viewers.

In addition to YouTube, there are many more ways learners are interacting with videos through web-based providers, subscription services, and social media. There are increased opportunities and ease by which to incorporate live-streamed and on-demand shows, movies, episodes, recorded events, talks, and so much more for learning goals. One of the popular platforms is TED Talks. TED speakers hail from all over the world and present talks to share ideas on a myriad of subjects and to inform and inspire people. For teachers who want to infuse lessons with videos there is TedEd, a free platform that allows educators to use digital tools and resources to engage students with TED Talks as well as videos from YouTube. Once teachers have signed up for a free TED-Ed account, they have the ability to search the

TED-Ed library of digital lessons and use an existing one or create their own customized lesson. The TED-Ed activity for students includes a window to watch the video, prompts to help the student think about the content with context supplied by the lesson author, multiple choice and short answer questions, and sections for discussion and reflection. Using this platform, teachers can incorporate video content created by their preferred source, which could also be their own multimedia, and share the online experience with their students and the rest of the TED-Ed community.

One TED Talk, in particular, has been used by educators to help learners think about stereotypes and the role that media play in how people view others. Recorded at TEDGlobal 2009, novelist Chimamanda Ngozi Adichie talks about "the danger of a single story" (Adichie, 2009). Her words powerfully communicate her experiences and realizations about how narrow the portrayals of others are when there is a lack of diversity in the messages shared. She describes "how to create a single story, show a people as one thing, as only one thing, over and over again, and that is what they become" (Adichie, 2009). Showing Adichie's TED Talk during professional learning sessions that I have facilitated in the United States has sparked interesting reflections, discussions, and takeaways. Participant reactions include a female educator who wears a head covering sharing the experiences that she has had, and a high school teacher telling the story of a student in her class who came to the United States from another country seeking political asylum and how the other students have related to him. The video and conversations have been excellent starting points for using the lens of global education to drive content and skills learning.

Born out of the ideas from this TED Talk, two community arts groups, one in Detroit and the other in Washington, DC, created and led The 524 Project over a three-month period in spring 2014, with a driving question: "How can we as educators use the tools of connected learning to empower students to take their stories into their own hands and speak out on behalf of the places and people they call home?" (Gilliland, 2014). In this collaborative project, a high school class from Detroit and a high school class from Washington, DC partnered to learn about their cities and share their stories with the use of mobile digital tools. With the guidance of their community arts educators, students in the classes researched the histories and local stories of both cities and participated in activities that incorporated writing, poetry, film-making, and performance. Students used iPads to produce videos and participate in live videoconference exchanges to get to know each other and communicate their ideas and insights. At the end of the project, both classes and their communities came together for a live, simultaneous broadcast of their work that was also recorded and shared on YouTube. The feedback and results from the project experience show the teens' shifts in thinking, and also reveal the personal connections that the students made. This is an example of an exemplary project that puts students' voices at the center, giving them opportunities to use new tools and methods to create and engage in learning experiences to help promote new understandings.

Mobile movie-making technologies give students and teachers the tools needed to produce their own media for various purposes. Most smartphones and tablets are equipped with high-quality cameras that record still and moving images. Microphones are built in to the devices and can also be easily plugged in to achieve improved sound quality. Picture, video, and sound recordings are saved right on the device and may also be sent to an online storage account such as Dropbox, Google Drive, or iCloud. There are a number of applications that allow users to edit and enhance their digital work and put media elements together to form movies and digital stories. Examples of applications that provide the ability to produce customized movies include iMovie, Videolicious, and Animoto.

Educators have many options to consider when implementing video-based projects that support the development of 21st-century skills and global capacities. Students can create documentaries, news broadcasts, skits, commercials, public service announcements, and other creative forms of digital storytelling. When planning a project, key components include determining the intended audience and the purpose of the media message. Is the movie aiming to share a persuasive message, to encourage taking action to help a cause? A story that will build empathy and communicate a powerful idea to shift thinking? Projects can be individual or carried out in groups of various sizes. Each student does not necessarily have to have his or her own device, and it is not necessarily better to have access to more devices. When students think of their own ways to execute their projects, by taking into account the resources they have, including human, technical, and content-related, desired skills and competencies for the 21st century are fostered in the process. Collaborative projects may include contributors from other locations who can participate and connect through social sharing platforms. Upon completion of the movies, teachers can display them on a screen or interactive whiteboard for the class to view together and reflect on the process and finished products. Produced media may also be posted on the class and school website, blog, or YouTube channel. Teachers must be sure to secure permissions for students' privacy by school leadership and parents when sharing images and names on the Internet. Some educators face challenges when trying to get approvals for online dissemination of student work. It is helpful to connect with and learn from those who have successfully used policies and informative measures to ensure student safety while publishing their work online. Once any barriers are overcome, giving students the opportunity to have authentic audiences beyond their school expands the possibilities for exchanging ideas and engaging as global citizens.

A motivating and exciting way to involve students in video production is through competitions. The nonprofit organization Next Vista for Learning regularly hosts movie-making contests. A current contest promoted on the website (http://www.nextvista.org) is the Service via Video Project. This competition encourages youth from all over the world to submit video stories about members of their communities who are serving others. Guidelines, rules, and resources are provided on the website for those who want their videos entered in the contest. Videos selected by judges as finalists are promoted on the site for a worldwide audience to view, and winners receive prizes and funds donated to their causes. Contests like these offer benefits to those creating and submitting the videos, as well as the audience watching the movies. Students producing the videos have a real-world purpose and goal to achieve, and knowing that the project is for the public typically adds motivation to produce high-quality work. And the viewers benefit from new information, perspectives, and insights gained through others' personal experiences.

The Next Vista for Learning website hosts a growing video library that includes past contest submissions and educationally-focused content produced by students and teachers. All of the movies on the site are previewed and geared to a school-aged audience. Some of the specific categories include "The Seeing Service Collection," videos about people doing good and charitable deeds; "The Global Views Collection," movies produced in different regions that can help students better understand many different places around the world; and "Light Bulbs," short videos offered on a wide variety of topics such as careers, culture, world languages, and science. Some of the ways teachers are incorporating these types of videos are to provide entry points for discussion and writing, to introduce new perspectives from people who have passions and ideas to share, and to inspire their students by watching others take action and helping others.

Viewing and creating multimedia offers exciting opportunities to learn and share ideas. Free video content providers and movie creation tools support dynamic ways to engage learners. Educators and students can use media to develop thinking skills, advance understandings, and bring learning to life.

Conclusion

The development of modern literacies and skills in today's students is increasingly important to prepare them for success as world citizens and next-generation workers. Building understanding of core content while fostering 21st-century skills and global competencies can be achieved within the contexts of authentic, transdisciplinary themes that engage students with real world problems and tools. Mobile technologies used to connect people and ideas, and to create media for sharing perspectives, can offer exciting possibilities for learning, and empower students in meaningful learning endeavors.

References

Adichie, C. N. (2009, July 23). Chimamanda Ngozi Adichie: The danger of a single story [Video file] Retrieved from http://www.ted.com/talks/chimamanda_adichie_the_danger_of_a_single_story?language=en

ASCD. (2015, June 3). *The whole child*. Retrieved June 3, 2015, from http://www.wholechildeducation.org/

Asia Society. (2010). *Ready for the world: Preparing elementary students for the global age*. Retrieved from http://asiasociety.org/files/Ready%20for%20the%20World.pdf

Austin, N. (2015). On campus: Breaking news—no, just making it over for next edition on Facebook, school desks. *The Modesto Bee*. Retrieved May 31, 2015, from http://www.modbee.com/news/local/education/nan-austin/article21013797.html

Boix Mansilla, V., & Jackson, A. (2011). *Educating for global competence: Preparing our youth to engage the world*. Asia Society and Council of Chief State School Officers. Retrieved from http://asiasociety.org/files/book-globalcompetence.pdf

Buturian, L., & Solheim, C. (2012). *Digital media: Giving voice to students and fostering global learning*. The Board of Regents of the University of Wisconsin System. Retrieved May 30, 2015, from http://www.uwex.edu/disted/conference/Resource_library/proceedings/63428_2012.pdf

CAST. (2015, June 3). *About universal design for learning*. Retrieved from http://www.cast.org/our-work/about-udl.html#.VW8eC2RVhBc

Gilliland, J. (2014). iPads and arts education: Rewriting cultural narratives with The 524 Project. Retrieved May 31, 2015, from http://www.edutopia.org/blog/ipads-arts-education-524-project-jeff-gilliland

Jacobs, H. H. (Fall 2014). Activating digital-media-global literacies and learning. *Independent School Magazine*. Retrieved May 23, 2015, from http://www.nais.org/magazines-newsletters/ismagazine/pages/activating.aspx

New Jersey Revised Statutes. (2013). Instruction on Holocaust, genocides required in elementary, secondary school curriculum. NJ Rev Stat § 18A: 35–28.

Newsela. (2015a). *How Newsela inspired Janet Jeffries' 5th graders to become activists.* Newsela Blog. Retrieved May 31, 2015, from http://blog.newsela.com/2015/05/08/how-newsela-inspired-janet-jeffries-5th-graders-to-become-ac
tivists

———. (2015b). *An update from Watsonville.* Newsela Blog. Retrieved May 31, 2015, from http://blog.newsela.com/2015/05/29/inspiring-students-to-take-action

Perkins, D. (2014). *Future wise: Educating our children for a changing world.* San Francisco, CA: John Wiley & Sons.

Project Tomorrow. (2014). *Ten things everyone should know about K–12 students' digital learning.* Retrieved May 29, 2015, from http://www.tomorrow.org/speakup/pdfs/SU14_Flyer_StudentTop10_Print.pdf

———. (2015). *Speak up: Digital learning 24/7: Understanding technology-enhanced learning in the lives of today's students. Speak Up 2014 national findings from K–12 students.* Retrieved May 29, 2015, from http://www.tomorrow.org/speakup/pdfs/SU14S-tudentReport.pdf

Townsend, J. C. (2012). Why we should teach empathy to improve education (and test scores). *Forbes online.* Retrieved June 2, 2015, from http://www.forbes.com/sites/ashoka/2012/09/26/why-we-should-teach-empathy-to-improve-education-and-test-scores/

World Economic Forum. (2015). New vision for education: Unlocking the potential of technology. Retrieved June 2, 2015, from http://www.weforum.org/reports/new-vision-education-unlocking-potential-technology

7. *Enhancing Media Literacy in Bosnia and Herzegovina: Toward Utilization of IT Tools in Teaching Media and Digital Literacy*

Vanja Ibrahimbegović-Tihak

Introduction

Media literacy education for the 21st century should be about teaching citizens to be active participants in society by becoming critical, analytical thinkers, able to evaluate, re-think, and question, as well as use media to express themselves creatively. It should incorporate new technologies in the learning process—which, among other things, would challenge education in Bosnia and Herzegovina as we know it.

In the Bosnia-Herzegovina (B-H) education system, media (traditional or digital) are hardly a part of the curricula (Ibrahimbegović-Tihak, 2015; Tajić, 2013). The research and empirical data on almost all aspects of media literacy issues are very modest. Teachers' training on digital and media literacy skills has never been provided and is not commonly available now. In the old approach to teaching—in which no or a limited amount of questions are welcome—the teachers play the role of information giver, and the students are expected to reproduce the information in the form in which it was given to them. This approach to teaching still dominates the elementary as well as high school classrooms in B-H (Ibrahimbegović-Tihak, 2015).

The introduction of media and digital literacy in the B-H curricula has the potential to transform the stagnant education system in B-H into one promoting critical thinking, questioning authority, and problem solving skills, by teaching students to be creative, effective communicators using media and ICT. It would also ensure that they are analytical and critical toward media content. In other words, media and digital literacy education in B-H provides a chance for the education system in B-H to democratize itself, which would result in (further) democratizing the society as a whole.

In this context, this paper examines the current conditions under which media literacy education takes place in B-H, exploring the elementary school teachers' skills in media and digital literacy, and elementary school students' media use for education purposes. In the second part of the paper, two case studies regarding the use of digital technology in B-H schools are presented and briefly analyzed, in an attempt to point to opportunities for advancing this practice.

The sources used are comprised of limited available research and analysis on B-H media education and digital technology use in schools, interviews with educational policy makers, and primary research (a survey) on the elementary schools teachers' media and digital skills and their use of media and ICT in the classrooms. In addition, the current work on media literacy education by European and U.S. authors has been consulted, in order to put this chapter into a comparative perspective and position B-H in the global context.

The mentioned survey was conducted among 202 elementary school teachers from 19 schools in 19 cities[1] all around B-H. The survey participants were not selected by a random sampling. They were participating at the USAID-funded Teachers' Training Program within the Education for Social Justice Project. The Project is implemented by the Center for Educational Initiatives Step by Step. Therefore, the surveyed teachers do not represent the average teachers of elementary schools in B-H. Rather, they belong to a selection of highly motivated teachers, as they applied for the non-obligatory, in-service education program and passed the selection process. This fact should be kept in mind when generalizing the survey results and making assumptions regarding the whole population of teachers.

Background Information on Bosnia-Herzegovina and Its Education Development Environment

Bosnia-Herzegovina is a country located in the southern part of the European continent, in the heart of the Balkans peninsula. It is an ethnically diverse country, with three main ethnic groups: Bosniaks, who are Muslims; Serbs, who are Orthodox Christians; and Croats, who are Catholics. It is populated by around 3.8 million inhabitants,[2] and is still recovering from a severe interethnic conflict that came about after the dissolution of Yugoslavia in the early 1990s.

The current political system of B-H came into place as a part of a conflict resolution mechanism—the Dayton Peace Agreement—signed in December 1995 in Dayton, Ohio, which includes the country's constitution. The peace agreement, including the constitution, was created by international community representatives, and accepted as a compromise solution by all sides involved in the war: representatives of the three ethnic groups from B-H, and representatives of neighboring countries Serbia and Croatia. The "Dayton Constitution" sets up a highly decentralized political system of power sharing, in order to accommodate the interethnic conflict, as well as to keep the country together. The disproportionally extensive bureaucratic apparatus—the result of the power sharing system—which is additionally burdened by corruption, has proven itself to be an obstacle for any progress in the state- and democracy-building process that has been underway for the last 20 years.

How does this translate into the educational system(s) and educational policy? There are 14 ministries in B-H with jurisdiction over education—namely, the state-level Ministry of Civil Affairs, which plays a general, coordinating role, and two Entities Ministries for Education and Science, which have several key differences in scope of responsibilities.

The Ministry of the Republic of Srpska acts as a central body for the whole area, whereas the Ministry of Education and Science of B-H Federation has more of a coordinating role among 10 cantonal ministries of education. In the Federation, cantons hold the real power over the education process. In addition, the Brčko District has its own government, with a section for education.

In terms of legal framework, there is a Framework Law on Primary and Secondary Education at the state level. Accordingly, each entity, district, and canton has its own laws regulating education. In theory, they should be synchronized. In practice, they often are not. Similarly, the law enforcement agencies are often not well coordinated themselves.

According to Nadija Bandić, the Federal Ministry of Education Official, the coordination role among the cantonal ministries represents a serious limitation to the jurisdiction of the Federal Ministry. She emphasizes the problem of lack of expertise in the field of media literacy in the governmental education institutions. She sees partnering with the emerging experts operating outside of the formal education system as the solution to this problem (Interview, March 14, 2014).

The lack of coordination between the educational institutions has resulted in many vastly different educational practices across B-H. In addition, according to Magill, the complex educational policy structure has had negative effects on the professional advancement of teachers, because it is done on

12 different levels (Republic of Srpska, 10 cantons, and Brčko District—the state- or federal-level institutions do not have jurisdiction here). This is why it is difficult to give an overarching comment on the quality of training for teachers, when it comes to media education (Magill, 2010).

Marija Naletilić, a representative of the educational policy-making body the Agency for Development of Primary and Secondary Education of B-H (APOSO),[3] is in agreement with this judgment. Naletilić, the head of the Common Core Curricula Department of APOSO, was asked about teachers' training in regards to media and digital literacy skills. The most encouraging part of her answer had to do with awareness of the importance of teachers' training issues in regards to media and digital skills, within the institution she is representing. However, no concrete action is taking place to address it. Naletilić explained that the agency has formed a working group composed of experts from schools and pedagogy institutes to develop Guidelines for the Continued Professional Development of Teachers, which would enable the path toward a quality education in B-H (Interview, March 3, 2014). However, no practical verification of the commitment to move on systematic teachers' training in media and digital literacy is evident.

Elementary School Teachers' Competencies in Media and Digital Literacy

The skills of teachers will be evaluated here on the grounds of the survey conducted among the 202 teachers from 19 cities across Bosnia and Herzegovina, and other available research. The survey was aimed at understanding teachers' media habits on a day-to-day level, as well as their media use in the classrooms. Those skills will be examined against students' skills and media habits, mapping the discrepancy between the two groups.

Surveyed teachers were asked to evaluate their own media literacy skills. Ninety-one percent of them explicitly stated that they needed and wished for more information and training in the field, before they would feel comfortable using it in the classroom.

The teachers were asked to assess the frequency (once a day, at least once a week, less than once a week, never, or I don't know) of their interactions with different media (watching TV, listening to radio, reading the press, reading books, going to the cinema, using smartphones, browsing the Internet using smartphones, browsing the Internet using computers or tablets), within the three months prior to answering the survey questions.

The survey results demonstrate that TV is the primary daily-used media among the respondents. Seventy-three percent of them use it every day. On the other hand, 49% responded that they used the Internet every day, accessing it via computer or tablet, whereas 41.6% said they have been accessing the Internet on a daily basis via smartphone. The survey shows that over one quarter of respondents (26.5%) have not used the Internet via smartphones.

In terms of using media as a news source, this survey's results are in line with other available research for B-H (Džihana, Ćendić, & Tahmaz, 2012). Namely, TV again dominates as a news source, but web portals and social networks (mainly Facebook, with 65% users among the respondents, followed by Twitter, with 10% users within the surveyed group of teachers) are becoming more and more utilized for this purpose as well.

The research on children's media habits in B-H is rather limited. The study ordered by the state Ministry of Security and supported by Save the Children International looked into school children's behavior online, in order to evaluate some government programs directed to online security[4] (Muratbegović, Mujanović, & Kepeš, 2013).

Using focus groups, the study was aimed at assessing the Internet use habits among elementary and secondary school pupils in B-H. The research showed that 90% of children and youth aged 7–18 with access to the Internet use it for their own purposes. Asked what those purposes are, most of them (46.2%) answered schoolwork. The second-ranked response (30%) was "to communicate with friends." The same study points to Facebook as the most-used social network among this group. All of the children and youth aged 7–18 who participated in these focus groups use Facebook (Muratbegović, Mujanović, & Kepeš, 2013).

Moreover, the students emphasized that they had no formal (nor informal) training on Internet use in school, neither instructions for the use of technology nor for the development of critical attitude toward digital media content and potential risks (Criminal Policy Research Centre, 2013).

The survey also explored the teachers' PC gaming skills and/or habits, in the light of the contemporary educational practice trend of including PC games in the education process. At the annual Media and Learning Conference, in Brussels in November 2014,[5] PC gaming was the hottest topic. The majority of presented and awarded projects focused on gaming as an educational tool.

Similarly, the 2015 conference Media Meets Literacy in Warsaw focused on presenting positive practices in teaching media literacy across Europe, also putting the spotlight on educational games, awarding first and second prizes for best educational media and digital practices to two games: one for primary education,[6] and one aimed at older learners dealing with online privacy issues.[7]

The survey results however show that in B-H this trend is not followed. Around 56% of survey respondents did not use PC games at all in the three months prior to participation in the survey. Therefore, the readiness of the majority of B-H teachers to engage in "technological challenge in the classroom," in the current environment, seems rather questionable.

The teachers' and students' media habits, especially the use of ICT and social media as presented above, should be given a closer look, in order properly to address the training and education needs of both groups. This task asks for more comprehensive research, specifically targeted. However, in terms of social media use, it seems that Facebook could be a starting point for uniting these two groups in the "digital learning process."

Regarding media use in the classrooms, the survey showed unsatisfactory results, even for the use of traditional media. Though 87% of surveyed teachers find it possible and desirable to use media in their work, not many of them have actually used it. The survey showed that 22% of respondents used TV programs in the classroom in the school year 2013–14, whereas 21% used newspapers. Regarding the frequency in both cases, all of the respondents stated that they used media for 1–5 classes throughout the year.

The teachers were also asked how often (always, often, sometimes, never) they encourage their students to use ICT for learning and research. Only 12% of them responded always; 46.3% responded often; 37% responded sometimes; and 4.2% of surveyed teachers said they never encourage their students to use ICT for educational purposes.

Furthermore, according to the survey, 40.6% of respondents had never used the Internet during their classroom work. This fact is even more disturbing, knowing that all the schools the surveyed teachers work for have Internet access. Moreover, as it emerged in conversations with respondents, schools tend not to allow Internet access to students. The access is coded and the passwords are given to the staff only.

The majority of surveyed teachers consider this a good practice. The general attitude was that if children were granted access, it would distract them from class. The fact that the majority of teachers did not even consider the possibility of taking advantage of it to use in class, is rather alarming. It points to a shortage of up-to-date perspective on the learning process, and to issues with the education system.

According to Elisabeth Thoman and Tessa Jolls, the new technologies are "challenging the very foundation of education" (Thoman & Jolls, 2008). The role of teachers in the 21st century is radically changed in comparison to 19th- and 20th-century teachers' roles. Earlier, the teachers were information and knowledge sources, not unlike textbooks as a source for learning. Not anymore. Today, children and youth, but also adults, need the ability to both "critically interpret the powerful images of a multimedia culture and express themselves in multiple media forms" (Thoman & Jolls, 2008).

Thus, the role of teachers becomes ensuring that students gain the critical process skills to confront the information overload of today's information society. Their role is to help their students reach a new literacy, needed for living, working, and being a citizen in the 21st century. This includes mastering the skills of lifelong learning (Thoman & Jolls, 2008). According to the attitudes of surveyed teachers from B-H, as well as their current skills, they don't seem ready to respond adequately to today's challenges to education.

Several Issues to Be Emphasized

The teachers recognize the importance of media use in the classrooms, as well as being aware of its insufficient presence at the moment. They, just like their students, do acknowledge the need for additional education in this regard. The vast majority of teachers predominantly use traditional media. Though there is a visible trend of increase in the use of ICT, their digital skills are not adequate to respond to the needs of their students belonging to the 2.0 generation.

Therefore, an urgent issue for the education policy in B-H is to create a systematic solution in terms of bridging the gap between the digital skills of teachers and students, and equipping current as well as future teachers to be competent, media- and digitally literate citizens and teachers of the 21st century. However, the interviews with the policy makers at different levels of B-H government did not provide much reassurance that this important issue is being taken seriously.

Charting Media and Learning in Europe, the series of three annual reports that are part of the European Commission-funded MEDEA.net project, has been dealing with the question how media is used to support teaching and learning in different parts of Europe from 2012 to 2014. The third report (2014) was focused on teachers' training in the seven European countries[8] participating in the project. This report's findings show that even much more developed countries than Bosnia and Herzegovina are also struggling with the issue of setting up efficient teachers' training systems to include media in education (Vos & Terryin, 2014).

The report says that although more and more attention is given to media literacy and media-based learning in various countries, it was discovered that future teachers are not (yet) trained in exploiting the potential of media in education. Overall, high-quality teacher training is crucial to make sure a large number of future teachers know how to integrate media (literacy) in their daily teaching practice, to enable them to act as change-makers in education. This is, however, an ongoing process (Vos & Terryin, 2014).

The Use of ICT in B-H Schools Despite the Curricular Obstacles

Lea Tajić's analysis on media literacy in B-H shows that media education represented in the curricula for the primary and secondary education is insufficient. For instance, media literacy as such does not appear in primary or secondary school curricula. It is somewhat represented within other subjects. In primary schools it is to a limited extent taught under the name of media culture, within the curricula of Bosnian/Serbian/Croatian language. In secondary schools, some elements of it can be found within information and computer science programs (Ibrahimović, 2015; Tajić, 2013).

Content-wise in primary schools, the teaching of media culture does not go beyond discussing film, theater, TV shows, and literature. The focus is on understanding the language that respective media use. Other important aspects for the development of media literacy skills, such as access to different media content, critical approach to it, and the development and production of media content, are completely neglected. Internet, social media, and ICT in general are not even mentioned within the subject of media culture (Tajić, 2013). However, despite the out-of-date curricula that fairly consistently ignore ICT, there are two optimistic examples of different models of introducing ICT in primary educational practice in different parts of Bosnia and Herzegovina. These were developed from two different approaches.

Case 1: The School of the Future Project with the Sarajevo Canton and Microsoft

Several years ago, an enthusiastic and a tech savvy elementary school teacher Dzenita Arbak Demir, along with a fellow teacher, decided to change something in her day-to-day teaching. The intention was to influence the way students have been using technology. According to Demir's testimonial, up to that point it was limited to social media and (not educational) PC games.

The idea for the School of the Future Project came after Demir learned about the SOLE (Self-Organized Learning Environment) concept of education, created by Sugata Mitra. This is a learning process led by child learners, using online tools for self-organized, motivated, socially engaged, and team-based work, searching for answers to "big questions." A small group of four learners uses one connected device. They choose the group, and a question to research. They can move freely, look at what other groups are doing, and use that information in their group, and at the end each group shares its findings. The teacher's role is to support the group work and provide the structure, not the answers. This approach encourages children's natural curiosity; supports students' critical thinking, communication, and information search skills; and helps develop self-confidence. Learners are more motivated and collaborative, and the learning process becomes fun (Mitra, 2013).

Demir piloted a SOLE-based class with her students in an improvised environment, using the modest technical equipment the school had at the time:

> The SOLE concept has proved itself a great success. It was interesting and good not only for our students, who were more motivated than usual, but also for the teachers. We ended up strengthen our own capacities, as we had to learn new methodology to teach our classes this way. All of this happens without changing the current curriculum; it actually fits very well into our current educational goals. And it saves resources: time and financial. (Interview, April 21, 2015)

After this pilot, the Ministry of Education of Sarajevo Canton approved the method and supported the idea in principle, but no funding was available. Nonetheless, the idea was recognized as worth funding by private, for-profit companies. Funding was secured from Microsoft.[9] The project, named "The School of the Future," was expanded to eight other schools in the Sarajevo Canton (nine in total), which received technology donations (hardware, including one laptop and four tablets per school, and software). This meant equipping one e-classroom per school. In addition, the School of the Future project includes training of educators who will be implementing the School of the Future project based on the SOLE concept.

The project has officially been launched in April 2015. All participants in the program are obligated to do a SOLE-based class twice a month, and post about it on SharePoint and Yammer for the purpose of implementation and impact monitoring.

Case 2: The Dositej Project in the Republic of Srpska: A top-down approach

This project represents an attempt, in at least one part of Bosnia and Herzegovina, systematically to integrate the use of ICT in primary school education, introduced by the Ministry of Education and Culture of the Republic of Srpska (RS). It has been implemented in the primary schools of RS, which includes 49% of B-H territory, since 2012, when the first stage was completed and 65 schools were newly equipped. By November 2014, the second stage was completed and another 60 schools had received new IT equipment. The RS Ministry of Education and Culture, with the local IT company, has thus far equipped 125 out of 187 primary schools in this part of the country, according to the official RS government website.

"The Dositej Project," as it is called, provides technology (hardware and software) that supports one-to-one e-learning, in which each learner has the use of a connected device or laptop, and each e-classroom has 20–25 devices. This process is controlled by the teacher, who is able to see from his or her device what each of the learners is doing on- or offline. The teachers have the power to disconnect any of the students' devices in any given moment. The system also enables easier scoring of tests, recording student attendance logs, etc. It overall assists in many teachers' administrative tasks. However, it does not by itself provide an innovative approach to the process of teaching.

The project, in addition, oversees the teacher training, to be offered by the same IT company that provides the technology. Each school that received the equipment was supposed to send teachers to get trained on how to use it. The number of trained teachers per school was to be at least equal to the number of equipped e-classrooms per school (which varies in accordance to the size of the school and number of pupils). This rule was to ensure that the e-classroom is being used by at least one teacher per school. However, the research conducted in order to evaluate the project implementation and impact thus far, shows that new equipment, and even initial training, is not nearly enough for efficient technology integration into education and competent media and digital literacy classes. Only 68 out 125 schools, in fact, responded to the survey questions. Out of those 68, in 15 schools the e-classrooms are not in use (the number of teachers using the classrooms is smaller than the number of e-classrooms in the school), whereas in other schools the average number of users of the e-classrooms is 2–3 teachers per school. These data were collected in December 2014 (Stanković, 2015).

Therefore, technology available to the teachers in schools in RS is not utilized to its full potential. This is due to several reasons, mainly the lack of teachers' competencies and motivation. Radmila Dakić, a teacher in one of the schools in which the Dositej project is being implemented, who looked into the teachers' ICT competencies, argues for more substantial and consistent teacher training programs, first for developing the ICT skills and then for incorporating them into the classroom work (Dakić, 2015).

Comparative Analysis and Concluding Remarks

These two models for integrating technology into B-H schools differ in various aspects. Let us first put attention on the ways they came into place, and how they were implemented. The project in the Sarajevo Canton was developed by a few committed and self-driven individuals, on the margins of educational policy making. On the other hand, the project in the Republic of Srpska was approached by a top-down system.

The first model was introduced by committed and savvy teachers willing to work extra to learn new methodology and approaches to teaching. Therefore, its further expansion is limited, as it depends on fundraising and additional engagement of teachers. It seems, however, promising in terms of the impact that it might achieve—that is, for developing students' media and digital literacy skills—as it provides the framework for collaborative work, research skills, and critical thinking development. All of these skills, as noted earlier, are only sporadically, if at all, part of the current curricula in the majority of B-H classrooms. However, the Ministry of Education had only an immaterial role in this process. This challenges the successful implementation of the model. Though it is encouraging that there are motivated professionals, ahead of the system they work in, it is not realistic to expect that they bear responsibility for the entire reform process. Moreover, it is even less feasible to expect a global IT company to continue providing the financial support to what should be the task of the governmental institutions. As long as the institutional involvement is missing, it is not likely that this model of technology integration in education can be fully developed. Moreover, there are other cantons of B-H that did not get involved in the process at all.

On the other hand, the second model was introduced as systematic educational reform. However, in a way it was imposed on the teachers. They took it on as additional work that they were not equipped to implement to full capacity, according to research and evaluation after almost two years of e-classrooms in practice in RS (Dakić, 2015).

In addition, introduced reforms in the schools of RS provide for merely a technologically advanced version of what is, in fact, the same old-fashioned way of teaching. It provides no guarantees that the technology used this way will contribute to the development of more complex media and digital skills, other than perhaps improved user skills. This conclusion is additionally supported by the fact that the teachers' trainings were not conducted by education experts, but exclusively by IT engineers, who could only focus on developing basic user ICT skills among teachers. The next step required for successful educational technology integration, according to Radmila

Dakić—developing the teachers' skills to incorporate technology in their classrooms—was not even addressed by the mentioned trainings.

The availability of funds to support technology integration in the education process should be the next evaluation criteria for successful implementation. A comparison between a small-scale project such as the first model, which spent up to 35,000 BAM[10] encompassing 9 schools, and the one aimed at nearly 200 schools, which has currently spent over 18 million BAM[11] for the implemented two-thirds of the project, might seem unrealistic. However, it is important in terms of evaluating the investment over its (possible) impact. Having in mind the status of B-H as a developing country, it becomes even more important.

The critics of the Dositej project claim that the investment in it, worth four times more than the annual education budget of Republika Srpska, is irrational and too big of a challenge for underdeveloped B-H and RS (Kurtović, 2015). Having in mind all the above-mentioned information on the project's implementation, this criticism seems to be more than reasonable.

The first model, on the other hand, has not really been tested in practice. It was only piloted and is currently being implemented for a very short time, in order to produce significant results for analysis. But the most significant downside of this model is the lack of B-H federal and cantonal institutions' collaboration, in order to incorporate technology in education. However, there are two essential elements of this first model that make it a much more appropriate choice for which to argue. One is the innovative SOLE-approach to the classroom work, which not only develops students' critical thinking and collaborative learning skills, along with research techniques and technology use, but also affects teachers and supports their professional development as well. The other is an economic argument. It is logical to support the first model due to its significantly lower price than the alternative. But it also seems to be a better fit for the current B-H educational system, which, as shown in the example of RS, cannot absorb overwhelming technology integration. The slower pace of integrating technology into teaching practice should inevitably be combined with intense teacher training, as well as viable institutional support, for the best results.

Notes

1. Bihać, Velika Kladuša, Sanski Most, Odžak, Jablanica, Mostar, Kupres, Goražde, Gradačac, Zenica, Kiseljak, Sarajevo, Gradiška, Derventa, Istočno Sarajevo, Novi Grad, Foča, and Banja Luka. These cities belong to both entities in B-H.

2. According to the still-preliminary results of the last census held in 2013, Agency for the Statistics of Bosnia-Herzegovina.
3. APOSO is a state level institution with the mission to "initiate and partake in the reform processes on developing the quality education system that ensures the full development of an individual and the society." The Agency is responsible for monitoring, promoting, and developing the Common Core Curricula (CCC). According to the Framework Law on preschool, elementary, and secondary education in B-H, CCC is the minimum curricular content over which the three main ethnic groups in B-H have a consensus. One of the remnants of the ethnic conflicts is disagreement on the nature of the conflict. In terms of education, it means disagreement on the history of the conflict, such that children in different parts of B-H, of different ethnicities, are learning different histories, especially related to 20th- and 21st-century events, national language and literature, and geography. The education system is based on the ethnicities. Therefore, CCC has been agreed upon by political representatives, rather than experts, in order to pass a state-level law, which turned out to be very general and broad.
4. The purpose of the study was to evaluate the government's program for protecting children from online pornography (Muratbegović, Mujanović, & Kepeš, 2013), focusing on identifying behavioral risks in children's use of ICT, and the possible role of education. The study and its purpose show the dominant protectionist approach to media and digital literacy in B-H, when (if) present at all.
5. This conference is organized annually by the Flemish Ministry of Education. It gathers experts and organizations (governmental and nongovernmental) promoting active use of media in the education and learning process, as well as media literacy. See http://media-and-learning.eu
6. The Evens Prize for media education was awarded to a Dutch media education organization, mediawijzer.net, for its game Media Masters.
7. The Saustrian Institute for Critical Digital Culture's Cracked Labs, was awarded the runner-up prize for its online game Data Dealer.
8. The countries that participated in the MEDEA.net project are: Belgium, Germany, Greece, Austria, Romania, Bulgaria, and Estonia.
9. Eight Sarajevo schools were equipped by a donation from Microsoft, and the same equipment for a ninth school was secured through funds from the publishing company Sarajevo Publishing. Microsoft in B-H, within its CRS (corporate social responsibility) policy has a history of supporting the use of ICT in education, through the Partner in Learning Forum and similar programs, organizing competitions and conferences, safer Internet days, etc. Stating the obvious would be to say that the interest of both companies in investing in technology for public schools is primarily economic. However, this does not change the fact that this particular collaboration made innovative educational practice in Sarajevo schools available.
10. The currency of Bosnia-Herzegovina.
11. Data from the official website of the government of the Republic of Srpska: http://www.vladars.net/sr-SP-Cyrl/Vlada/Ministarstva/mpk/media/vijesti/Pages/Dositej-drugi.aspx

References

Dakić, R. (2015). Kompetencije ucitelja za kompjuterizovanu nastavu. *Dositej* [E-magazine]. Banja Luka, Bosnia-Herzegovina: LANACO. Retrieved from http://caso pisdositej.eucionica.com/images/casopisBroj5/dositejBroj5.pdf

Džihana, A., Ćendić, K., & Tahmaz, M. (2012). *Mapping digital media in Bosnia and Herzegovina*. Report by the Open Society Foundations. Retrieved from http:// www.opensocietyfoundations.org/sites/default/files/mapping-digital-media-bos nia-20120706.pdf

Ibrahimbegović-Tihak, V. (2015). Kompetencije nastavnog kadra u Bosni i Hercegovini kao element razvoja medijske pismenosti. In V. Ibrahimbegović-Tihak (Ed.), *Medijska pismenost u digitalno doba*. Sarajevo, Bosnia-Herzegovina: Internews in BiH.

Ibrahimović, N. (2015). Mediji i medijska pismenost u osnovnoj skoli. In V. Ibrahimbegović-Tihak (Ed.), *Medijska pismenost u digitalno doba*. Sarajevo, Bosnia-Herzegovina: Internews in BiH.

Interview. (2014, March 3). Marija Naletilić. Head of the Common Core Curricula Department of the Agency for Development of Primary and Secondary Education of B-H (APOSO). Sarajevo, Bosnia-Herzegovina.

Interview. (2014, March 14). Nadija Bandić. Federal Ministry of Education Official. Sarajevo, Bosnia-Herzegovina.

Interview. (2015, April 21). Dženita Arbak Demir. Teacher. Sarajevo, Bosnia-Herzegovina.

Kurtović, E. (2015). Dosije Dositej: Informatizacija obrazovanja u Republici Srpskoj. Sveti Sava na zidu, Dositej u ormaru. In *Školegijum*. Sarajevo, Bosnia-Herzegovina: FOD B-H.

Magill, C. (2010). *Education and fragility in Bosnia and Herzegovina*. Paris, France: UNESCO.

Mitra, S. (2013). *SOLE (Self-organized learning environment) Toolkit. An online resource designed to help educators and parents support kids (8–12 years old) as they tap into their innate sense of wonder and engage in child-driven learning*. Retrieved from http:// www.ted.com/prize/sole_toolkit#intro

Muratbegović, E., Mujanović, E., & Kepeš, N. (2013). *System for protection of children against child pornography and other forms of sexual abuse and exploitation through Information and Communication Technologies in Bosnia and Herzegovina: Evaluation of activities implemented from 2010 to 2012*. Retrieved from http://www.cprc.ba/ en/biblioteka/EvaluationofActionPlanENG.pdf

Stanković, A. (2015). Realizacija nastave u elektronskim učionicama kojima su osnovne škole u Republici Srpskoj opremljene u okviru projekta Dositej. *Dositej* [E-magazine]. Banja Luka, Bosnia-Herzegovina: LANACO. Retrieved from http://casopisdositej. eucionica.com/images/casopisBroj5/dositejBroj5.pdf

Tajić, L. (2013). *Medijska pismenost u Bosni i Hercegovini*. Sarajevo, Bosnia-Herzegovina: Internews in BiH.

Thoman, E., & Jolls, T. (2008). *Literacy for the 21st century: An overview and orientation guide to media literacy education.* Los Angeles, CA: Center for Media Literacy.

Vos, I., & Terryin, D. (Eds.). (2014). *Charting media and learning in Europe.* MEDEA. net report. Retrieved from http://www.medeanet.eu/sites/default/files/MEDEA-net_Deliverable_4.3_Annual_Report_2013/index.pdf

8. Contextualizing Global Media Literacy in the Standards-Based Classroom: Moving Beyond the Culture of the Dichotomous "Like"

Kelly McNeal

The context of evaluation of media in and outside of school differs. If students in the United States are to be successful in a global world, they need to comprehend that evaluation in a professional or school context is a high-level analytical activity with a complex rationale, and is beyond subjectivity. A significant chasm exists between the type of media evaluation students are conducting outside of school and the type of learning the Core Curriculum State Standards (CCSS) is asking them to master for college and career readiness. In social media in which students engage, such as Instagram, Twitter, and Facebook, students can quickly evaluate their peers' or strangers' posts and "tweets," by "liking" or taking a related action. In social media, no further explanation or justification is needed when something is "liked." Users of social media consider themselves expert evaluators merely by participating in the evaluative liking of something. The word *like* implies that the opposite would be not to like something. Thus, only two evaluative choices are possible. This makes liking something a dichotomous choice and a low-level evaluation—one that is proliferating in modern society but is contrary to the type of high-level analytical and evaluative skills being asked of students to master in the CCSS.

In order to aid students' development of high-level analytical and evaluative skills, this chapter reviews the CCSS anchor standards and the skills students need to master. The chapter then discusses facets of critical literacy and culturally relevant pedagogy—namely, ideas that should be discussed with students if they are uncomfortable discussing global issues from different perspectives. Finally, the chapter discusses Bloom's Taxonomy and verbs related to it. Although Bloom's Taxonomy has been utilized by teachers for curriculum and lesson planning, the discussion in this chapter proposes that these verbs be taught to students, so they can use them to discuss, analyze, and research what could otherwise be polarizing issues. Polarizing issues, such as ISIL and Palestinian independence, are become increasingly difficult to discuss in classrooms, because teachers might lack the necessary strategies to teach students about these topics. Indeed, teachers themselves might also have polarizing views about topics, leading them to avoid informational global texts. However, the CCSS requires that students be able to read, write, research, speak about, and critique a wide range of media. Thus, both teachers and students must develop lifelong strategies that they can use professionally to move beyond the culture of the dichotomous like. Utilizing the verbs associated with Bloom's Taxonomy will aid students in meeting the CCSS standards, building critical literacy skills, building their global awareness, and avoiding arguments and the dichotomous like.

Anchor Standards

Forty-three of the 50 states in the United States have adopted the CCSS in English language arts and literacy, as a means of setting attainment levels of what students should know at different benchmarks during their schooling. The ELA and Literacy CCSS are standards for what kindergarten through grade 12 students should know and be able to do in the areas of language arts and literacy, history and social studies, science, and technical subjects. They are "designed to prepare all students for success in college, career, and life by the time they graduate from high school" (Common Core State Standards, 2014a, para. 1). The standards are broken down into bands by grade level, for grades kindergarten through 8, and then by two-year bands for the high school years, to provide more flexibility. The focus is on achievement or outcome rather than means, thereby creating a great deal of flexibility for districts and states in terms of how to achieve these means. The standards focus on a holistic or integrated model of literacy (Common Core State Standards, 2014a). The model is divided into strands of reading, writing, speaking and listening, and language.

The K–12 English/Language Arts CCSS have "anchor" standards, which are the overarching K–12 standards in reading, writing, speaking and listening, and language. These anchor standards are broad standards, providing teachers a broad concept of what all K–12 students need to learn. Standards are then broken down in a detailed manner by grade level or grade band, based on these anchor standards, in a grade-appropriate manner.

Several of the anchor standards focus on reading, writing, speaking about, and analyzing diverse media formats (see Figure 1). These anchor standards are a focus of this chapter. These K–12 literacy/language arts standards prepare students to live in a global society. The selected anchor standards indicate that students need to demonstrate skills in finding digital media, evaluating this media, and presenting information about this media in a clear and logical manner in formal English, when appropriate. These standards also detail the importance of the types of media students must be able to understand, analyze, and critique, including but not limited to visual and digital media.

The CCSS support the tone of this chapter, as well as the innate needs of students, by noting the importance of "demonstrating command of formal English when indicated or appropriate" (Common Core State Standards, 2014b, para. 1). Thus, the purpose of this chapter is not to suggest that students should stop "liking" things in a dichotomous way, either in or outside of school contexts, but rather to encourage them to realize that the dichotomous like is not a school or professional evaluation.

Figure 1: Anchor standards focusing on working with diverse media formats.

Core Curriculum Reading Anchor Standards
CCSS.ELA-LITERACY.CCRA.R.7 Integration of Knowledge and Ideas: Integrate and evaluate content presented in diverse media and formats, including visually and quantitatively, as well as in words. (seventh grade standard)
CCSS.ELA LITERACY CCRA.R.8 Delineate and evaluate the argument and specific claims in a text, including the validity of the reasoning as well as the relevance and sufficiency of the evidence. (eighth grade standard)
CCSS.ELA-LITERACY.CCRA.R.9 Analyze how two or more texts address similar themes or topics in order to build knowledge or to compare the approaches the authors take. (ninth grade standard)

Core Curriculum Writing Anchor Standards
CCSS.ELA-LITERACY.CCRA.W.8 Gather relevant information from multiple print and digital sources, assess the credibility and accuracy of each source, and integrate the information while avoiding plagiarism. (eighth grade standard)
CCSS.ELA-LITERACY.CCRA.W.9 Draw evidence from literary or informational texts to support analysis, reflection, and research. (ninth grade standard)

Core Curriculum Speaking and Listening Anchor Standards
CCSS.ELA-LITERACY.CCRA.SL.2 Integrate and evaluate information presented in diverse media and formats, including visually, quantitatively, and orally. (second grade standard)
CCSS.ELA-LITERACY.CCRA.SL.4 Present information, findings, and supporting evidence such that listeners can follow the line of reasoning and the organization, development, and style are appropriate to task, purpose, and audience. (fourth grade standard)

CCSS.ELA-LITERACY.CCRA.SL.5 Make strategic use of digital media and visual displays of data to express information and enhance understanding of presentations. (fifth grade standard)
CCSS.ELA-LITERACY.CCRA.SL.6 Adapt speech to a variety of contexts and communicative tasks, demonstrating command of formal English when indicated or appropriate. (sixth grade standard)

Critical Pedagogy, Culturally Relevant Pedagogy, and the CCSS

I would be remiss if I did not call attention to the fact that I am writing about the CCSS, a polarizing topic in itself. However, when I read the language of the CCSS, I do not feel pulled to one side or the other; instead, I see these standards as another change in the course of our nation's educational history. I recognize certain flaws in them, particularly in their implementation and assessment. However, while reading them, I view them as what they are: a vision for a minimum attainment by students nationwide, at set times during their education. I do not see methods imposed, although I do see glimpses of concepts perhaps grounded in rationale from world-renowned theorists. As the standards do not mandate methodologies, they do not have to be oppressive, unless a district forces teachers to utilize scripted, pre-packaged materials that have been marketed to them as "standards-based."

Freire and his theory of critical pedagogy support the idea of students thinking critically and reflecting upon their reality—namely, the idea of praxis (Freire, 1986, p. 36). The idea of praxis refers to when oppressed people become aware of their oppression by thinking critically about their oppression and then struggling for liberation. Many types of oppression exist. We in America tend to think of oppression in terms racial or economic issues, but another form of oppression relates to access to different types of education or media. We in the United States are intolerant of other countries who do not allow their citizens to access our news, our popular culture, or our Internet sources, yet it is rare that students in mainstream American classrooms study international news sources, learn about international popular culture, or visit international news sources. The CCSS mandates that students gather evidence from multiple sources and evaluate these sources. In order for our students to be competitive in a global world, it is necessary for them to be aware of media and news sources outside of the United States. Not being aware of these sources and consciously or even subconsciously limiting students' access to them is a form of oppression. Freire introduced the concept of "conscientization, a process that invites learners to engage the world and others critically" (McLaren, 1989, p. 195). The CCSS anchor standards support students' mastery of conscientization.

Ladson-Billings (1995) built on Freire's idea and developed the theory of culturally relevant pedagogy, which links schooling and culture. Ladson-Billings developed this theory based on research she conducted with African American students who wanted to maintain their own culture while succeeding academically. This theory has become renowned in multicultural education.

When students are faced with information from cultures other than their own, they might get defensive before they even read or view the information from the source. Therefore, students' own cultures should be recognized and valued while they are being taught to master the CCSS. For example, students have told me that they feel it is "anti-American" to read an article on the Al Jazeera website. When this happened, as a class, we explored what it means to be "an American" and then read parts of the Constitution and the Declaration of Independence. We also discussed if citizens in other countries should be allowed to read our newspapers and go to our news media websites. The class further brainstormed about what "freedom" meant to them. I explained that it was my job to teach them and that they needed to learn certain objectives; I had planned the activity to help them master these objectives.

I explain this to you, the reader, because understanding students' culture and resistance is important, and it relates to culturally relevant pedagogy. Three tenets of this theory relate to practice. First of all, students must have academic success, cultural competence, and critical consciousness. Academic success in a culturally relevant classroom means focusing on the positive and making ideas relevant. Ladson-Billings (1995) pointed out that this does not mean making students "feel good": "There is a difference. Students must choose academic success" (p. 160). The second tenet is cultural competence. Ladson-Billings's research pointed to African Americans, who might lose their own culture in order succeed academically, and then are called "White." Teachers, parents, and students need to understand that a school's culture asks for different competencies than social media do; although the "like" is not necessarily appropriate in a professional or academic context, students' own cultures and out-of-school usage of media are to be valued. The last aspect of culturally relevant pedagogy—critical consciousness—relates to the CCSS. The first two tenets, of students being academically successful and culturally aware, are not enough if the students are not also critically conscious. A classroom grounded in culturally relevant pedagogy supports the anchor CCSS.

Bloom's Taxonomy and the Linked Verbs

Benjamin Bloom, a psychologist and educational theorist, is best known for the creation of "Bloom's Taxonomy" and his work in the area of mastery learning. Bloom and other curriculum and measurement specialists began work on the Taxonomy in the late 1940s and completed their work in 1956 (Bloom, Englehart, Furst, Hill, & Krathwohl, 1956). The goal of the Taxonomy was to create a common language and statements regarding what students were to learn, so that exams could be utilized uniformly across universities. Bloom himself served as a professor at the University of Chicago, and he worked on the Taxonomy with his colleagues nationwide. The original Taxonomy sought also to serve as a means to discuss common learning goals, to provide a basis for facilitating broad curriculum goals, and to aid in creating questions and learning activities.

The cognitive Taxonomy consists of six categories: knowledge, comprehension, application, analysis, synthesis, and evaluation (Bloom et al., 1956). The Taxonomy was revised in 2001 by Bloom's students and educational researchers (Anderson & Krathwohl, 2001). The most significant changes to Bloom's Taxonomy were that nouns became verbs and some of the categories were switched. The revised categories are as follows: remember, understand, apply, analyze, evaluate, and create. The significance of this revised Taxonomy lies in the use of verbs in the categories and the idea that verbs need to be utilized in the dynamic process of learning. This significant change provided a way to apply Bloom's Taxonomy in practical usage settings. Bloom's Taxonomy verbs are now frequently utilized in curriculum development by teachers, when they write their objectives, and they are seen throughout the CCSS. See Table 1 for Bloom's Taxonomy verbs.

While it is becoming more and more commonplace for Bloom's Taxonomy verbs to be utilized in curriculum planning, lesson planning, and assessment development, students themselves are not generally familiar with these verbs. The students may see the verbs in the standards or on the board in the objectives, but they are not commonly taught to consult routinely with the Taxonomy when completing their work or creating projects. The Taxonomy spans the demonstration of lower-level knowledge such as defining and describing, mid-level knowledge such as demonstrating and diagraming, and higher-level knowledge such as creating and judging. There is some overlap in the verbs, and this can be confusing to students and teachers alike if Bloom's definitions are not carefully consulted. For example, under both evaluation and comprehension is the verb *describe*. In order to demonstrate that a student has comprehended a concept, he or she could describe the facts

Table 8.1. Bloom's Taxonomy Verbs. (Texas A&M University at Galveston, n.d.).

Definitions	Knowledge	Comprehension	Application	Analysis	Synthesis	Evaluation
Bloom's Definition	Remember previously learned information.	Demonstrate an understanding of the facts.	Apply knowledge to actual situations.	Break down objects or ideas into simpler parts and find evidence to support generalizations.	Compile component ideas into a new whole or propose alternative solutions.	Make and defend judgments based on internal evidence or external criteria.
Verbs	Arrange Define Describe Duplicate Identify Label List Match Memorize Name Order Outline Recognize Relate Recall Repeat Reproduce Select State	Classify Convert Defend Describe Discuss Distinguish Estimate Explain Express Extend Generalized Give example(s) Identify Indicate Infer Locate Paraphrase Predict Recognize Rewrite Review Select Summarize Translate	Apply Change Choose Compute Demonstrate Discover Dramatize Employ Illustrate Interpret Manipulate Modify Operate Practice Predict Prepare Produce Relate Schedule Show Sketch Solve Use Write	Analyze Appraise Breakdown Calculate Categorize Compare Contrast Criticize Diagram Differentiate Discriminate Distinguish Examine Experiment Identify Illustrate Infer Model Outline Point out Question Relate Select Separate Subdivide Test	Arrange Assemble Categorize Collect Combine Comply Compose Construct Create Design Develop Devise Explain Formulate Generate Plan Prepare Rearrange Reconstruct Relate Reorganize Revise Rewrite Set up Summarize Synthesize Tell Write	Appraise Argue Assess Attach Choose Compare Conclude Contrast Defend Describe Estimate Evaluate Explain Judge Justify Interpret Relate Predict Rate Select Support Value

relating to that concept, verbally or in writing. In order to evaluate a concept, a student would have to describe a judgment based on some type of external criteria. Posting the verbs in classrooms and encouraging students to have printouts of the verbs, as well as to look them up on the Internet, can remind students of the types of low to high tasks they can do for activities and projects.

Putting Bloom's Verbs into Action: Moving Away from the Dichotomous "Like"

Students must learn to demonstrate skills such as finding digital media, evaluating these media, and presenting information about these media in a clear and logical manner, in formal English when appropriate, in order to meet the CCSS. A learning environment based on critical and culturally relevant pedagogy can aid students as they try to evaluate and reflect upon global media and move beyond the dichotomous "like," which is prevalent in 21st-century pop culture. The practical strategy of utilizing Bloom's Taxonomy verbs can guide students, and dissuade them from utilizing polarizing vocabulary in the classroom.

The majority of media, texts, and visuals that students will encounter when they enter college or their careers are informational texts. It is therefore imperative that they be comfortable reading, writing, speaking about, and evaluating informational text and garnering it from multiple sources. One source not commonly utilized to access informational media is foreign websites. This source is therefore a focus of this chapter. As we prepare students to live in a global society, we must help them become aware of global media sources and become capable of accessing and evaluating them in a strategic manner.

To begin to or to further expose students to foreign media sources, I recommend that teachers themselves select foreign news sources. At first, such news can be in the form of an article, and then the same strategy can be utilized for videos or live news broadcasts. For example, Al Jazeera has print material on its website (www.aljazeera.com), and Euronews offers informational videos (www.euronews.com). The individual teacher can decide what type of material to select; the goal is to teach the students strategies for reading, writing about, analyzing, discussing, presenting, reflecting on, evaluating, and eventually researching, using foreign news sources.

To demonstrate this strategy, I selected an article from www.aljazeera.com that compares and contrasts ISIL and the Mexican drug cartels, and a video from www.euronews.com that discusses how politicians in Italy support the recognition of Palestine as a state. In a hypothetical teaching scenario, a similar strategy would be utilized for both media sources. Students would be instructed to use Bloom's Taxonomy to read, write about, and present a presentation about the article or video. The activities developed for the article were created by me, based on Bloom's Taxonomy. For the purpose of this chapter, examples will be given based on the general anchor standards, but different grade levels would align activities to specific standards. I recommend that, whenever a new strategy is utilized in the classroom, it first be directed by the teacher. This means that, in this case, the teacher would select the material for reading, and the class would complete the first activity together. The next time the class does the activity (for example, for the video), the teacher can differentiate the activity by having students work in groups and have students brainstorm some of their own tasks based on the Bloom's Taxonomy verbs. After students are familiar with this activity, I suggest that the teacher have students select their own article or video, and then write their own tasks for a project, using the Bloom's Taxonomy verbs.

The first article selected is drawn from www.aljazeera.com, titled "Mexican Drug Cartels Are Worse than ISIL," by Musa Al-Gharbi (Al-Gharbi, 2014). While it may be considered a controversial article, the activities designed around this article are consciously focused and derived from Bloom's Taxonomy verbs. This is an example of the content of the article:

Mexican drug cartels are worse than ISIL

Western obsession with the Islamic State is fueled more by bigotry than any genuine assessment of risk or atrocities

by Musa al-Gharbi

The horrific rampage of the Islamic State of Iraq and the Levant (ISIL) has captured the world's attention. Many Western commentators have characterized ISIL's crimes as unique, no longer practiced anywhere else in the civilized world. They argue that the group's barbarism is intrinsically Islamic, a product of the aggressive and archaic worldview that dominates the Muslim world. The ignorance of these claims is stunning.

While there are other organized groups whose depravity and threat to the United States far surpasses that of ISIL, none has engendered the same kind of collective indignation and hysteria. This raises a question: Are Americans primarily concerned with ISIL's atrocities or with the fact that Muslims are committing these crimes?

For example, even as the U.S. media and policymakers radically inflate ISIL's threat to the Middle East and United States, most Americans appear to be unaware of the scale of the atrocities committed by Mexican drug cartels and the threat they pose to the United States.

Cartels versus ISIL

A recent United Nations report estimated nearly 9,000 civilians have been killed and 17,386 wounded in Iraq in 2014, more than half since ISIL fighters seized large parts on northern Iraq in June. It is likely that the group is responsible for another several thousand deaths in Syria. To be sure, these numbers are staggering. But in 2013 drug cartels murdered more than 16,000 people in Mexico alone, and another 60,000 from 2006 to 2012—a rate of more than one killing every half hour for the last seven years. What is worse, these are estimates from the Mexican government, which is known to deflate the actual death toll by about 50 percent.

This article would be selected for middle or high school students, because of its potential for high-interest content and details as well as the seriousness of its subject matter. Based on the Bloom's Taxonomy verbs (Table 1), as well as the general CCSS Anchor Standards (Figure 1), the activities for the article would require students as a whole class to:

1. **Define** ISIL and Muslim and then **identify** Syria, Iraq, and Mexico on a world map. (Knowledge)
2. **Summarize** the article in one paragraph. **Discuss** your summary with a peer. (Comprehension)
3. **Illustrate** the death totals in graphs. **Predict** future death tolls for ISIL and Mexico based on the evidence in the article. (Application)
4. **Compare** and **contrast** ISIL with the Mexican drug cartels utilizing a Venn diagram. (Analysis)
5. The Al Jazeera article has direct links to sources within the text. Click on the links from one paragraph and **rewrite** one paragraph based on the source material you find in the direct links. (Synthesis)
6. **Evaluate** the article utilizing the *Critically Analyzing Information Sources: Critical Appraisal and Analysis* (Research & Learning Services, 2015). **Justify** your evaluation to the class in a formal presentation. (Evaluation)

These activities focus on building students' critical reading, writing, listening, thinking, reflection, researching, and evaluation skills, as well as global awareness, and prevent students from thinking in dichotomous terms. After being consciously directed through activities such as these, students will become acquainted with the Bloom's Taxonomy verbs and begin to be comfortable with creating their own activities.

In the next set of activities I would do with students, I would utilize a video, "Italy urges recognition of Palestinian state" (Euronews, 2015). The video offers the following description:

Italian MPs have backed a non-binding resolution that urges the government to recognize Palestine as a state.

Italy's Chamber of Deputies voted by 300 to 45 to pass the motion presented by Prime Minister Matteo Renzi's Democratic Party.

But they failed to back a move supported by the left wing Left Ecology and Liberty party that would have "fully and formally recognized the Palestinian State."

While most developing countries recognize Palestine as a state, most Western European nations do not, supporting the Israeli and US positions that an independent Palestinian state should emerge from negotiations with Israel.

Ireland, Britain and France have held similar parliamentary votes on the status of Palestine in recent months. Sweden went further, officially recognizing Palestine.

Earlier, pro-Palestinians activists clashed with Israeli troops in the West Bank town of Bilin. Hundreds of Palestinian protesters gathered to mark the 10th anniversary of weekly demonstration against the construction of the Israeli separation barrier.

After reading this description as a class and watching the video, I would write the six domains of Bloom's Taxonomy on the board and instruct the class to brainstorm possible activities that they could complete under each category. I would then allow students to select one activity from each domain and work in groups, pairs, or individually to complete them. There would still be a great deal of oversight during this activity, as I would be controlling the media and facilitating the creation of the activities, but this type of brainstorming would aid students in understanding the process they need to go through to create their own activities with Bloom's Taxonomy.

For example, within the Knowledge domain, I would ask students to look at the verbs under the heading "Knowledge." First, I would ask them whether they know what all the verbs mean. If they do not, I would ask them to look up the verb, read the definition, use it in a sentence, and think of a synonym for the verb. If they still do not understand, I would ask a peer to help them do this. All students would be asked to take notes during this exercise. Next I would ask the students the following question: "When you think about the video, what knowledge do you think is important for you to know in the video, not just now but five years from now?" I would explain that this is the type of information that needs to be memorized, and that it is low-level knowledge. While it is important knowledge, sometimes a person must simply memorize it. For example, this is the case for an important date, a definition, or a place on a map. If a debate or discussion about something ensued, related to the Knowledge domain and directly related to the article (as long as it involved a Bloom's Taxonomy verb), I would write it down as an activity. When brainstorming ideas about a controversial topic such as this one, I find that I must make sure that I am paying attention to what the students are saying and that they are meeting the guidelines. For example, "define Palestine" would be an acceptable activity or "identify Palestine or Italy on the world map;" but "define terrorists or anti-Semitics" would not be acceptable activities, as terrorists and anti-Semitics are not mentioned in this video or write-up. It is important to be familiar with the articles and videos you are presenting, so that the classroom environment becomes one in which the students investigate multiple perspectives directly related to the media source, as opposed to a classroom environment that perpetuates polarity of thinking. We would then do this type of brainstorming for each of the Bloom's categories. Once the brainstorming was finished, the students would do the activities and then present selected ones to the class.

Looking to the Future

I purposely chose articles that are controversial, not because I want students to have polar opinions about controversial topics, but because I think that, due to the rise in social media, a polarity of opinions is already a strength of the current generations. Therefore, the strategies in this chapter focus on teaching students how to view articles beyond thinking in dichotomous terms, by using the lens of Bloom's Taxonomy. Technological changes have been dramatic in the last decade; they have caused shifts in the way we do everything, including learning, communicating, and assessing students. The changes in technology have provided new ways to communicate, which has introduced a dichotomy in the way things are evaluated and viewed. This technology has significantly influenced culture and created a polarization in the way students think about people, issues, and concepts. It also has benefitted schools in society, as it has given schools direct access to foreign new sources and media. While strong opinions can be an asset, students whose opinions are not supported by facts and a wide range of knowledge may be a great malady in America's 21st century. If American students are going to be competitive in a global society, it is imperative that they are media savvy and do not view issues in a polarizing way. The CCSS mandates that students need to demonstrate skills in finding digital media, evaluating these media, and presenting information about these media in a clear and logical manner, in formal English when appropriate. Teachers who are open to having students access foreign media sources and utilize the strategy of Bloom's Taxonomy verbs can support students in learning the CCSS, in a way that is linked to critical and culturally relevant pedagogies.

References

Al-Gharbi, M. (2014, October 20). Mexican drug cartels are worse than ISIL. *Al Jazeera*. Retrieved from http://america.aljazeera.com/opinions/2014/10/isil-vs-mexican drugcartelsunitedstatesislamophobia.html

Anderson, L. W., & Krathwohl, D. R. (Eds.). (2001). A taxonomy for learning, teaching, and assessing: A revision of Bloom's Taxonomy of Educational Objectives (Complete edition). New York, NY: Longman.

Bloom, B., Englehart, M., Furst, E., Hill, W., & Krathwohl, D. (1956). *Taxonomy of educational objectives: The classification of educational goals. Handbook I: Cognitive domain*. New York, NY: Longmans, Green.

Common Core State Standards. (2014a). *English language arts*. Retrieved from http://www.corestandards.org/ELA-Literacy/

Common Core State Standards. (2014b). *English language arts standards, college and career readiness anchor standards for speaking and listening*. Retrieved from http://www.corestandards.org/ELA-Literacy/CCRA/SL/6/

Euronews. (2015, February 27). *Italy urges recognition of Palestinian state*. Retrieved from http://www.euronews.com/2015/02/27/italy-urges-recognition-of-palestinian-state/

Freire, P. (1986). *Pedagogy of the oppressed*. New York, NY: Continuum.

Ladson-Billings, G. (1995). But that's just good teaching! The case for culturally relevant pedagogy. *Theory Into Practice, 34*(3).

McLaren, P. (1989). *Life in schools*. White Plains, NY: Longman.

Research & Learning Services. (2015). *Critically analyzing information sources: Critical appraisal and analysis*. Ithaca, NY: Cornell University Library. Retrieved from http://guides.library.cornell.edu/criticallyanalyzing

Texas A&M University at Galveston. (n.d.). *Bloom's Taxonomy Verbs*. Retrieved from http://www.tamug.edu/faculty/Blooms_Taxonomy_Action_Verbs.pdf

9. Project Censored: Building a Global "Networked Fourth Estate" in a Digital Age

ROB WILLIAMS

"All that the sharpest critics of democracy have alleged is true, if there is no steady supply of trustworthy and relevant news."
—Walter Lippmann, "Journalism and the Higher Law," 1920

"There seems to be more news than ever before, but it isn't worth as much as it used to be."
Carl Jensen, Project Censored founder, 2001

"Journalism Is Dead! Long Live Journalism!"[1]

This two-sentence rallying cry neatly summarizes both the promise and peril of the U.S. "news" industry as it moves into a brave new 21st-century world marked by creative uncertainty. The so-called "crisis in journalism" is by now well known to even casual observers. Our alluring digital media age has dealt a near-death blow to the traditional model of advertising-supported, print-exclusive, professionally sourced news. As so-called "objective" news reporting has withered during the past decade, U.S. citizens seeking real, in-depth, and vital information about current events (beyond Buzzfeed, "Bieber Fever," the Twitterverse, or the 2016 presidential election "horse race") have had to turn elsewhere to find reliable data to fuel reasonable decision-making about the future of the United States, currently the planet's richest and most powerful nation and empire.

Before going any further, it is worth providing a brief summary of the two-decades-long, dramatic transformations reshaping U.S. news culture that have accompanied the transition from the analog to the digital age. To rewind for a moment, it is safe, if somewhat simplistic, to say that U.S. professional news culture enjoyed a reasonably successful century-long run from the late 19th-century professionalization of the field to the 1980s, led by flagship organizations like the *Washington Post*, *New York Times*, and *Wall Street Journal*, a national network of daily and weekly presses, and a robust national corporate commercial broadcasting network (both radio and television).

U.S. news' troubles began with the arrival of the digital age, when the Internet's speed, immediacy, expanding reach, and aggressive disaggregation of traditionally bundled news content quickly began eroding traditional revenue sources, as well as packaging information and deploying news in novel and unpredictably disruptive ways. Take one example: the invention of Craigslist alone siphoned off billions of dollars from classified news listings, print journalism's traditional "cash cow." Corporate commercial newspaper CEOs scrambled to respond to declining profits in the digital age by firing editors, downsizing newsrooms, shrinking news beats (especially labor, foreign policy, and state/local news), and repackaging news as more "user friendly," which loosely equates to deploying whatever content will maximize profits in an age of declining revenue—moving from analog dollars to digital dimes, as the popular adage goes, and now, perhaps, pennies. Aggregation is replacing research, PR is supplanting hard news, and opinion is challenging fact—all troubling trends to veteran news watchers. "21st century journalism now seems to be about keeping people stupid," explains former broadcast-journalist-turned-media-professor Traci Griffith. "It's about the Twitter mentality—tell me everything I need to know in 140 characters or fewer."[2]

Indeed, news observers can sometimes seem erratic, when considering the pros and cons of the state of U.S. "news" in our digital age. On the surface is the hype. The Internet's arrival appears to be one big pro-news phenomenon, the e-enthusiasts explain, making the gathering, distributing, and consuming of 21st-century "news we can use" more easy and efficient than ever before. On the other hand, more astute observers challenge such cyber-cheerleading, seeing instead a complex constellation of new opportunities and challenges for news in the Digital Age. "By unbundling the newspaper and making advertising cheaper and more efficient, the Internet has led to a drastic drop in newspaper employment and the Internet has increased the supply of rubbish in and around journalism: content farms, recycled PR (known as 'churnalism'), stories that are cheap rewrites of other stories, lists, and 'charticles' with no purpose other than pushing up page views" (popularly called "clickbait"), explains

New York University professor of journalism Jay Rosen. The good news? The Internet, Rosen concludes, is improving journalism for many reasons. For instance, it "drives down the cost of getting journalism to people who want it" and "opens the market up to more players allowing more ideas to be tried." In addition, it "gives new tools to anyone who wants them," like online databases, Skype, RSS, Google Alerts and Hangouts, as well as mobile publishing options like ubiquitous social media platforms. The Internet, furthermore, "alters the balance of power between users and journalists," "replacing a system in which a small number of gatekeepers employed by a heavily capitalized industry that tended towards monopoly held almost all the powers of the press."[3]

What is the big picture summary for news in the age of digital? "The digital revolution," explains Pulitzer Prize–winning media scholar and sociologist Paul Starr, "has weakened the ability of the [U.S.] press to act as an effective agent of public accountability by undermining the economic basis of professional reporting and fragmenting the public."[4] Beyond the accelerating collapse of traditional news production and delivery, the shiny happy promise of the new digital age of an "information superhighway" has given way to the tyranny of social media selling, as traditional corporations who have consolidated older news platforms compete with powerful new global media corporations—think Google, Facebook, Amazon, Apple, and other "Lords of the Cloud"—whose primary job is aggregating millions and millions of personal users' data for purposes of "sharing" surveillance, "liking" content, and creating "click-through" commercialism.

Make no mistake. What Starr calls a "serious long-term crisis" in U.S. journalism is very real. And yet, while many observers wail, gnash their teeth, and wring their hands, independent media activists and journalists have been busy rolling up their sleeves, and the results at the grassroots level are cautiously encouraging. Perhaps the biggest untold news story of the new century (so far) for the troubled state of U.S. journalism is this: as embattled U.S. newspapers scratch their heads, slim down their offerings, and shutter their doors, new and more democratic models of participatory citizen journalism are being seeded and beginning to sprout across the country.

Beyond Analog: Trends Framing "News" in Our Digital Age

In their now-classic but somewhat forgotten critique of U.S. news entitled *Manufacturing Consent: The Political Economy of the Mass Media* (1988), Edward S. Herman and Noam Chomsky provided perhaps the most provocative analog age critique of traditional mainstream news in the United States. Rather than playing to the much-celebrated stereotype of the U.S. journalist as a tenacious if gritty gumshoe unearthing scandal in the name of truth, justice, and the American way, Herman and Chomsky studied *New York Times* coverage across a host of important stories and applied political economic theory, linguistics, and a deeper structural approach to construct what they famously called "a propaganda model of news." In this influential model, *Manufacturing Consent*'s authors argued that, in a culture of journalism shaped in a corporate commercial matrix, "all the news" deemed "fit to print" must first pass through a series of elite-massaged "filters"—advertising, ownership, news shapers, news makers, and "flak" (negative criticism)—before managing to see the light of day. In this way, Chomsky and Herman concluded, U.S.-based socioeconomic and political elites maintained hegemony over the structural creation and curation of news in the United States, massaging, suppressing, and distorting the "news" to reflect back to the U.S. news-consuming public a narrow range of stories friendly to U.S. elite interests.

As the analog age news gives way to a new digital generation, it is tempting to dismiss Chomsky and Herman's critique as outdated, a relic of an earlier era, particularly in light of the simplistic celebratory rhetoric that has accompanied the arrival of the so-called Information Age. Interestingly, however, the Digital Age has ushered in new trends in journalism that embody both promise and peril for U.S. news in the 21st century. "Is the Internet making journalism better or worse?" asked Matthew Ingram in a 2011 Gigaom article. The answer is "Yes."[5]

So, how do we support better-quality U.S. journalism in the digital age? Several solutions and some innovative experiments are already underway.[6] Some suggest public subsidies for traditional news gathering organizations; others advocate for philanthropies and foundations to pick up the slack. A third solution involves the investor-funded founding of new or existing investigative sites and news channels such as Glenn Greenwald's anchoring of *The Intercept,* Facebook darling Chris Hughes's kickstarting of the *New Republic,* or Amazon founder Jeff Bezos's acquisition of the *Washington Post.* And there is yet another way, combining face-to-face and virtual modes, town and gown communities, analog and digital platforms, amateurs and professionals, and news gathering methods involving both research and primary interview cultivation. Perhaps the best term for this emerging model of news is "the networked fourth estate."[7]

Project Censored: Crowdsourcing Independent News

On the leading edge of this exciting new trend is Project Censored, one of the oldest and most visible independent news reporting initiatives in the United

States, and a powerful example of "crowdsourcing" at work. "We aim to be a model of media democracy in action," observes Project Censored associate director Andy Roth. "Our main objectives are to train students in media literacy and First Amendment issues, while bringing to light information that has been under-reported or censored in some way. We think that free press rights are imperative for a democratic culture to function, and, with our students, faculty, and community members, we advocate for those rights."[8] (Full disclosure: I have provided pro bono work and writing for Project Censored for many years, and am a long-time supporter and reader.)

Here is a quick snapshot of its history: Sonoma State University journalism professor Carl Jensen founded Project Censored in 1976, as a single, semester-long sociology class focused on media censorship. More than three decades later, with indefatigable leadership from Jensen and his successors Peter Phillips, Mickey Huff, and Andy Roth, Project Censored has grown into an independently funded organization boasting a presence on nearly two dozen U.S., European, and South American college campuses, an annual book publication that features the "Top 25 Censored Stories of the Year," a multimedia website, a weekly radio show on Berkeley-based KPFA/Pacifica Radio, and an emerging global online presence, thanks to the Internet's democratic reach. "We are funded by individual donors and accept no corporate money," explains Project Censored director Mickey Huff. "Due to the controversial nature of some of our research, many of the grants we used to receive are no longer available, so we rely on generous individuals and book sales to fund our efforts."[9]

U.S. News: Censorship and Solutions

Before we go any further, I know what you may be thinking. "Censorship"? Really? In the United States of America? Aren't we a democratic society sporting a national media landscape marked by hundreds of television stations, thousands of radio stations, and millions of websites? To understand Project Censored's mission and approach, let's begin with their definition of "censorship." When most thinking Americans hear the word "censorship," they probably call to mind a country with a state-sponsored news system like, say, the People's Republic of China (PRC), a society marked by a single governing party with a monopoly on official news sources (i.e. Xinhua News Agency—the national media mouthpiece for the Chinese Communist Party, which distributes state-approved news through print, television, radio, and Internet channels). This narrow form of censorship is known in Project Censored circles as "direct censorship," referring to "direct government control of news."[10]

The Project Censored team defines "censorship" of the U.S. news more broadly, as a "form of propaganda"—"deceptive communication used to influence public opinion to benefit a special interest," marked by "the subtle yet constant manipulation of reality by mass media, including the intentional omission of a news story, or an important aspect of a news story, based on anything other than a desire to tell the truth."[11] News manipulation, Project Censored explains in a nod to Chomsky and Herman's propaganda model of news, takes many forms, including political pressure (from government officials and agencies), economic pressure (from advertisers and corporations), and legal pressure (from well-funded lobbying groups and their allies). "Censorship is not limited to overt intentional omission," observes the Censored team, "but also includes anything that interferes with the free flow of information in a society that purports to have a free press system."[12] In sum, our fabled 21st-century new media age presents us with seemingly infinite news choice, but the reality is much more circumscribed, as what passes for U.S. news and reporting is heavily influenced by commercial, corporate, and political players. "In the digital media age, we are presented with a seemingly infinite amount of information, and yet much of it is either superfluous or slanted to hide the truth," explains Censored student journalist Michael Kolbe. "Project Censored provides its participants and readers with the filters necessary to sift through the morass of junk news that billows out of the corporate media smokestack."[13]

In delivering independent reporting, Project Censored claims no political affiliation or stance, and the organization states that it works hard to avoid being labeled with the mainstream media-manufactured liberal/conservative dualism so popular in the U.S. corporate press. "Our readers span the political spectrum, from left to right, largely because the news stories we highlight call into question abuses of power wherever they occur," observes Roth. "During the Bush years, we ran stories critical of the Bush administration's 'war on terror,' but not because they were Republicans. We are equally critical of how President Obama, a Democrat, is employing deadly drone strikes and targeted killings to pursue U.S. military objectives globally."

Independent observers, including crowd-sourced Wikipedia, claim that Project Censored has a leftist slant, based on the types of news stories they highlight—"big business, economic inequality, the Pentagon, damage to the environment, and the misdeeds of conservative politicians"[14]—as well as the involvement of national-profile progressive scholars, including (now-deceased) Howard Zinn, Noam Chomsky, Michael Parenti, Normon Solomon, and Robert Jensen, in the organization's annual work. Several years ago, in a public debate with Project Censored's Mark Lowenthal, conservative commentator

Jack Shafer complained that Project Censored has an "overbearing left-wing bias." But Roth takes issue with these criticisms, stating that "our goal is to speak truth to power, without the obsessive concern for the usual political distinctions, such as liberal versus conservative, that corporate media emphasize again and again."[15]

The Censored team's grassroots generative approach to news creation also supports critical thinking and media literacy education, two skill sets vital to discerning citizens and healthy democracies in the digital age. "Even in a society with strong free speech protections, if powerful elites can significantly manipulate public opinion, then free speech may actually serve the interests of those in power more effectively than traditional censorship," explains Andy Roth. "For this reason, the development of students' critical thinking capacities is crucial to democracy—especially for millennials who are bombarded with digital media that aim to colonize their attention through 'clicks' and 'likes.'" Roth lists a number of critical thinking and media literacy skills vital to effective news gathering within the Censored arena: "to formulate vital questions clearly and precisely; to gather and assess relevant information; to formulate well-reasoned conclusions and solutions that can be tested against relevant criteria and standards; to think open-mindedly across alternative systems of thought, while identifying underlying assumptions; and to communicate all of this effectively—these are elementary critical thinking skills that make free speech meaningful and robust democracy possible," Roth explains. "Researching Validated Independent News (VINS) stories provides students with direct, hands-on opportunities to engage and hone these skills."[16]

The VINS Approach: Crowdsourcing and Vetting Independent News

Since 1993, Project Censored's "Top 25 Censored News Stories of the Year" publication has served as the organization's annual flagship project, representing a powerful example of independent news "crowdsourcing" and reporting in action. "Our approach to news encourages participation," explains Roth. "The corporate media treat their audience as consumers first, and citizens a distant second. This makes sense—after all, corporate media are in the business of selling a product (the audience) to a customer (advertisers)." By contrast, Project Censored extends a direct invitation to interested citizens to participate in the new gathering process. "We encourage our readers and supporters to be more than passive consumers of news. We teach people (especially our students) to be active, critical readers of news, and we encourage people to become the media themselves," concludes Roth.[17]

The stories that end up being published by Project Censored's annual print publication go through a rigorous, annual, five-step vetting process. "Every year we receive as many as 1,000 article submissions, each of which must be read and evaluated for inclusion at the Project Censored website and, ultimately, for the annual book of the year's top 25 censored stories," notes Roth, summarizing the challenge. Step #1 involves fall semester student researchers and faculty evaluators at various colleges identifying "candidate stories" and vetting each one for "importance, timeliness, strength of its sources, and corporate media coverage." College teams send edited lists of news stories to Project Censored headquarters, and the same process is repeated. Stories that pass this second filter (Step #2)—usually 300 or so—are published on the Media Freedom International website (mediafreedominternational.org) and marked as "Validated Independent News" (VIN) stories for an international readership.[18]

Come spring, Project Censored affiliate campus student-faculty teams and Censored's international panel of judges cull the 300 semi-finalists down to 25 final stories (Step #3). At this point, classes led by Peter Phillips, Mickey Huff, and several affiliates conduct extensive LexusNexus and ProQuest database research and review for each final story (Step #4), then send the stories to be ranked 1–25 (Step #5) by a panel of judges comprised of media studies scholars, professional journalists, and one former FCC commissioner. The "Top 25" list is published in book form each autumn by award-winning Seven Stories Press in New York City (they've carried Censored's annual book since 1996), and co-published in alternative and independent news journals and websites globally. "Although the stories that Project Censored brings forward may be socially and politically controversial—and sometimes even psychologically challenging," observe Roth and Huff of the final result, "we are confident that each is the result of serious journalistic effort."[19]

A "Déjà Vu" section, meanwhile, provides updates on previous years' censored stories, while the "Junk Food News" section (a term coined by Project Censored founder Carl Jensen three decades ago) focuses on "infotainment" stories, the annual *ad nauseam* coverage of which (in addition to making us nauseated) pushed out legitimate news (think incessant 2013 "news" coverage of McDonald's new McRib sandwich, football player Tim Tebow, and weekly TV show "The Voice," to name three), as well as highlighting examples of "news abuse," reporting in "partial ways that make the story distracting, titillating, and even confusing, often at the expense of the story's fundamental facts and overall significance."[20]

Finally, Project Censored explores what Peter Phillips and Mickey Huff call the "truth emergency" (a phrase they coined in 2008) embedded in our largely complicit U.S. culture of news, which is so often silent on vital stories of economic wealth and political power. The annual 2013 book concludes with an international "unhistory" section that considers how stories of media justice around the country and across the world go ignored, falling into the "black hole" of U.S. cultural memory—the Kent State shooting, Guantanamo Bay, Fukushima, and attacks on American immigrants of Middle Eastern origin—to name but four featured in the 2013 collection.

The result is an impressive independent grassroots effort to crowd-source and publish vital news stories of import for all U.S. citizens interested in educating themselves about what is really going on beyond the commercial walls erected by the corporate "news" media. "Corporate news media are largely for-profit, top-down organizations that exercise hegemonic control over information," explains Censored intern Michael Kolbe. "Project Censored provides an opportunity for college students to research issues and news stories in which they have an interest, offering a uniquely democratic and community based approach to news gathering and research."[21]

Conclusion: News the United States Can Use—Building a "Networked" Fourth Estate

Reading Project Censored sometimes feels like occupying a parallel universe, especially if one is conditioned to accept the "news" (can you say "infotainment"?) served up by the U.S. "establishment" media as content that can be considered at all useful or relevant. As the Censored team reminds us, "Independent media—not their corporate counterparts—constitute both the 'mainstream' of healthy U.S. journalism and the sturdy foundation of authentic democratic self-government."[22] As the professional journalism industry continues to implode and reinvent itself piecemeal, Censored's work grows ever more vital in an era marked by the dumbing down of "news" in favor of increased infotainment, public relations fluff masquerading as legitimate journalism, and helped along by the waning of collective public attention in the age of Twitter and Snapchat.

"Information these days is so quickly glossed over, with the short attention span of viewers and the ever-diminishing availability of print media," concludes Censored intern Kira McDonough. "The bright side is that more people are able to connect, research, and share news in this new digital age, and organizations such as Project Censored can reach many more people now. This is the time that many more people seem to be seeking out the truth, so 'truth tellers' like Project Censored need to remain vigilant and relevant."[23] Indeed, as the great 19th-century civil rights activist Wendell Phillips famously observed, "Eternal vigilance is the price of liberty."[24]

"Project Censored can thus be understood as part of what Yochai Benkler describes as the newly-emerging 'networked fourth estate,'" explains Andy Roth. "More diverse and organizationally decentralized, the networked fourth estate challenges the previous dominance of an elite-controlled, centralized, top-down mass media," Roth summarizes, drawing on Benkler. Features include "agility, scope, and diversity of sources and pathways that allow it to 'collect and capture information on a global scale that would be impossible for any single organization to replicate by itself.'"[25] As this chapter goes to press, Project Censored is partnering with the Action Coalition for Media Education to create a new initiative called the Global Critical Media Literacy Project (GCMLP), which envisions expanding Project Censored's decades-long work into more communities in more countries over the next several years. "By fusing ACME's media literacy approach with Project Censored's VINS news gathering experience, we aim to create a more powerful and robust networked approach to independent news gathering and deployment in the Digital Age," explains GCMLP co-founder Nolan Higdon. "Our 21st-century world is in dramatic need of thinking and reflective citizens, accurate independent news, and a fresh infusion of energy into democratic discourse, and we believe that GCMLP can provide all three."[26] With Higdon's words and vision in mind, let us celebrate and support Project Censored: our 21st-century world of independent news is fortunate to have their team on the global news beat.

Notes

1. The title of the June 2012 national Journalism That Matters conference, meeting in Denver, CO before the 5th National Conference on Media Reform, sponsored by the Free Press.
2. T. Griffith, professor in the department of Media Studies, Journalism & Digital Arts at Saint Michael's College (personal interview, May 20, 2015).
3. Ingram, 2011.
4. Quoted in Huff & Roth, 2012, p. 21.
5. Ingram, 2011.
6. For example, Massing, 2015.
7. This term is explored fully in Benkler, 2013.
8. A. Roth, associated director of Project Censored (personal interview, November 8, 2014).
9. M. Huff, director of Project Censored (personal interview, November 14, 2014).
10. Huff & Roth, 2012, p. 30.
11. Huff & Roth, 2012, p. 30.

12. Huff, forthcoming.
13. M. Kolbe, student intern at Project Censored (personal interview, November 16, 2012).
14. See www.Wikipedia.org, "Project Censored."
15. Shafer quoted in Roth, Interview, ibid.
16. Roth, forthcoming.
17. Roth, Interview, ibid.
18. All VINS can be found at http://www.projectcensored.org/category/validated-independent-news/
19. Huff & Roth, p. 31.
20. Huff & Roth, p. 164.
21. Kolbe interview.
22. Huff & Roth, p. 23.
23. K. McDonough, student intern at Project Censored (personal interview, November 18, 2012).
24. Attributed to W. Phillips, from a speech in Boston, MA, on January 28, 1852. In (1853) *Speeches Before the Massachusetts Anti-Slavery Society*, p. 13.
25. Roth, forthcoming.
26. N. Higdon, assistant director of Project Censored (personal interview, May 15, 2015).

References

Benkler, Y. (2013). WikiLeaks and the networked fourth estate. In B. Reveni, A. Hints, & P. McCurdy (Eds.), *Beyond WikiLeaks: Implications for the future of communications, journalism and society* (pp. 11–34). New York, NY: Palgrave Macmillan.

Brock, G. (2013). *Out of print: Newspapers, journalism, and the business of news in the digital age*. London, UK: Kogan Page.

Frechette, J., & Williams, R. (2016). *Media education for a digital generation*. New York, NY: Routledge.

Herman, E. S., & Chomsky, N. (1988). *Manufacturing consent: The political economy of the mass media*. New York, NY: Pantheon Books.

Huff, M., & Roth, A. (2012). *Censored 2013*. New York, NY: Seven Stories Press.

Ingram, M. (2011, July 21). Is the Internet making journalism better or worse? Yes. *Gigaom*. Retrieved from https://gigaom.com/2011/07/21/is-the-internet-making-journalism-better or-worse-yes/

Massing, M. (2015, Summer). Digital journalism: How good is it? *New York Review of Books*. Retrieved from http://www.nybooks.com/articles/archives/2015/jun/04/digital journalism-how-good-is-it/

McChesney, R. (2014). *Digital disconnect: How capitalism is turning the Internet against democracy*. New York, NY: New Press.

Peters, C., & Broersma, M. (2012). *Rethinking journalism: Trust and participation in a transformed news landscape*. New York, NY: Routledge.

Phillips, P., & Huff, M. (2010, June 9). *Analysis of Project Censored: Are we a left-leaning, conspiracy-oriented organization?* Projected Censored. Retrieved from http://www.pro

jectcensored.org/top-stories/articles/analysis-of-project-censored-are-we-a-left-lean
ing-conspiracy-oriented-organization/

Roth, A. (forthcoming). Breaking the corporate news frame: Project Censored's networked news commons. In J. Frechette & R. Williams (Eds.), *Media education for a
digital generation*. New York, NY: Routledge.

Schiffrin, A. (2014). *Global muckraking: 100 years of investigative journalism from around
the world*. New York, NY: New Press.

Stevens, M. (2014). *Beyond news: The future of journalism*. New York, NY: Columbia
University Press.

10. Developing Students' Pedagogical Media Competencies and Intercultural Competencies through a U.S.-German Partnership

Maria Boos
Jennifer Tiede
Silke Grafe
Petra Hesse

Introduction: Research Objectives and Collaboration

The rapid development and spread of digital media in the last several decades have had a powerful impact on most societies and individuals worldwide. One of the positive effects has been that it has become remarkably easy to connect with people from all over the world and to work, chat, and socialize regardless of country borders. However, certain skills are required to use media effectively and responsibly (Buckingham, 2003; Hobbs, 2011; Tulodziecki & Grafe, 2012), especially in communications across cultures and languages. Media and intercultural competencies are generally considered core competencies by researchers in this area. Media competencies enable individuals to handle media appropriately toward their intended use, and to understand the societal role and impact of media (Hobbs, 2011; Tulodziecki, Herzig, & Grafe, 2010). While children and youth acquire some media competencies in informal learning settings, they have to be taught others more explicitly in school. The teachers themselves need training and skills to teach these media competencies successfully, appropriately, and comprehensively (Tulodziecki, 2012). The teachers' skills will be referred to as *pedagogical media competencies* in the following chapter. *Intercultural competencies* help people reflect on cultures other than their own, broaden their own perspectives, and successfully communicate with members of other cultures (Byram, 1997). Both competencies are necessary, but not sufficient, to achieve media-enabled cross-cultural communication.

The authors are interested in enhancing pre-service teachers' pedagogical media competencies and intercultural competencies at institutions of higher education. The German members of the team developed a seminar for German university students, which grew out of the collaboration of U.S. and a German media education professor. The seminar uses a multi-pronged approach to enhance students' media and intercultural competencies, including a media-assisted joint session of U.S. and German students.

In this chapter, the authors will introduce the project in some detail and share some preliminary findings. They will provide a brief sketch of the theoretical framework in order to introduce relevant terms and constructs and to delineate the intended goal. They will go on to describe the collaboration between the U.S. and German instructors, as well as the seminar, in more detail. They will discuss the empirical survey, report some of the findings, and interpret the results. They will conclude with some final reflections on the limitations of the current project, and an outline of perspectives for the future.

Theoretical Framework

As already stated, the main purpose of this project was to help students acquire and develop both *pedagogical media competencies* and *intercultural competencies.*

Pedagogical media competencies

Given the infusion of information and communication technologies into daily life and their importance for children and youth, teachers should have specific skills and competencies to meet the demands and challenges posed by new technologies (e.g., Wilson, Grizzle, Tuazon, Akyempong, & Cheung, 2011). However, there is no clear consensus on the definition of such pedagogical media competencies.

In U.S. scholarship, a basic distinction is made between "teaching *with* media and technology" and "teaching *about* media and technology"; the latter is also referred to as *media literacy* or *media education* (Tiede, Grafe, & Hobbs, in press). The TPACK ("technological, pedagogical, and content knowledge") model is well established as a framework for some of the competencies in question. Developed by Mishra and Koehler (2006) and building on the work of Shulman (1986), it highlights seven components of pedagogical media competence that are likely "to facilitate teachers' successful integration of technology into the classroom" (Mishra & Koehler, 2006, p. 1017). Based on Shulman's work on content knowledge, Mishra and Koehler added technological knowledge, technological content knowledge, technological pedagogical knowledge, and technological pedagogical content knowledge. In the process, they created a comprehensive and widely used framework for teaching *with* media and technology. Ever since its conception, this framework has been subject to extensive research. Most recently, it was studied by Crompton (2015), and new scales were developed for its validation (Horzum, Akgün, & Öztürk, 2014). The TPACK model was amended by adding several new components and theoretical considerations. Sang, Tondeur, Chai, and Dong (2014) considered cultural differences and developed the new CTPACK model. Tzavara and Komis (2015), as well as Bachy (2014), reconsidered TPACK with regard to subject-specific contexts (Technological Didactical Content Knowledge (TDCK), and Technopedagogical Disciplinary Knowledge (TPDK)).

A second U.S. approach to defining the pedagogical media competencies required of teachers can be found in the National Educational Technology Standards (NETS), issued by the International Society for Technology in Education (ISTE, 2008). In compliance with the TPACK model, some of the NETS refer to aspects of teaching *with* media, such as designing digital learning environments, and some also address issues of teaching *about* media, like the legal or ethical aspects of media use. Additionally, a third dimension is introduced, as some of the standards refer to on-the-job training and leadership competencies (ISTE, 2008; Tiede et al., in press).

A slightly different focus can be found in other guidelines, such as the Core Principles of Media Literacy Education, issued by the National Association for Media Literacy Education. These principles also suggest important skills and competencies, but they mainly refer to aspects of teaching *about* media, such as the role of media in culture and the importance of critical thinking about media, technology, and culture (NAMLE, 2008).

Germany and other German-speaking countries have also been witness to intense academic debates about pedagogical media competencies. Tulodziecki and Blömeke (1997) identified five target areas of pedagogical media competencies for teachers. These five areas are (1) using media in a competent way; (2) understanding and sensitively considering the meaning of media for children and youth socialization; (3) analyzing and assessing media content with regard to aspects of teaching and learning; (4) fulfilling media-related educational and advisory tasks in lessons and projects; and (5) understanding and influencing personal, equipment-specific, organizational, and school-related conditions for media education at school (see also Blömeke, 2000; Tulodziecki, 2012). This work was continued and further specified and amended, most significantly by Gysbers (2008), Siller (2007), and Tulodziecki (2012) (Tiede et al., in press).

Recently, the project "Modelling and Measuring of Pedagogical Media Competencies" (M³K), funded by the German Federal Ministry of Research and Education, pioneered a new approach in this field. A new and comprehensive model was developed that relies on the aforementioned German academic discourse but also considers international experts' reviews and a number of international models. As a result, pedagogical media competencies have been redefined as the interplay of media didactics, media education and school reform. *Media didactics* refers to teaching *with* media, i.e. the design and use of media content for educational purposes; *media education* addresses media-related educational and teaching tasks such as considering the ethical impact of media on individuals and society; and *school reform* deals with the integration of media into school on a cross-curricular and systemic level (Tiede et al., in press; Tulodziecki et al., 2010, p. 41). Five competency aspects further specify these three main areas: (1) understanding and assessing conditions; (2) describing and evaluating theoretical approaches; (3) analyzing and evaluating examples; (4) developing one's own theory-based suggestions; and (5) implementing and evaluating theory-based examples. From the combination of these five competency aspects with the three core areas of media didactics, media education, and school reform, two standards per combination result, for example, Standard ME2.1: "Student teachers are able to describe concepts of media education and related empirical findings appropriately," and Standard ME2.2: "Student teachers are able to assess concepts from an empirical, normative or practical perspective" (cf. Tulodziecki, 2012).

As these different models from the United States and Germany show, the exact definition of pedagogical media competencies is subject to debate from multiple theoretical points of view, and their content differs, particularly in international comparison. However, in spite of the differences, there are essentially three core areas: *media didactics* (teaching *with* media), *media education* (teaching *about* media), and media-related *school reform*. The significance attributed to each of these areas varies, but evidence for the importance of all three can be found in the academic discourse of both countries.

Intercultural competencies

Understanding languages and cultures other than one's own becomes more and more important in industrialized societies (Garrett-Rucks, 2012) because of an increase in international cooperation in politics, business, and science (Loboda, 2003). Acquiring intercultural competencies becomes desirable as well as necessary.

The authors define intercultural competencies as "the ability to communicate effectively in cross-cultural situations and to relate appropriately in a variety of cultural contexts" (Bennett & Bennett, 2004, p. 149). They agree with European and U.S. colleagues who consider Byram's model (1997) groundbreaking (Garrett-Rucks, 2012; Wiest, 2013). Byram, Gribkova, and Starkey (2002) assume that the foundation of intercultural competence lies in the attitudes of the intercultural speaker and mediator. An intercultural speaker does not adjust to a culture, but stands between cultures and tries to mediate between them (Byram, Gribkova, & Starkey, 2002). According to this model, the process of acquiring intercultural competencies includes five elements (Byram, 1997), which are defined as follows:

- Intercultural attitudes, that is, "curiosity and openness, readiness to suspend disbelief about other cultures and belief about one's own."
- Knowledge "of social groups and their products and practices in one's own and in one's interlocutor's country, and of the general processes of societal and individual interaction."
- Skills of interpreting and relating, defined as the "ability to interpret a document or event from another culture, to explain it and relate it to documents or events from one's own."
- Skills of discovery and interaction, that is, the "ability to acquire new knowledge of a culture and cultural practices and the ability to operate knowledge, attitudes and skills under the constraints of real-time communication and interaction."
- Critical cultural awareness, defined as the "ability to evaluate, critically and on the basis of explicit criteria, perspectives, practices and products in one's own and other cultures and countries." (Byram et al., 2002)

The model shows that in order to develop intercultural competencies, individuals need to gain knowledge about countries and cultures, but they also need to be given opportunities to reflect on their own culture and their attitudes toward others.

In the project described here, this was attempted by creating a small seminar where German and U.S. students had the chance to reflect jointly upon their own media biography and their media use today.

The Collaboration

Including German and U.S. students in this collaborative project held a number of promises. Both countries have a rich tradition of educational research and discourse about pedagogy, particularly with regard to media pedagogy. Even though the discourse in both countries evolved fairly independently, there are important congruencies of central concepts and beliefs (Grafe, 2011; Tiede et al., in press). As a result, the collaboration of a German and a U.S. institution of higher education seemed worthwhile and made sense on theoretical grounds.

At the Ruhr-University Bochum in Germany, a new curriculum was implemented in the winter term 2013–14. Students of all subjects were given the opportunity to elect the class "Media Education in Germany and the US in Comparison," as an elective subject as part of their bachelor's degree course. Eleven students from different fields of studies joined the class, which took place three hours a week over the course of 15 weeks. The class cooperated with a class on "Children and the Media" at Wheelock College in Boston, Massachusetts. This 15-week course for undergraduates majoring in Psychology and Human Development, communications, or American studies met for 3 1/2 hours per week, and has existed since the mid-1990s. Students explore children's (mis)understanding of the media and the effects of media (violence; representations of race, gender, and class) on children's development. They also learn about media ownership, and the impact of growing up in consumer society. As future teachers and human service professionals, Wheelock students discuss how they can address children's fascination with the media as teachers, social workers, counselors, and future parents. In the process, they explore a wide range of responses, from media literacy education, to parent education, to the creation of media policies, and to media activism. Considering the course in light of the above definitions of pedagogical media competencies, it is primarily an example of "teaching *about* media and technology;" but students also practice what it means to "teach *with* media and technology."

As indicated earlier, the main goal of the collaboration between the two institutions of higher education was to help students gain and develop both *pedagogical media competencies* and *intercultural competencies*. As both constructs are very complex, selected competency areas were chosen for the development of the course curriculum:

Pedagogical media competencies:

- Media education
  - o Understanding and assessing conditions:
    - Media use of German and U.S. children and teenagers
    - Media biographies of German and U.S. children and teenagers
    - Media effects on German and U.S. children and teenagers
  - o Describing and evaluating theoretical approaches:
    - Different concepts of media education in Germany and the United States
    - Digital literacy in a participatory culture
    - Cyberbullying research in Germany and the United States
  - o Analyzing and evaluating examples:
    - Cyberbullying interventions in Germany and the United States
    - Teaching material on different media education topics
- Media didactics
  - o Describing and evaluating theoretical approaches:
    - Functions of media in the classroom

Intercultural competencies:

- Intercultural attitudes, skills of interpreting and relating, critical cultural awareness:
  - o Stereotypes of people in the United States and Germany
  - o Stereotypes of Turkish people in Germany
- Knowledge:
  - o Definition of intercultural competencies
  - o Byram's model of intercultural competencies

These topics were covered in weekly sessions with the German students. Additionally, the exchange with students and a teacher from the United States was supposed to extend the intercultural competencies of the students, especially their "intercultural attitudes" and "skills of discovery and interaction."

Furthermore, e-learning was an important element of the class: students created animated videos; found all information about the course on the software learning management system "Moodle"; used web conferencing software for seminar sessions; and collected, documented, and reflected on different assignments in their own e-portfolios. Tulodziecki, Herzig, and

Grafe's (2010) action-oriented approach is compatible with such activities and provided the didactic orientation for the whole seminar. This involved giving students a complex task at the beginning of the learning process, then discussing specific goals and the significance of the topic. After further planning of the learning process and gathering of information, students solved the task in groups. At the end of each session, results were presented, compared, discussed, and summarized, and the students reflected on the whole learning process. Two sessions that involved international exchange are described in further detail in the following.

The international collaboration consisted of a synchronous online meeting with the American professor who gave a lecture about the state of the art of cyberbullying research in the United States. During the session, German students had a chance to ask questions and to discuss cyberbullying interventions in the United States and in Germany. They also described and reflected on their own experiences with cyberbullying. They went on to apply their new knowledge by creating an animated video about cyberbullying as a homework assignment. In addition, students of the two media classes in both countries had an online conference meeting. They had been given two tasks in preparation for the meeting: to keep a diary of their own media use and to create their own media biographies using an e-portfolio. One main goal of this joint session was to discuss and to reflect on stereotypes of Germans and Americans.

Methodology

The goal of this collaborative project was to extend the pedagogical media competencies and intercultural competencies of the participating students. In order to document which competencies students demonstrated at the end of the semester, a combination of quantitative and qualitative research methods was used.

Questionnaire

At the German university, a research study was conducted about course outcomes, following a pre-test/post-test design with control group. A questionnaire was administered at the beginning and at the end of the semester, to measure changes in students' pedagogical media and intercultural competencies. The questionnaire consisted of 13 questions, 9 measuring pedagogical media competencies and 4 assessing intercultural competencies. The questionnaire followed a mixed-methods approach: 2 of the 9 questions about media pedagogical competencies were closed-ended, 4 of the questions were open-ended, and 3 of the questions were semi-structured. The 4 questions referring to intercultural competencies were closed-ended (multiplechoice or yes/no).

The seven questionnaire items assessing students' pedagogical media competencies were derived from Tulodziecki et al.'s (2010) theoretical framework. Additional questions were taken from earlier studies by Blömeke (2000), Loboda (2003), and the Medienpädagogischer Forschungsverband Südwest (2012).

The sample size is n $_{TG}$ = 11 German students, 7 of whom completed both the pre-test and the post-test at the beginning and end of the winter semester 2013–14. The test group consisted of 4 male and 7 female students aged 21 to 30 (x $_{Age\ TG}$ = 24.36, SD $_{Age\ TG}$ = 1.8). Most of the students majored in English (4 students) and history (3 students). The remaining students majored in many other liberal arts disciplines (German, French, Slavic languages and Russian culture, philosophy, comparative literature, theater, linguistics, culture and society), as well as business, communications, and physical education.

The sample size of the German control group was n $_{CG}$ = 20 German students, with 11 participants completing both pre- and post-test. The control group was composed of 5 male and 14 female students (one student did not answer the question about gender) aged 20 to 45 (x $_{Age\ CG}$ = 24.42, SD $_{Age\ CG}$ = 2.79). The members of the control group were comparable to the test group, in terms of their undergraduate majors.

Interviews

For a deeper qualitative analysis of the intercultural competencies, semi-structured interviews (Friebertshäuser & Langer, 2010) were conducted with seven German and three American students drawn from the population of participants in the joint session at the end of the term. The 14 open-ended interview questions were based on Byram's (1997) five aspects of intercultural competence. Two questions addressed the competency aspect "intercultural attitude," 2 questions covered the aspect "knowledge," 1 question explored the aspect "skills of discovery and interaction," 6 questions addressed the aspect "skills of interpreting and relating," and three questions focused on the aspect "critical cultural awareness."

To evaluate the qualitative data (open-ended questions in the questionnaire and the interviews), a frequency analysis was conducted. Frequency analysis is a form of content analysis where text elements and their frequency are counted (Schnell, Hill, & Esser, 2008). Thus, references to Byram's model of intercultural competencies were identified and quantified. To do so, all five aspects of Byram's model were assigned a maximum number of points, depending on their composition. For example, four points could be achieved in the field of intercultural attitudes, if references to all of the following four aspects were detected in the students' answers: (1) curiosity (being interested in the other country's culture); (2) openness (being ready to learn something about the other culture); (3) knowledge about the fact that one's own attitudes and values are not the only ones possible; and (4) the ability to decenter (being aware how one's own values, attitudes, and behavior might be perceived by other cultures or people) (Byram et al., 2002).

Results

As indicated above, the main goals of the data collection were twofold: to measure changes in German students' intercultural and pedagogical media competencies using a pre-test/post-test design; and to further explore students' intercultural competencies by conducting interviews after the joint session of German and U.S. students.

Questionnaire

The following table indicates the findings of the questionnaire. The items referring to pedagogical media competencies are labeled *PMC*; items relating to intercultural competencies are labeled *ICC*.

Table 10.1. Descriptive results of the questionnaire.

		Test group		Control group	
Item No.	$x_{maximum}$	$x_{pre\text{-}test}$	$x_{post\text{-}test}$	$x_{pre\text{-}test}$	$x_{post\text{-}test}$
PMC1	4	0.44 (SD 0.53)	1.29 (SD 1.11)	1.10 (SD 0.79)	0.73 (SD 1.10)
PMC2	2	0.33 (SD 0.5)	0.43 (SD 0.79)	0.05 (SD 0.22)	0.09 (SD 0.30)
PMC3	3	0.89 (SD 0.78)	1.86 (SD 0.90)	0.30 (SD 0.57)	0.36 (SD 0.67)
PMC4	3	0.67 (SD 0.5)	0.43 (SD 0.79)	0.30 (SD 0.47)	0.55 (SD 0.82)

Item No.	X maximum	Test group		Control group	
		X pre-test	X post-test	X pre-test	X post-test
PMC5	2	0 (SD 0)	1.00 (SD 0.82)	0 (SD 0)	0 (SD 0)
PMC6	2	0.89 (SD 0.78)	1.00 (SD 0.82)	0.60 (SD 0.75)	1.09 (SD 0.83)
PMC7	2	1.00 (SD 0.71)	1.57 (SD 0.53)	0.85 (SD 0.59)	0.82 (SD 0.40)
PMC8	3	0 (SD 0)	0.86 (SD 0.38)	0.05 (SD 0.22)	0.18 (SD 0.40)
PMC9	4	0.22 (SD 0.44)	0.43 (SD 0.79)	0.15 (SD 0.37)	0.18 (SD 0.40)
ICC1	1	0.22 (SD 0.44)	0.71 (SD 0.49)	0.45 (SD 0.51)	0.36 (SD 0.50)
ICC2	1	0.44 (SD 0.53)	0.14 (SD 0.38)	0.15 (SD 0.37)	0.27 (SD 0.47)
ICC3	1	0.33 (SD 0.50)	0.43 (SD 0.53)	0.40 (SD 0.50)	0.45 (SD 0.52)
ICC4	1	0.67 (SD 0.50)	0.57 (SD 0.53)	0.40 (SD 0.50)	0.36 (SD 0.46)
Σ	29	6.11 (SD 1.51)	10.71 (SD 2.9)	4.8 (SD 2.48)	5.45 (SD 2.73)

The overall results of the test group improved between pre- and post-test, with the exception of three items, which deserve particular attention. First of all, item PMC4 ("Which media educational approach does the following lesson example represent?") requires factual knowledge about media education and the ability to apply that knowledge. A decline can be noted in the test group's results from pre-test to post-test. The same applies for item ICC2 about intercultural competence (a situation of clashing cultural habits is described, and the participants are expected to choose the correct rationale from a choice of four given answers), and for item ICC4, about intercultural competence (a situation is described in which the habits of members of different cultures collide, expectations are not met, and the participants are expected to choose the correct rationale from a choice of four given answers).

Students' answers to the other eight items did not yield any surprising findings. The results revealed a moderate increase in measured competencies in the test group from pre-test to post-test.

Interviews

The interviews were conducted in order to amend the survey data on intercultural competencies. The frequency analysis revealed the following results.

Table 10.2. Descriptive results of qualitative explorative analysis of intercultural
competencies.

Competency aspect	$X_{maximum}$	$X_{German\ students}$	$X_{U.S.\ students}$
1. Intercultural attitudes	4	2.86 (SD 0.49)	1.33 (SD 0.44)
2. Knowledge	3	1.86 (SD 0.24)	2 (SD 0.67)
3. Skills of interpreting and relating	3	2 (SD 0.57)	1.67 (SD 0.44)
4. Skills of discovery and interaction	3	2 (SD 0.57)	1.33 (SD 0.44)
5. Critical cultural awareness	3	1.57 (SD 0.59)	2 (SD 0)
Σ	16	10.29	8.33

According to this data, the German sample performed better in the area of
intercultural attitudes. Critical cultural awareness was the area where the students' answers showed the fewest references to the model. The U.S. sample,
on the other hand, performed better in the areas of knowledge and critical
cultural awareness. Their lowest results were noted in the field of intercultural
attitudes. All in all, the German sample on average achieved a higher score
than the U.S. sample.

Discussion

The main goal of this study was to develop a university seminar, based on relevant theoretical frameworks, with the intention of increasing students' pedagogical media competencies and intercultural competencies. The descriptive
data analysis indicates that this goal was achieved with moderate results.

Limitations of the study

It should be noted that the reported study is exploratory and that some limitations have to be considered when interpreting the results. Most importantly, the test instrument was not fully validated at the time of use. Hence,
the results ought to be understood as reflecting trends in the data, instead
of reliable and valid assessments of the competencies in question. Moreover,
the sample size of the test group was rather small, and the size of the U.S.

comparison group was even smaller—hence, the descriptive presentation of the results, because a statistical evaluation would not be appropriate (Rost, 2005). Furthermore, the circumstances of the project did not allow for a pre-test/post-test design with control group for the qualitative, interview assessment of intercultural competencies.

Questionnaire results

Despite the limitations, the results can be understood to point to trends in the data. Nine of the items were concerned with pedagogical media competencies. PMC5 and PMC8 were affected rather directly by the seminar, as the students could not solve them at all at the beginning of the seminar, but were much more successful at the end of the seminar. The conclusion seems warranted that the sessions of the seminar that referred to media education competency Aspect 2 (describing and evaluating theoretical approaches) and Aspect 3 (analyzing and evaluating examples) were successful and led to an increase in knowledge in these content areas. This makes sense given the strong emphasis of the seminar on the first aspect.

Six additional items measuring pedagogical media competencies showed a moderate increase from pre-test to post-test, and thus further illustrate students' improvements on items PMC5 and PMC8. PMC4 showed a trend in the opposite direction, even though the students should have been able to solve the task by applying skills in the context of media education, competency Aspect 3 (analyzing and evaluating examples). Unclear instructions or wording, misunderstandings in the learning process, or gaps in the coverage of relevant facts may be to blame for this result.

Of the four items assessing intercultural competencies, two revealed a slight decline in the test group. The other two items showed a moderate increase in scores. This can be explained by the curriculum of the seminar, which primarily focused on pedagogical media competencies. Due to time constraints, intercultural competencies were covered only in one lesson and in the joint session with the U.S. students.

Interview results

The differences between the German sample and the U.S. sample were notable (Table 2), but small. The strongest difference between the two groups appeared in their "intercultural attitudes." German students may have an advantage, because they are surrounded by so many other European countries and practice intercultural competencies through travel and daily encounters with members of other national groups. The German students also chose to participate in this seminar on "Media Education in Germany and the U.S. in Comparison." As a group, they may have been particularly interested in intercultural attitudes. Wheelock students' higher scores on "knowledge" and "critical cultural awareness" make sense because of a strong emphasis on diversity and cultural awareness throughout the Wheelock curriculum. The sample sizes were much too small to draw any conclusions about more general differences between the two cultures. Additional research is called for, with larger samples of students and more similar courses and interventions, to draw more definitive conclusions.

Future perspectives

To avoid the limitations of the current pilot project, professors in the United States and Germany, and in other countries, will have to team up even more deliberately. Various obstacles to collaboration will have to be taken into account, most prominently differences in semester schedules, time differences, and structural differences in the undergraduate curriculum. In the ideal future project, professors in two or more countries will agree to plan and teach identical courses, as well as conduct pre- and post-tests with all of their students, to assess their pedagogical media competencies and intercultural competencies at the beginning and at the end of the semester. To do so, a validated test instrument will be required to improve the reliability of the results and to enable sounder comparisons. Furthermore, the combined use of qualitative and quantitative methods should be expanded, as well as the use of methods of comparative research (Blömeke & Paine, 2008). Only then will it be possible to draw more definitive conclusions about broader cultural differences and similarities in pedagogical media competencies and intercultural competencies, and their origins in cultural practices.

References

Bachy, S. (2014). TPDK, a new definition of the TPACK model for a university setting. *European Journal of Open, Distance and E-Learning 17*(2), 15–39.

Bennett, J. M., & Bennett, M. J. (2004). Developing intercultural sensitivity: An integrative approach to global and domestic diversity. In D. Landis, J. Bennett, & M. Bennett (Eds.), *Handbook of intercultural training* (3rd ed.) (pp. 147–65). Thousand Oaks, CA: Sage.

Blömeke, S. (2000). *Medienpädagogische Kompetenz. Theoretische und empirische Fundierung eines zentralen Elements der Lehrerausbildung.* München, Germany: Kopaed.

Blömeke, S., & Paine, L. (2008). Getting the fish out of the water: Considering benefits and problems of doing research on teacher education at an international level. *Teaching and Teacher Education, 24*(4), 2027–37.

Buckingham, D. (2003). *Media education: Literacy, learning and contemporary culture.* Cambridge, UK: Polity.

Byram, M. (1997). *Teaching and assessing intercultural communicative competence.* Clevedon, UK: Multilingual Matters.

Byram, M., Gribkova, B., & Starkey, H. (2002). *Developing the intercultural dimension in language teaching: A practical introduction for teachers.* Strasbourg, France: Council of Europe.

Crompton, H. (2015). Pre-service teachers' developing technological pedagogical content knowledge (TPACK) and beliefs on the use of technology in the K–12 mathematics classroom: A review of the literature. In C. Angeli & N. Valanides (Eds.), *Technological pedagogical content knowledge: Exploring, developing, and assessing TPCK* (pp. 239–50). New York, NY: Springer.

Friebertshäuser, B., & Langer, A. (2010). Interviewformen und Interviewpraxis. In B. Friebertshäuser (Ed.), *Handbuch qualitative Forschungsmethoden in der Erziehungswissenschaft* (3rd ed.) (pp. 437–55). Weinheim, Germany: Juventa.

Garrett-Rucks, P. (2012). Byram versus Bennett: Discrepancies in the assessment of learners' IC development. *Proceedings of Intercultural Competence Conference, 2* (2), 11–33. Retrieved from http://cercll.arizona.edu/_media/development/confer ences/2012_ICC/garrett_rucks_byram_versus_bennett_ic2012.pdf

Grafe, S. (2011). 'Media literacy' und 'media (literacy) education' in den USA: Ein Brückenschlag über den Atlantik. In H. Moser, P. Grell, & H. Niesyto (Eds.), *Medienbildung und Medienkompetenz* (pp. 59–80). München, Germany: Kopaed.

Gysbers, A. (2008). *Lehrer – Medien – Kompetenz. Eine empirische Untersuchung zur medienpädagogischen Kompetenz und Performanz niedersächsischer Lehrkräfte.* Berlin, Germany: Vistas.

Hobbs, R. (2011). *Digital and media literacy: Connecting culture and classroom.* Thousand Oaks, CA: Corwin.

Horzum, M. B., Akgün, O. E., & Öztürk, E. (2014). The psychometric properties of the technological pedagogical content knowledge scale. *International Online Journal of Educational Sciences, 6*(3), 544–57.

International Society for Technology in Education (ISTE). (2008). *The ISTE NETS and performance indicators for teachers (NETS-T).* Retrieved from http://www.iste.org/ docs/pdfs/20–14_ISTE_Standards-T_PDF.pdf

Loboda, J. (2003). *Entwicklung eines Tests zur Erfassung interkultureller Handlungskompetenz (TIHK).* Diplomarbeit an der Universität Regensburg. Retrieved from http://www.uni-regensburg.de/Fakultaeten/phil_Fak_II/Psychologie/Thomas/ lehre/PWP_IK/DALoboda_Gesamt.pdf

Medienpädagogischer Forschungsverband Südwest [mpfs]. (2012). *JIM-Studie 2012: Basisuntersuchung zum Medienumgang 12-bis 19-Jähriger.* Stuttgart, Germany: Medienpädagogischer Forschungsverband Südwest.

Mishra, P., & Koehler, M. J. (2006). Technological pedagogical content knowledge: A framework for teacher knowledge. *Teachers College Record, 108*(6), 1017–54.

National Association for Media Literacy Education (NAMLE). (2008). *Core principles of media literacy education*. Retrieved from http://namle.net/publications/core-prin ciples/

Rost, D. H. (2005). *Interpretation und Bewertung pädagogisch-psychologischer Studien*. Weinheim, Germany/Basel, Switzerland: Beltz.

Sang, G., Tondeur, J., Chai, C. S., & Dong, Y. (2014). Validation and profile of Chinese pre-service teachers' technological pedagogical content knowledge scale. *Asia-Pacific Journal of Teacher Education*, 1–17.

Schnell, R., Hill, P. B., & Esser, E. (2008). *Methoden der empirischen Sozialforschung* (8th ed.). München, Germany: Oldenbourg Wissenschaftsverlag.

Shulman, L. S. (1986). Those who understand: Knowledge growth in teaching. *Educational Researcher, 15*(2), 4–31.

Siller, F. (2007). *Medienpädagogische Handlungskompetenzen: Problemorientierung und Kompetenzerwerb beim Lernen mit neuen Medien*. Mainz, Germany: Universität.

Tiede, J., Grafe, S., & Hobbs, R. (in press). Pedagogical media competencies of pre-service teachers in Germany and the United States of America: A comparative analysis of theory and practice. *Peabody Journal of Education*.

Tulodziecki, G. (2012). Medienpädagogische Kompetenz und Standards in der Lehrerbildung. In R. Schulz-Zander, B. Eickelmann, H. Moser, H. Niesyto, & P. Grell (Eds.), *Jahrbuch Medienpädagogik 9* (pp. 271–97). Wiesbaden, Germany: Springer VS.

Tulodziecki, G., & Blömeke, S. (1997). Zusammenfassung: Neue Medien—neue Aufgaben für die Lehrerausbildung. In G. Tulodziecki & S. Blömeke (Eds.), *Neue Medien—neue Aufgaben für die Lehrerausbildung* (155–60). Tagungsdokumentation. Gütersloh, Germany: Verlag Bertelsmann Stiftung.

Tulodziecki, G., & Grafe, S. (2012). Approaches to learning with media and media literacy education: Trends and current situation in Germany. *Journal of Media Literacy Education, 4*(1), 44–60.

Tulodziecki, G., Herzig, B., & Grafe, S. (2010). *Medienbildung in Schule und Unterricht. Grundlagen und Beispiele*. Bad Heilbrunn, Germany: Julius Klinkhardt.

Tzavara, A., & Komis, V. (2015). Design and implementation of educational scenarios with the integration of TDCK: A case study at a department of early childhood education. In C. Angeli & N. Valanides (Eds.), *Technological pedagogical content knowledge: Exploring, developing, and assessing TPCK* (pp. 209–24). New York, NY: Springer.

Wiest, B. (2013). *Byrams Modell der interkulturellen kommunikativen Kompetenz*. Retrieved from http://school-partnerships.eu/de/m1_2-cultural-iceberg-and-byrams-framework/

Wilson, C., Grizzle, A., Tuazon, R., Akyempong, K., & Cheung, C.-K. (2011). *Media and information literacy curriculum for teachers*. Paris, France: United Nations Educational, Scientific and Cultural Organization.

11. Breaking Down Barriers: Digital Media and Universal Design

VICTORIA BROWN

Background

Within any classroom, students have various abilities for using the material presented in the classroom to achieve learning outcomes. In those same classrooms are students who come from a variety of cultural backgrounds. Disparities in levels of technical skill can be attributed to differences in primary language and uses of digital media in the home. Differences in primary language and uses of digital media in the home can be attributed to varying technical skills. Principles of universal design implemented in a global classroom invested in rich digital media experiences assist the teacher in meeting the needs of children with diverse needs.

Issues of Access

Access to digital media has been correlated to student achievement through several studies. Students scored better on the Program for International Student Assessment (PISA) if they used computers at home for educational purposes (Organisation for Economic Co-Operation and Development, 2005). The same study also identified that longer periods of time for students using the computer correlated with higher PISA scores on the mathematics assessment. In another study, similar results were found, that the more time students spent using informational technology, the better their grades and grade point averages were (Jackson et al., 2008). Apparently, the longer students spend on the computer, the greater the diversity of activities in which they engage, such as gaming, reading websites, and writing, all of which are academic-type activities (Jackson et al., 2008).

Ensuring access to digital-rich classrooms can mitigate the lower achievement rates due to reduced technology access within the home. Cultural background of the students can be a factor in the lack of exposure to technology in the home. The Internet primarily supports approximately 800 million English users, resulting in the dominant language being English (Miniwatts Marketing Group, 2015). This leads to non-English-speaking families not valuing the use of technology. Because fewer websites are available to non-English-speaking families, they are less likely to understand the importance of access to the Internet. As a result, these families, if they have Internet access, use older computers with slower Internet connection speeds (Garland, 2009–10). The older computers and lower bandwidth with slower speeds, combined with lack of access to digital tools, resources, and services and the opportunities to use that technology, impact the students' ability to increase their digital knowledge, awareness of the world, and academic skills (Davis, Fuller, Jackson, Pittman, & Sweet, 2007).

Universal Design for Learning Guidelines

Variations in students' abilities occur in several different domains. For example, students have varying perceptual abilities, cognitive abilities, cultural understandings, and linguistic backgrounds that exist along a continuum. At one end of the continuum, students could be gifted with exceptional abilities to access the information presented in the lesson. Others require assistance, such as glasses, hearing aids, and cognitive structural aids in order for them to be successful. Finally, some students experience extreme challenges in these areas, requiring extensive support or alternative approaches to allow them to achieve a level of success.

Experience Challenges	Typical Skills and Abilities	Exceptional Talent

Increasingly, teachers are required to reach all of the students in the classroom. Universal Design for Learning (UDL) gives guidance for accommodating the varying needs of the students in the classroom. The principles of universal design provide a variety of strategies, which can be embedded throughout a unit of study. Below is a description of the principles the National Center on Universal Design for Learning has developed over time to guide teachers in designing instructional experiences that meet the needs of their diverse classrooms. The Center's website has additional information than what is provided here (http://cast.org).

The guidelines for UDL were developed as the usability of digital content emerged in the mid-1980s (CAST, 2015). The Center for Applied Special Technology (CAST) was formed to explore ways in which technology could be used to support the needs of diverse children, of whom many experience learning challenges due to a disability. The guidelines give educators a pedagogical framework in which to evaluate, select, and implement the technology tools in the support of learning.

Multiple means of representation

This guideline, multiple means of representation, addresses differences in the ability to comprehend material; decipher language, expressions, and symbols; and use the senses for perception. By providing different options for students to select from in understanding and comprehending the lesson, the chances for success in achieving the learning outcomes increase. Ideas for multiple representations include cognitive scaffolding, use of multimedia to enhance the understanding of definitions, access to translations for different languages, and alternatives for auditory or visual information (National Center on Universal Design for Learning, 2012).

Multiple means of engagement

The multiple means of engagement guideline promotes the development of purposeful, motivated learners. Students in the classroom have varying levels of motivation based upon their interests and abilities. The options in this guideline use individual choice and utilize students' values to create individualized goals and objectives to match the students' unique perceptions. At the same time, the options teach students coping strategies and reflection skills to improve their metacognition (National Center on Universal Design for Learning, 2012).

Multiple means of action and expression

To guide students into becoming strategic, goal-directed learners, the guideline for multiple means of action and expression again suggests options for students. This guideline allows students the opportunities to express what they have learned and the ideas they have developed, in creative ways. By setting individualized goals that match student abilities, the students are motivated to achieve at the level of their capabilities. The individualized goals allow students to create projects using multimedia tools that match their preferences. Finally, teachers can provide various methods to respond to the learning outcomes by using technology tools (National Center on Universal Design for Learning, 2012).

Digital Media Skills

Digital media skills are becoming important as more media options are available to students. Through accessing digital media, students are able to access, evaluate, and analyze information. Digital tools are used by students to create and share new digital media products (Heick, 2014; Media Smarts, n.d.; US Digital Literacy, 2014). Students are empowered as they engage in learning activities, when they are able to select the media that best matches how they learn. Through the use of collaboration tools, students discuss the information they are accessing and evaluate the accuracy of that information. The last skill set is producing media to be shared with others. Through the discussions the students have, they create products that demonstrate the new knowledge they have acquired (Media Smarts, n.d.; US Digital Literacy, 2014).

Digitally Rich Instructional Unit

In the past, extraordinary claims were made in predicting changes in the classroom due to new technology like motion pictures, radio, and television (Cuban, 1986). These technologies did not revolutionize the classroom, because the media used did not have a social component. Film and radio are consumable products that are one-directional, creating a passive learning experience. Similar claims were made as the computer made its way into the mainstream of society. At first, the machines provided very limited, isolated experiences, because they were not connected to each other. With the development of the Internet, the computers became bridges to new social activities with social networking programs. Students now drive their learning, by selecting content in which they are interested. Tools became available to communicate in both synchronous and asynchronous formats. Social media tools enhance communication abilities. Finally, social media impact becomes more powerful with computers small enough to fit into the hands of the smallest learners. Today, digital and media literacy skills are considered necessary 21st-century skills (Partnership for 21st Century Skills, 2011).

A digitally rich instructional unit increases access to a broader range of instructional materials. The additional breadth of instructional material allows for more varied interactions with the material, creating deeper learning experiences. Pairing the digital media with principles of universal design, the students have multiple ways of learning the material. A digitally rich instructional unit would include three different stages: (a) introducing the content/multiple means of presentation; (b) interacting with the world/multiple means of engagement; and (c) creating and sharing ideas/multiple means of action and expression.

Stage 1: Introducing the content/multiple means of presentation

A digitally rich unit uses digital media to introduce the students to the content in which they will later engage. A variety of methods could be used to build context for what the students are about to learn. Approaches include the introduction of problems for the students to solve, projects for the students to build, or questions the students themselves have generated about the world. Once the context for the unit is understood, students are ready to access the digital resources.

Through network and wireless connections, the world becomes the classroom. Students are able to reach outside the classroom in ways never possible before. The static two-dimensional book pages come to life with digital media. Through these connections, students become better world citizens by developing a holistic view of the commonalities across cultures and recognizing their responsibilities to participate positively in the global community (Carter, 2014). The best way for students to begin to understand others is to explore different perspectives (Banks, 2006). Digital resources on the Internet allow students to be exposed to the different perspectives through digitized primary sources and digital current event outlets.

The technology that connects students to these resources is providing access for those who are the most vulnerable. The digitized resources allow for multiple means of representation. Students are able to select the media that matches their perceptual preferences or to accommodate visual or auditory deficits to enhance their understanding of the material. Groups interested in promoting their points of view often provide resources for students to use, to enhance their understanding of the issues. Screen readers read aloud the material from electronic print resources, allowing access by students with poor reading skills or visual impairments. Interactive games or demonstrations appeal to kinetic learners. Visual learners may prefer video presentations.

Students whose primary language is not English access the digital curriculum options using screen translators or apps that translate words and phrases, broadening their access to information. The WordLens app allows the student to use the camera in mobile devices to "view" the text, by converting the words into the preferred language of the user. Translator Speak and Translate becomes a virtual translator that converts speech into 100 different languages. Google Translate provides a textbox in which to paste the text requiring translation. The student is able to select the language preference, before the program provides the translation. A great additional feature is a list of definitions for single words that are immediately displayed.

Primary sources

Primary source information is valuable for developing perspectives, since conflicts are often rooted in the past. Primary sources are artifacts, documents, recordings, or other items created during the time period the students are studying. With high-resolution digital cameras, artifacts and documents are quickly replicated and made available on the Internet. Film can also be converted into a digitalized format, as video casts and audio recordings are posted as podcasts. Through the digitized artifacts, students are able to read and see for themselves the newspaper clippings, diaries, letters, and other artifacts from the past, without the filter of opinions from those writing textbooks. Students' ability to explore past historical events through the perspectives of different ethnic groups allows them to develop a deeper understanding of the causes and the effects of those events upon the different groups involved.

A variety of primary source documents are available for teachers through museums. Museums have digitized archives of artifacts and made these available online. National museums often have artifacts that they do not have room to display. Smaller museums want to share the viewpoints of the groups represented. For these museums, the online collections are designed to entice viewers to their museums and to share their stories. The Smithsonian pulls together online collections of digitized primary source artifacts to expand the audience viewing the vast archives of historical artifacts available. To further enhance the accessibility of these collections, games and simulations are available to allow another way of engaging with historical information.

Current events

Another way to develop an understanding of different perspectives is through current events. News organizations, both print-based and media-based, are creating content that is accessible by students. In some cases, these news organizations have suggestions for educators as to how to use their content in the classroom. Using these resources, students build awareness of current events of the day and the impact of these events. Bringing the events into the classroom allows them to watch history unfold in real time. At the same time, students develop an understanding of the multiple viewpoints that surround current issues. Exposure to the differing points of view allows them to form their own opinions on these topics. Examples of the current events resources are the CBBC Shows for Kids, DOGO news, Time for Kids, SNN Student News, KidsPost, The Learning Network, and PBS News Hour for Kids.

Stage 2: Interacting with the world/multiple means of engagement

Once the students have the content material, digital tools allow them to collaborate with each other, connect with experts, or interact with other classrooms to evaluate, analyze, and apply the knowledge they are learning to produce products to share with others. As the students are engaging with the content, teachers identify individual goals for students based upon their ability levels, strengths, and weaknesses.

Collaboration tools pave the way for students to interact with experts or other students from around the world. Collaboration tools have been evolving. At the same time, collaboration enhances accessibility by providing alternate methods for engagement with the curriculum. The skills taught in the classroom become connected to activities the children are doing in their own lives. Social media is engagement. Through social media, students contribute to the discussion in active ways by adding their own opinions or creating their own products to share with others for comment.

Web 2.0

The web 2.0 tools emerged with advancements in the Internet browsers that allowed interactions rather than static presentation of information. The first of these tools, blogs, are a form of online personal journals typically written by an individual or a group with a special interest. Once the authors share their thoughts or ideas, others comment on the value of or add to the concepts presented. Experts, today, blog on different topics. Several blogging sites are available for education, such as Blogger, Wordpress, Edublog, Kid-Blog, and Glogster.

Although written blogs are still popular, video blogging is an evolution of this form of technology. This form of blogging allows students to record themselves using mobile devices or webcams and then post the recording to a site for others to respond to. Again, video blogging is a great way to engage students in a variety of different ways with the curriculum. SchoolTube is a great resource for classroom teachers interested in using video in their classrooms. Teachers are able to create a channel for their classrooms, and to control the content that is posted to the channel by the students, by previewing the videos before posting. Another alternative is VoiceThread. For a fee, teachers establish a class blog that allows students to post text, audio, and video blogs.

Social media

Social media are a collection of tools used to create online communities that allow the sharing of information, ideas, and creations with a larger audience. Social media tools work by providing online discussion spaces. Within those spaces, students share documents they create, pictures they take or find, and videos they locate or create. Teachers use social media to post educational content they want students to use. Students become engaged as they add to those resources through their own searches.

A variety of different tools are available for teachers depending on what their needs may be. Learning management systems are providing safe online spaces for students by requiring a class code to establish their accounts. The systems allow the teacher to communicate with the class and provide a place for turning in homework, as well as sharing thoughts and reflections. Some of the learning management systems are free, while others cost the teacher or the district. Different learning management systems to consider are twiducate, NEO, Edmodo, and Blackboard.

Connecting to other groups of students is important in global classrooms. At the same time, the teachers will want to be sure the social media resources in which the students work are safe environments. Two popular companies, PenPals Schools and ePals, assist teachers in connecting their classrooms in safe online environments. Both companies have blogging sites, document sharing, and email. Assistance is available for teachers to locate and pair pen pal classrooms together based on common interests. Once the classrooms are connected, tools are available to promote planning collaborative lessons together. Resources are available for premade instructional material as well.

Online collaboration

Real-time collaboration is becoming easier with the latest versions of software products being brought to the market. Google documents are stored in a cloud, which promotes sharing with collaboration partners anywhere in the world. As authors and creators edit the shared documents, the changes are seen by the collaborators in real time. Google documents also tracks changes to the documents and those who make changes, which is helpful in the collaboration partnerships. Packaged with Microsoft Office Suite is a cloud-based storage system. This allows the originator of a document to share it with other collaborators, who, in turn, edit the document with the Track Changes feature. With Track Changes, the edits can be accepted or rejected by the other collaborators. Changes made offline are synced to the document as soon as the user becomes connected. Apps are also available for mobile devices.

To embrace completely the social aspects of the Internet, instantaneous connections are available with videoconferencing. The first conferencing tools used a webcam attached to the computer. This technology is currently available today using both hardwire and wireless connections. Smartphones or tablets use the cellular or wireless networks to connect with real-time video. The advantage to this approach is that hardwired Internet connections are not needed.

Videoconferencing tools have other advantages. For example, many embedded tools allow sharing of computer screens and shared control over the workspace, to work synchronously on documents or presentations. Experts can be brought into the discussion, since these tools allow multiple connections simultaneously. Google Hangouts are included in the Google educational suite, making it an easy-to-use videoconferencing tools for classroom use. Skype is part of the Microsoft Office Suite, allowing for easy integration with the products being used for collaboration in creation by students. Both Google Hangouts and Skype work for computer, telephone, and cell phone, allowing flexible connections to collaboration sessions.

Collaboration classrooms

Emerging classroom technology is becoming available that allows students to interact with each other and the world. Interactive boards are available that allow up to six students to gather and share learning activities on a table. These tables are bringing engagement with instructional material to a new level, by integrating kinetic interactions with the social aspects of learning together. For older students, the large interactive boards connect to other boards at other locations, using business software rather than the educational software package. The large boards have enough room for two individuals to share ideas on the same board. Connected, the interactions reach four students. The interactions of the boards are very similar to that of a tablet, using touch technology, making them easy to learn how to use. Connecting through videoconferencing software just enhances this experience.

Another form of collaboration tool that is emerging is stations that allow sharing of devices. Two forms of this technology exist. One consists of a device with several dongles that connect to an HD monitor. Using the USB dongles, laptops and tablets are displayed on the monitor. The user downloads a small program on the portable device. By pressing a button on the dongle, the portable device desktop is displayed on the monitor. The software displays up to four devices on the same screen. The other form is a variation using a URL to allow the devices to connect to an HD monitor. Because the software uses a URL, the collaboration extends to students in another class-room or connects with an expert on a particular topic. This approach also allows smartphones to connect and be displayed. Imagine the collaboration taking place, with the sharing of information through this form of technology in the hands of students.

The next technology combines upgrades to software videoconferencing software and sound systems, to make collaboration classrooms less expensive to build than in the past and more ubiquitous. When videoconferencing tools are connected to a larger video camera, classroom activities are shared in real time and recorded for later views by students. The newer speaker systems have microphones with noise-cancelling software, along with careful place-ment of speakers that allow conversations in the classroom to be sent with clear audio to off-site locations, such as another classroom or to students at home. By using Skype or Google Hangouts, the classroom is extended by connecting to an off-site classroom or to students in other locations in instan-taneous, natural ways.

Stage 3: Creating and sharing ideas/multiple means of action and expression

Once the students have worked through the solutions to the projects or problems, they are now ready to demonstrate their new knowledge through expression and to take action. The media-rich classroom has many ways in which students can express themselves. Traditional classrooms would use tests or written papers for the expression of knowledge. In the media-rich class-room, students present their new knowledge to audiences that reach beyond the teacher.

Advancements in technology are allowing students to capture and create high-quality video and multimedia quickly and easily. The technology has become ubiquitous, making it naturally integrated in our everyday lives. Social media sites are allowing students to quickly share their creations with family and friends. The camera built into mobile devices has made it easy to capture pictures and video. Computer platforms come with basic editing soft-ware that is easy to learn. Students create their own movies and post them to social media sites. Presentation tools (Keynote, PowerPoint, and Prezi) pro-vide ways to organize the video, images, and audio that the students gather to communicate their ideas.

For multimedia creations, students have several choices requiring different levels of technology skills. Kid Pix 3D is an example of easy-to-use multimedia products that allow the students to create an animated, three-dimensional story to share their creativity and knowledge with others. Stories can also be created with animation tools that students enjoy using. Voki has a product that allows the animated figure to talk on behalf of the student. Comic Creator takes this same concept a step further. Using this tool, students develop a comic strip to tell their story or to promote an idea. OfficeMix is an add-on to PowerPoint that allows the creator to add interaction into the presentation.

More complex tools are available for creative students to develop their own worlds of imagination and interactivity. MinecraftEdu is a great resource for teachers to adapt a popular game software (Minecraft), allowing students to build worlds and to incorporate basic storylines. To take the storyline development to yet another level, Project Spark allows students to develop their own gaming world. Then the students share the world they have created with others. Students with more advanced technical skills may want to experiment with professional-level tools such as Camtasia, Captivate, or Flash. These tools convert presentations into interactive multimedia showcasing students' knowledge.

Students have great tools to share their creations with others, with easy-to-develop websites. Google Sites are free websites available for educational uses that allow students to quickly build persuasive content or knowledge-sharing sites. The next evolution of presentation software is evident in Sway, an app available through Office 365. Sway allows the integration of the office products with media sources YouTube, Facebook, and Twitter, into one attractive display that resembles a website.

Conclusion

Combining the digital media with the principles of UDL through digital-rich instructional units creates a powerful learning experience for all students in the classroom. For students who experience access challenges to traditional text-based instruction, due to a disability or by not having access in their home to technology, the digital-rich media environment produces windows to the world outside the classroom. Primary and secondary source data honor cultural diversity in the classroom at the same, allowing students to make their own decisions. Presenting the information to students in different digital media promotes students taking charge of their learning by selecting the options that work best for them. Digital social media tools offer many options for students to engage with the content and to collaborate with others. The choices available assist all students in interacting with the content through their best learning modalities. Finally, through the newer digital tools available for creating new content, students have many options for sharing what they have learned.

References

Banks, J. A. (2006). *Cultural diversity and education: Foundations, curriculum, and teaching* (5th ed.). Boston, MA: Pearson/Allyn and Bacon.

Carter, A. (2014). *Tear down that wall: Joining the global classroom community to instill global citizenship.* Edutopia. Retrieved from http://www.edutopia.org/blog/tear-down-wall-global-classroom-adam-carter

CAST. (2011). *Universal design for learning guidelines version 2.0.* Wakefield, MA: Author.

—— (2015). *CAST timeline: CAST through the years: One mission, many innovations.* Retrieved from http://www.cast.org/about/timeline.html#.VTJpLv5FCbM.

Cuban, L. (1986). *Teachers and machines: The classroom use of technology since 1920.* New York, NY: Teachers College Press.

Davis, T., Fuller, M., Jackson, S., Pittman, J., & Sweet, J. (2007). *A national consideration of digital equity.* Washington, DC: International Society for Technology in Education. Retrieved from http://www.iste.org/digitalequity

Garland, V. E. (2009–10). Emerging technology trends and ethical practices for the school principal. *Journal of Educational Technology Systems, 38*(1), 39–50.

Heick, T. (2014). *The definition of digital literacy.* Te@chthought. Retrieved from http://www.teachthought.com/technology/the-definition-of-digital-literacy/

Jackson, L. A., Zhoa, Y., Kolenic, A., Fitzgerald, H. E., Harold, R., & Von Eye, A. (2008). Race, gender, and information technology use: The new digital divide. *CyberPsychology and Behavior, 11*(4), 437–42.

MediaSmarts. (n.d.). *Digital literacy fundamentals.* Retrieved from http://mediasmarts.ca/digital-media-literacy-fundamentals/digital-literacy-fundamentals.

Miniwatts Marketing Group. (2015). *Internet world users by language: Top 10 languages.* Retrieved from http://www.internetworldstats.com/stats7.htm

National Center on Universal Design for Learning. (2012). *Guidelines: Theory & practice version.* Retrieved from http://www.udlcenter.org/print/371

Organisation for Economic Co-Operation and Development. (2005). *Are students ready for a technology-rich world? What PISA studies tell us.* Paris, France: OECD Publications.

Partnership for 21st Century Skills. (2011). *Framework for 21st century learning.* Retrieved from http://www.p21.org/storage/documents/1.__p21_framework_2-pager.pdf

US Digital Literacy. (2014). *Digital and media literacy for today's learners.* Retrieved from http://digitalliteracy.us

Part 3
Practice, Assessment, Action

12. Global Education Projects

MELDA N. YILDIZ

"We are all connected. To each other, biologically. To the earth, chemically. To the rest of the universe, atomically."

—Neil DeGrasse Tyson

Introduction

This chapter provides both theoretical frameworks and best practices for designing and implementing the *global media literacy education* (GMLE) curriculum, and discusses innovative and transdisciplinary teaching strategies for the global classroom. We argue that teaching and learning in the 21st-century classroom calls for (1) developing a transdisciplinary global media literacy education curriculum (GMLE); (2) implementing collaborative, globally connected projects that are multicultural, multilingual multimedia; and (3) rethinking learning and teaching through innovative and transformative classroom practices around the world. We showcase examples of online, collaborative, and innovative learning projects, and global education resources and networks. The chapter is a practical guide for educators who would like to rethink and transform their curriculum, and prepare their students for the ever-changing global economy.

In addition, we explore the role of educational technologies such as Global Positioning System (GPS), cell phone, and tablet PC technologies in developing global media projects. We outline creative strategies and possibilities for integrating learning technologies into the curriculum with limited resources and equipment, and demonstrate examples that integrate maps, mathematics, and media education using cell phones, tablet PCs, and GPS devices. In teacher education programs and professional development settings, we may be able to introduce these tools and frameworks to prepare globally connected and culturally and linguistically responsive pedagogy.

This chapter shares the insights from the P–20 classrooms. Teacher candidates and teacher educators participated in the Participatory Action Research (PAR) project. They identified innovative, transdisciplinary, and cost-effective strategies and tools for teaching and learning, and developed multicultural and multilingual curriculum, transdisciplinary project-based learning activities, and integrated math, maps, and media in their lesson plans.

The purpose of this chapter is twofold: (1) provide strategies for designing a "GMLE curriculum" for 21st-century learners; and (2) suggest innovative and free tools for designing collaborative learning activities for the online, global classroom. We use the term *global classroom* to illustrate the nature of learning where educators together with their students develop transdisciplinary learning environments and experience collaborative inquiry-based, project-based learning activities across different cultures and languages. We argue that the GMLE curriculum model provides teachers with the foundation, tools, and means to support learning in the global classroom of the 21st century.

Global Media Literacy Education (GMLE) Curriculum Model

The GMLE curriculum model promotes creativity, innovation, transdisciplinarity, and global citizenship. The GMLE model is based on several curricular frameworks and educational models: flipped learning (Bergmann & Sams, 2012), the Understanding by Design (UbD) Framework (Wiggins & McTighe, 2011), the Universal Design for Learning (UDL) framework (Rose & Meyer, 2002), the flattened classroom (Friedman, 2005), Technological Pedagogical Content Knowledge (TPACK) (Mishra & Koehler, 2006), the Partnership for 21st Century Learning (P21, 2014), the global competency matrix (Boix Mansilla & Jackson, 2011), and UNESCO's Media and Information Literacy (MIL) Curriculum for Teachers (UNESCO, 2011) and Global Media Literacy Assessment Framework (UNESCO, 2013). Each of these curriculum models provided us the research-based tools, strategies, frameworks, and approaches to help design the GMLE model, to prepare our students for the second half of the 21st century, for becoming global citizens and attaining the skills and resources for successful careers. The skills for students to develop within the GMLE curriculum model are: media and information literacy, global competency, critical thinking, problem-solving, critical autonomy, self-directed and adaptive learning, and 21st-century skills.

In addition to the curriculum models and skills, we would like to highlight several international networks and educational organizations. Global Competency Matrix is a collaborative effort by Council of Chief State

School Officers (CCSSO)[1]'s EdSteps Initiative & Asia Society[2] Partnership for Global Learning. The United Nations Educational, Scientific, and Cultural Organization (UNESCO)'s education initiatives are "committed to a holistic and humanistic vision of quality education worldwide."[3] The International Society for Technology in Education (ISTE)[4] provides educational technology resources and professional development, especially for K–12 teachers and teacher educators. The National Association for Media Literacy Education (NAMLE)[5] is a national organization that brings scholars, activists, organizations, and communities together in the field of media literacy education to provide a national forum for diverse views, visions, and voices. The Society for Information Technology and Teacher Education (SITE)[6] is dedicated to the advancement of the knowledge, theory, and quality of learning and teaching at all levels, with information technology. The American Educational Research Association (AERA)[7] is a national research organization that promotes educational research, encourages scholarly inquiry in the field of education, and serves the public good. The National Center on Universal Design for Learning[8] at the Center for Applied Special Technology (CAST)[9] outlines strategies, resources, and opportunities for every student, supports the effective implementation of UDL by connecting stakeholders, and provides checklists of innovative uses of new media and technologies. The Association for Supervision and Curriculum Development (ASCD)[10] promotes excellence in teaching and learning. ASCD creates innovative programs, products, and services that empower educators to support the success of all students. UNESCO, ISTE, SITE, AERA, CAST, and ASCD also provide resources, conferences, and publications in the field of education.

The Partnership for 21st Century Learning (P21) plays an active role in serving as a catalyst for global education and 21st-century learning, guiding policy and projects on 21st-century readiness for every student. Its mission is to build collaborative partnerships among educators and business, community, and government leaders to develop skills necessary for students to excel. Here are the "six beliefs that anchor P21's Framework for State Action on Global Education": 1) Focus on teachers: for students to be global, teachers must be global; 2) Transform and leverage language learning; 3) Use networks to share knowledge and build commitment; 4) Harness the power of global experiences; 5) Recognize partners are needed to make progress; and 6) Move past pilots: focus on scale, sustainability, and equity of access (P21, 2014, p. 3).

Teaching and Learning in the Global Classroom

New media and social media software (SMS) technologies have become integral parts of our daily lives and provided new challenges and opportunities for education. As digital media tools are more available and accessible, connecting classrooms around the world is becoming a reality. Through the current new media and technologies, our classes are ready to participate with the global community. One of the advantages of digital media is being able to reach out to students with diverse background and special needs. Classroom material can be provided in various formats. Small text can be enlarged, news articles can be adapted for students' reading levels, and the audio or video version of information can be provided. Flipped (blended) instructions and alternative assessment both have a huge potential to increase adaptive learning opportunities. Teacher candidates who have been using Khan Academy in my math and science courses mention how they are addicted to learning that is adaptive and individualized. One student said, "I wish I had had Khan Academy when I was in high school. Last night, I was up until 1 a.m. receiving more badges. It is quite addicting."

Global Education Is Transdisciplinary

Here are a couple of the GMLE project ideas that we would like to share. They are multilingual and multicultural, as well as integrating multimedia.

The first is called "Building a Zoo or Not." This project focused on animals and their habitats. Teacher candidates developed this 6th-grade unit integrating geography (a map of animals and their habitats around the world), mathematics (how to plan, create, and build a small-scale model zoo), science (animal habitats), language arts (reading books and magazines; watching documentaries and educational videos related to animals), world languages and cultures (how each animal sounds in other languages. e.g., a dog's bark is represented by *woof woof* in English, but *how how* in Turkish), art (building a prototype of a zoo using household items), and music (listening to and/or singing animal songs). The unit introduced at least two career options: veterinarian and zoo-keeper.

The second project is called "New Jersey across cultures throughout history." This 4th-grade curriculum unit made use of a gallery walk approach to teaching. Teachers and students studying the state of New Jersey co-developed a gallery walk, creating timelines that outlined important historical events for the state; maps showing major cities, historical sites, land formations, and statistics; interactive games based on fun facts about New Jersey; and students' research-based posters related to the state's economy, education, and culture. The lesson plan included research skills, critical thinking skills, and presentation skills. As a culminating activity, parents and other classes in the school were invited to experience and participate in co-creating the gallery walk by answering a few survey questions about New Jersey, and were given an exit ticket on the Garden State Highway.

Through innovative telecommunication tools such as Skype or Google Talk, global media literacy education projects and curriculum could connect classrooms around the world to discuss and take action on issues. Through dialogue, students can explore other perspectives, cultures, and languages, study different viewpoints on the issues, and experience how we are all interconnected (Tye & Tye, 1992). Through public, academic, and school libraries, students reach primary source materials and resources from other countries and regions. The GMLE curriculum expands the walls of the classroom. Educators bring scholars, scientists, and individuals from different backgrounds into their classrooms. Students interact and co-create content with other individuals around the world, using social media to share it with the world.

Neuroscience and Learning

The GMLE is based on the latest brain-based research by the National Center on Universal Design for Learning. Universal Design for Learning (UDL) is a framework first introduced by CAST in the 1990s in order to "guide the design of learning environments that are accessible and effective for all." (CAST, 2015). UDL is defined by CAST as a "research-based set of principles for curriculum development that give all individuals equal opportunities to learn."[11]

As Meyer, Rose, and Gordon (2014) say: "Now, instead of seeing the brain as a collection of discrete structures with specific functions, modern neuroscience views the brain as a complex web of integrated and overlapping networks. And learning is seen as changes in the connections within and between these networks" (p.3).

The UDL framework has been used in other educational settings: curriculum design, professional development, research, online course design, and flipped (blended) learning. Regardless of the students' ability, disability, linguistic and cultural background, age, gender, learning style, or motivations, UDL allows the learner to have alternative ways to access and complete to the curriculum. It provides educators with research-based principles and guidelines to customize the curriculum to serve all learners and address their diverse needs. It provides appropriate and flexible learning material for all types of learners and fosters instructional environments that maximize each student's ability to progress.

In addition to neuroscience and learning theories, UDL is in fact based on the Universal Design Movement in architecture. Ostroff et al. (2002) quoted Ronald L. Mace in their first chapter [12]: "Universal design is the design of products and environments to be usable by all people, to the greatest extent possible, without the need for adaptation or specialized design." For instance, ramps on the sidewalk are designed not only for people in wheelchairs but also to assist those with strollers and rolling bags. UDL in the context of global media literacy education simply provides educators a framework to rethink learning through neuroscience and progressive learning theories and to develop curricula that are inclusive and transformative.

The GMLE framework challenges "one-size-fits-all" curricula and identifies research-based curricula that are flexible, easy to use, cost-effective, and replicable. It challenges the curricula that are rigid, complicated, expensive, and only designed for the so-called "average" learner. The GMLE aims to provide every student with an equal opportunity to learn and co-create knowledge. It provides educators the opportunity to design a globally connected curriculum that addresses the needs of all learners with different abilities and backgrounds. It uses new media, innovative technologies, and tools that celebrate the stories of the global communities. It provides brain-based research and transdisciplinary approaches to learning.

This table was developed by our teacher candidates. It is based on CAST. org and Meyer et al. (2014).

Table 12.1

NETWORKS	LEARNING	SPECIALIZED	EDUCATIONAL PRINCIPLES[13]
Recognition	The "what" of learning; how we identify information and categorize what we see, hear, and read.	Sense and assign meaning to patterns we see to identify and understand information, ideas, and concepts to perceive information in the environment and transform it into usable knowledge.	Principle I: Provide Multiple Means of Representation.

By using multiple forms of media and technologies and offering combinations of audio and visual aids, individuals with special learning preferences, sensory disabilities (e.g., deafness), learning disabilities (e.g., dyslexia), and language or cultural differences will be able to grasp information more quickly and efficiently. Also learning, and the transfer of learning, occurs when multiple representations are used, because it allows students to make connections within, as well as between, concepts.

Strategic	The "how" of learning; our internally generated mental and motor patterns, actions and skills.	Generate and oversee mental and motor patterns to plan, organize, execute, and monitor actions and skills to initiate purposeful actions in the environment.	Principle II: Provide Multiple Means of Action and Expression.

Providing different means of interacting with the information, presenting what is learned in a different format, is essential. Alternatives to paper and pencil for students with challenges such as movement (e.g., cerebral palsy), strategic learning behaviors, poor organizational abilities (e.g., executive function disorders), or language barriers (ESL students). Some may be able to express themselves well in written text but not speech, and vice versa. Replacing writing with audio files, movies, or pictorial representations allows the students to express themselves, overcoming these challenges.

NETWORKS	LEARNING	SPECIALIZED	EDUCATIONAL PRINCIPLES
Affective	The "why" of learning; the feelings, values, or emotions that can influence attitudes toward learning.	Evaluate patterns and assign them emotional significance, to engage with tasks and learning and with the world around us, to monitor the internal and external environment, to set priorities, and to motivate and engage learning and behavior.	Principle III: Provide Multiple Means of Engagement.

Learners differ in the ways in which they can be engaged or motivated to learn. Factors that affect the willingness of students to engage with learning experiences including their interest, ability to sustain effort and persistence, and ability to self-regulate their learning. Other factors affecting learners' engagement include their neurology, culture, personal connection to the subject, subjectivity, and level of background knowledge. Some learners might like to work alone, while others prefer to work with their peers. In reality, there is not one means of engagement that will be optimal for all learners in all contexts. It may be beneficial for some learners to have multimedia choices, which may allow them to select how they are going to interact with the content area.

Educational Principles of Universal Design

Educators will be able to use these three principles and nine guidelines to make a decision about when to use technology to improve student learning in our globally connected curriculum. In our teacher education courses, our teacher candidates used learning technologies and the principles of UDL to design curricula that reflected global media literacy education. Teacher candidates explored a number of teacher-friendly examples, free resources, and lesson ideas that are outlined and evaluated by CAST.org for educational purposes. They used Lesson Builder[14] to create their own lesson plans implementing UDL in their curriculum projects.

Rose, Meyer, and Hitchcock (2005) explained the importance of digital media and technologies in the classroom to add flexibility and access to multiple display formats (text, image, sound, video, and subtitles in other languages) to enhance classroom activities. In a 21st-century classroom, students needs to be able to access, analyze, evaluate information, and become the producers of knowledge using digital tools (Rose, Meyer, & Hitchcock, 2005).

In addition to using Lesson Builder by CAST.org, teacher candidates explored examples and online resources and software on CAST principles and checkpoints. They were told to find resources as if they were part of an individual educational program (IEP) team for a student: How would you choose an educational program and/or assistive technology for a child with special needs? The team would examine the unique educational needs of the student. Here are a few resources we highlighted under each principle and checkpoint item listed by CAST.org, to help answer this question.

First, CAST.org Diigo resources can be searched by using tags such as grade level, subject, or type of resource.[15] Under "Principle I: Provide Multiple Means of Representation" (the "what" of learning), there are three checkpoint items: 1) Perception; 2) Language, Expression, and Symbols; and 3) Comprehension. Teacher candidates explored and integrated some of the technologies that support multiple means of representation. One of the challenges for multiple representation may be customizing the display of information and instructional materials, such as using magnifying tools for text and images, enlarging text with larger fonts, or using text readers to read the text aloud. Accessible instructional materials (AIM) can be designed in or converted into various formats (Braille, large print, audio, or digital text). Our teacher candidates also added the importance of integrating multilingual tools. They explored international keyboard options, and they tested the computers and set them on a language of their choice.

Checkpoint 1.1 under Principle I provides a link to the National Instructional Materials Access Center (NIMAC),[16] which converts instructional material into files in various accessible formats such as Braille, audio, and digital text. Under Checkpoint 2.1 ("Clarify vocabulary and symbols"), Visuwords, an online graphic dictionary, is listed.[17] It is an interactive dictionary providing word relationships that are illustrated by the color and pattern of the link between words.

Computers today are equipped with all sorts of accessibility options. Mobile apps provide many interactive dictionaries in the languages of the world. E-books with built-in audio options and various readability options (such as changing the background color, font, or size), as well as audio and video books, allow individuals to experience content on a variety of platforms.

Through library and media skills, students learn to search the web to explore and access primary source information through online museums (e.g., Google Art Project) and repositories (e.g., Merlot.org). Google Art Project gathers images of artifacts from numerous museums, providing details and background stories in online access.[18] The Smithsonian and Library of Congress are other examples of teaching and learning resources, making available their archives and collections of digitized primary sources that go beyond a textbook. Their sites include pictures, videos, animations for students, and links to lesson plans and grants for educators.

Under "Principle II: Provide Multiple Means of Action and Expression" (the "how" of learning), there are three checkpoint items: 1) Physical Action; 2) Expression and Communication; and 3) Executive Function. Communication is essential for students' success. From paint programs to other creative expression software such as Telegami[19] and Voki,[20] our teacher candidates used many apps and softwares to create animated characters that speak. With the help of new media and technologies, it is possible to have students at different levels learn to read and write. Word processors and Google Docs allow students to write and edit their work. Using speech-to-text software, the students can dictate what they want to write, and the software turns the words into text. Google Voice transcribes a spoken message and sends it as an email. For taking notes, students can use electronic pens, which also record audio and video versions of the lectures. Students with limited motor skills can write key words or symbols.

Under Principle II, there are various resources included for multiple means of action and engagement. For instance in Checkpoint 6.2 ("Support planning and strategy development"), brainstorming tools were introduced, such as Bubbl.us.[21] This is a simple and free web application that lets students brainstorm online and share their content. Under Checkpoint 6.3 ("Facilitate managing information and resources"), there are several resources for teachers such as RubiStar[22] and Teacher Vision.[23] RubiStar is a rubric-making tool that allows teachers to create, save, and share rubrics for their classes. It comes in an English and a Spanish version. The Teacher Vision: Graphic Organizers website comes with a collection of ready-to-use, printable graphic organizers. Graphic organizers are available for use across content, including reading, writing, science, math, and general use.

Checkpoint 6.4 ("Enhance capacity for monitoring progress") introduces the idea of creating charts and graphs[24] to support students in tracking their progress and to enhance teachers' capacity for monitoring progress.

Here are some of the resources our teacher candidates tested and integrated into their lesson plans to amplify learning: 1) Camera Mouse enables an individual to control the mouse pointer on a computer screen by moving his or her head.[25] 2) Boardmaker is another common software used as an assistive technology tools in schools.[26] Students use visuals for communication. 3) VoiceThread is a audiovisual tool for sharing and commenting on slides using text, audio, and video.[27] VoiceThread allows students to present and engage in discussions virtually. It can also be used as a videocast. 4) Animoto provides video and animation tools for making videos.[28] Students can upload images, pictures, and collage, and also upload and share videos. 5) Toondoo is a free website that allows students to create, share, and comment on comics or cartoon strips.[29] It comes with a library of ready-made pictures, or new pictures can be uploaded. 6) Scratch is designed to help students create and share multimedia projects and work collaboratively on games, stories that develop computer programming skills, and mathematical and computational thinking.[30] 7) Poetry Kit[31] is an online version of magnetic poetry.[32] Students choose words or phrases and create their own poetry.

Under "Principle III: Provide Multiple Means of Engagement" (the "why" of learning), there are three checkpoint items: 1) Recruiting Interest; 2) Sustaining Effort and Persistence; and 3) Self Regulation. Engaging students in their learning can take many different forms, such as simulations, animations, videos, games, and multimedia slides. New technology tools provide teachers with various multimedia tools to design their instructional materials to engage and motivate their students to make progress with complicated concepts. For example, preparing materials using a flipped learning model can increase accessibility and availability of the instructional materials from home, and allows students to review learning materials whenever and wherever they need.

Teachers can use the simple webcam to record and upload content and share video and audio insight about the learning material, as well as add formative assessment options, such as quizzes through Quizlet or Google Forms, to check comprehension and find out what to review for the following day. Teachers can create crossword puzzles, games, flash cards, and webquests to increase students' engagement in learning, as well as online badges for students to collect points and engage in completing tasks until they have achieved mastery. Most of the teacher candidates used Zunal.com for developing their own webquests. They found the website easy to use. It challenged the teacher candidates to rethink the delivery of instruction, how to engage the students in problem-based learning activities. One candidate proposed an alternative use of a webquest, saying: "My webquest can be used by a substitute teacher if I miss a day. I can still be part of their learning and assessment process."

Checkpoint 7.1 showcases a Tic-Tac-Toe model of providing students with a choice for their assignments. The concept of this checkpoint is to "optimize individual choice and autonomy." Students at Columbus East High School in Columbus, IN, worked on an Industrial Revolution unit, selecting three out of nine options for their class projects. They created a unique way for students to choose and present their projects on the Industrial Revolution. Two innovative teachers developed a transdisciplinary unit integrating subjects from health to economy, history to literature, and allowed their students to pick their topics, develop critical thinking and autonomy, and present their knowledge in different formats (public service announcements, DVDs, or a book).

Khan Academy, GeoGebra, Brain-pop, National Geographic, and TedEd can provide videos and animations for students to explore beyond the classroom material. Checkpoint 8.4 ("Increase mastery-oriented feedback") lists resources such as Carol Dweck's book *Mindset* (2007) that explains the difference between fixed versus growth mindsets. In order to increase mastery-oriented feedback, Dr. Dweck recommends developing a growth mindset, which requires effort, as opposed to intelligence, for learning.

For increasing global awareness and interest in global issues, students can read or watch news stories from websites such as Newsela,[33] which provides news at different reading levels. Our teacher candidates also explored several other news resources such as CNN Student News,[34] DOGO News,[35] National Geographic,[36] Time for Kids,[37] PBS News Hour for Kids,[38] and The Learning Network.[39] On some of these websites, students are invited to comment on the news stories and share their points of view, as well as provide feedback on the sites. For example, PBS News Hour for Kids includes Twitter feeds. CNN has a feature that invites students to be reporters.[40] Overall, most of these educational news resources are accessible in many ways. The online text can be translated into another language, and the text can be read aloud for struggling readers.

Through global education networks such as iEARN,[41] ePals,[42] PenPal Schools,[43] Global SchoolNet,[44] and Kids Go Global,[45] educators can connect students to other students around the world. They can share their stories and perspectives with each other in a safe online environment.

Classrooms connect using various telecommunication tools (e.g., webcams) and software such as Skype and Google Hangouts, which allow children to work collaboratively with each other. The only difficulty may be arranging face-to-face meeting times in different time zones. All of these telecommunication tools and resources allow students to participate in activities and interact with each other, without worrying about writing or reading disabilities, instead expanding the walls of the classroom to cultural experiences where the students learn to care about other cultures, share their own experiences, and develop global competencies.

For asynchronous communications, educators can encourage students to record and upload their videos and create digital stories. Digital storytelling encompasses multiple skill sets, especially group work and creative expression. Students can be encouraged to work together on writing a script, storyboarding ideas, filming the scenes, adding audio, pictures, and building transitions.

Global Education Network Organization

Our transdisciplinary collaborative projects aim to provide global education. Our teacher candidates identified and explored several Global Education Networks that provide transdisciplinary resources and offer project-based learning (PBL) platforms to promote collaborations among learners and educators around the world. For instance, teacher candidates examined how global education projects such as the Flat Stanley Project can provide transdisciplinary opportunities, involving various subjects from geography (in noting locations of Stanley's travels and destinations) to math (in measuring distances and times). The project focuses on connecting children to other children around the world through the "Flat Stanley" character model. It involves language arts, through journaling. Students share their stories and exchange ideas, questions, and images with students around the world.

Global Education Conference (GlobalEdCon) is an online network. Since 2010, it has run during the International Education week, connecting students, educators, parents, learning communities, and organizations around the world and exploring community initiatives, classroom practices, and global projects. It holds a week-long, free online conference in a webinar format, and presentations are archived for further dialogue. The conference is intended to connect classrooms across the world and recognizes diversity and educational access for all. The organization's wiki houses many curriculum-based, global education efforts. My teacher candidates and I had a chance to present each year, sharing our projects. As one of my teacher candidates said, "the best way to learn is to share."

TakingITGlobal.org (TIG) is a non-governmental organization that connects youth in order to access information, get involved, have a chance to connect and collaborate with one another through various telecommunication tools, and most importantly take action in their local and global communities. Its vision states "Youth around the world actively engaged and connected in shaping a more inclusive, peaceful and sustainable world." (TIG, 2015).

Classroom 2.0 provides a community-supported network for educators to share their ideas in various disciplines using collaborative online resources and technologies. The website hosts several networks, conferences, and events to support professional development and teacher collaboration. There are thousands of different special interest groups (e.g., STEM, ELL teaching, professional development, digital storytelling) to join in dialogue and collaboration.

The BoomWriter[46] and Write the World[47] are other transdisciplinary, collaborative, literacy-focused projects for students K–12. The BoomWriter's focus is to engage students in project-based learning that fosters critical thinking and 21st-century skills, while engaging in collaborative writing projects with other students in the school or around the world. Write the World is "dedicated to improving the writing of high school students through a global online community and guided interactive process." Its mission is to cultivate young writers to "develop their voices, refine their editing skills, and publish on an international platform."

iEARN (International Education and Resource Network) is one of the largest global network organizations, which connects over 40,000 schools, youth organizations, and young people worldwide. iEARN provides a safe and structured learning environment to link schools and students around the world through focused collaboration and dialogue, as well as contributing to the health and welfare of the planet and its people through experiential and transdisciplinary projects.

ePals is a collaborative and multilingual learning space that has self-paced and self-directed collaborative learning activities for K–12 students in 200 countries. For teachers, it provides curriculum resources to develop transdisciplinary projects, such as discussing and exploring holidays and festivals around the world. For students, it provides a safe platform for email, blogs, and mentoring. They can engage in cross-cultural exchanges and language-learning activities.

Facing the Future is a nonprofit organization that provides educators with the tools and resources for integrating global awareness and issues into the curriculum.[48] It aims to promote critical and creative thinking, systems thinking, problem solving, decision-making, collaboration, and cooperative learning, through building global connections and inspiring students to study global affairs and a sustainable world by taking on big issues like poverty, energy, and climate change.

Global Nomads Group (GNG) is a nonprofit education organization that fosters dialogue and understanding among the world's youth, by bringing the world to the classroom via new technologies.[49] It provides semester- or year-long virtual exchange programs between students in North America and sub-Saharan Africa, Central and Southeast Asia, the Middle East and North

Africa. Its mission is to connect students around the world to collaborate on projects and develop learning communities on global issues.

Global SchoolNet Foundation (GSN) is a nonprofit education organization that aims to prepare youth to be "productive and compassionate citizens in an increasing global economy" and "develop science, math, literacy and communication skills, [and] foster teamwork, civic responsibility and collaboration."[50] Its mission is to support 21st-century, brain-friendly learning, and improve academic performance through content-driven collaboration, while engaging educators and students in brain-friendly e-learning projects worldwide and helping youth explore community, cultural, and scientific issues.

Finally, we explored several collaborative projects focusing on science, technology, engineering, and mathematics (STEM). Here are a few worldwide, hands-on, K–12 projects focused on science:

1) The Center for Innovation in Engineering and Science Education (CIESE) hosts collaborative, project-based science activities, such as the Human Genetics Project and the Global Water Sampling Project, for K–12 students. Their mission is "to catalyze and support excellence in teaching and learning of science, technology, engineering, mathematics (STEM) and other core subjects through innovative, research-based instructional strategies and use of novel technologies."[51]

2) Global Learning and Observations to Benefit the Environment (GLOBE) is one of the U.S. government-sponsored programs that promote collaborative inquiry-based science investigations, to bring together students, teachers, and scientists around the world to study the dynamics of Earth's environment on local, regional, and global scales. GLOBE's mission is "to promote the teaching and learning of science; enhance environmental literacy and stewardship; and promote scientific discovery."[52]

3) Journey North: A Global Study of Wildlife Migration and Seasonal Change aims to engage students and citizen scientists around the globe in tracking wildlife migration and seasonal change.[53] The project is supported by the Annenberg Foundation. The project participants share field observations, play hide-and-seek games based on teaching seasons, explore interrelated aspects of seasons, and track seasonal changes while sharing their own field observations and data with their peers across North America.

Notes

1. http://www.ccsso.org
2. http://asiasociety.org
3. http://en.unesco.org/themes/education-21st-century
4. http://www.iste.org

5. http://namle.net
6. http://site.aace.org
7. http://www.aera.net
8. http://www.udlcenter.org
9. http://www.cast.org
10. http://www.ascd.org
11. http://www.udlcenter.org/aboutudl/whatisudl
12. http://humancentereddesign.org/adp/profiles/1_mace.php
13. http://www.udlcenter.org/aboutudl/whatisudl/3principles
14. http://lessonbuilder.cast.org
15. https://www.diigo.com/list/udlcenter/Guidelines-Examples-and-Resources
16. http://www.nimac.us
17. http://www.visuwords.com
18. https://www.google.com/culturalinstitute/u/0/project/art-project
19. https://tellagami.com
20. http://www.voki.com
21. http://www.bubbl.us/index
22. http://rubistar.4teachers.org/index.php
23. https://www.teachervision.com/graphic-organizers/printable/6293.html?de toured=1
24. http://nces.ed.gov/nceskids/createAgraph/default.aspx
25. http://www.cameramouse.org
26. https://www.boardmakeronline.com
27. http://voicethread.com
28. https://animoto.com
29. http://www.toondoo.com
30. https://scratch.mit.edu
31. http://play.magneticpoetry.com/poem/Original/kit/
32. http://magpo.com
33. http://newsela.com
34. http://www.cnn.com/studentnews
35. http://www.dogonews.com
36. http://kids.nationalgeographic.com
37. http://www.timeforkids.com
38. http://www.pbs.org/newshour/extra
39. http://learning.blogs.nytimes.com
40. http://ireport.cnn.com
41. http://www.iearn.org
42. http://www.epals.com
43. https://penpalschools.com
44. http://www.globalschoolnet.org/index.cfm
45. http://www.kidsgoglobal.net
46. http://www.boomwriter.com
47. http://writetheworld.com
48. https://www.facingthefuture.org
49. http://gng.org

50. http://www.globalschoolnet.org
51. https://www.stevens.edu/provost/research/centers/ciese
52. https://www.globe.gov
53. https://www.learner.org/jnorth

References

Bergmann, J., & Sams, A. (2012). *Flip your classroom: Reach every student in every class every day*. Eugene, OR: International Society for Technology in Education.

Boix Mansilla, V., & Jackson, A. (2011). *Educating for global competence: Preparing our youth to engage the world*. New York, NY: Asia Society. Retrieved from https://docs.google.com/viewer?url=http%3A%2F%2Fasiasociety.org%2Ffiles%2Fbook-globalcompetence.pdf

CAST. (2015). *Universal design for learning*. Retrieved from http://www.cast.org

Dweck, C. S. (2007). *Mindset: The new psychology of success*. New York, NY: Random House.

Friedman, T. L. (2005). *The world is flat: A brief history of the twenty-first century*. New York, NY: Farrar, Straus and Giroux.

Meyer, A., Rose, D. H., & Gordon, D. (2014). *Universal design for learning: Theory and practice*. Wakefield, MA: CAST Professional Publishing.

Mishra, P., & Kochler, M. J. (2006). Technological pedagogical content knowledge: A framework for teacher knowledge. *Teachers College Record, 108*(6).

Ostroff, E., Limont, M., & Hunter, D. G. (2002). *Building a world fit for people: Designers with disabilities at work*. Boston, MA: Adaptive Environments Center.

Partnership for 21st Century Learning (P21). (2014). *Framework for state action on global education*. Retrieved from http://www.p21.org/storage/documents/Global_Education/P21_State_Framework_on_Global_Education_New_Logo.pdf

Rose, D. H., & Meyer, A. (2002). *Teaching every student in the digital age: Universal design for learning*. Alexandria, VA: Association for Supervision and Curriculum Development.

———. (2006). *A practical reader in universal design for learning*. Cambridge, MA: Harvard Education Press.

Rose, D. H., Meyer, A., & Hitchcock, C. (Eds.). (2005). *The universally designed classroom: Accessible curriculum and digital technologies*. Cambridge, MA: Harvard Education Press.

TakingITGlobal (TIG). (2015). *About takingitglobal*. Retrieved from http://www.tigweb.org/about/

Tye, B. B., & Tye, K. A. (1992). Global Education: A study of school change. Albany: State University of New York Press.

UNESCO. (2011). *Media and information literacy (MIL) curriculum for teachers*. Retrieved from http://www.unesco.org/new/en/communication-and-information/media-development/media-literacy/mil-curriculum-for-teachers/

—— (2013). *Global media literacy assessment framework: Country readiness and competencies.* Retrieved from http://www.unesco.org/new/en/communication-and-information/media-development/media-literacy/unesco-global-mil-assessment-framework/

Wiggins, G. P., & McTighe, J. (2011). *The understanding by design guide to creating high-quality units.* Alexandria, VA: ASCD.

13. Media Assessment

Melda N. Yildiz

"Not everything that counts can be counted, and not everything that can be counted counts."

—Albert Einstein

Introduction

This chapter explores the use of innovative assessment in global media literacy education. It outlines innovative and transformative assessment models in developing global competencies, information literacy, critical thinking, and 21st-century skills among P–16 students, and showcases transformative, inclusive, multilingual, multicultural assessment models across content areas. It questions why and how we assess, and the role of assessment in the context of global media literacy education. The chapter explores differentiated approaches to adaptive assessment—assessing media work from e-portfolios to digital stories; from self-assessment to peer assessment. It invites educators to rethink assessment in preparing for teaching and learning in the second half of the 21st century.

A plague has been sweeping through American schools, wiping out the most innovative instruction and beating down some of the best teachers and administrators. Ironically, that plague has been unleashed in the name of improving schools. Invoking such terms as "tougher standards," "accountability," and "raising the bar," people with little understanding of how children learn have imposed a heavy-handed, top-down, test-driven version of school reform that is lowering the quality of education in this country. It has taken some educators and parents a while to realize that the rhetoric of "standards" is turning schools into giant test-prep centers, effectively closing off intellectual inquiry and undermining enthusiasm for learning (and teaching). It has taken even longer to realize that this is not a fact of life, like the weather—that is, a reality to be coped with—but rather a political movement that must be opposed.

—Alfie Kohn, 2015

Innovations in Assessment

Today, we live in an era in which "there is an app for everything." Of course, this is an exaggeration. There is only an app yet to be discovered for solving world hunger and peace. However, there are apps or online resources that assist us in teaching and learning, as well as assessing students' work. We can scan an algebraic problem from a textbook, and the solution shows on your phone (e.g. PhotoMath[1]). We can scan a text in another language, and it will be translated into English (e.g. WordLens). We can use an app to assist colorblind people (e.g. Colordetector[2]). We can provide authentic news articles that can be customized for various reading levels (e.g. Newsela[3]); and organizations such as Open Dyslexic[4] provide universal design solutions for readers at every level to be successful learners. We also have access to innovative assessment tools and content management systems (e.g. Taskstream[5]) and integrative learning tools and platforms (e.g. Brightspace[6]).

It is time to rethink assessment from process to product, and use it to celebrate learning and develop assessment frameworks for our globally connected classrooms. From PISA to TIMMS scores, international standardized tests and assessments have been in the public debate. The book *Surpassing Shanghai* (2011), edited by Marc Tucker, openly questioned the American education system, especially educational assessment.

Below is an assessment model for the global media literacy education framework we worked on in our teacher education classrooms.

Table 13.1

GMLE Assessment Framework
Developed based on Western and Northern Canadian Protocol for Collaboration in Education (2006).

Who assess(es)?	Assessment *for* learning/Diagnostic/Formative: The process of seeking and interpreting evidence.	Assessment *of* learning/ Summative: The process of assessing the final outcomes and performance.	Assessment *as* learning/Formative: Bringing learning into focus during the teaching activity.
Teacher	Engineering effective classroom discussions and other learning tasks that elicit information about student learning progress. Identifying and outlining learning concepts and lesson plans, goals, and success criteria. Engaging students as learning resources for one another. Cultivating students to become responsible for their own learning.	Providing final grade/summative evaluation.	Providing descriptive feedback that moves learners forward (i.e. outlining what was done well, what needs improvement, and how to improve).
Student(Self)	Outlining learning goals/rubrics/ checklists. Engaging in self-assessment and goal setting.	Reflecting on the final score, grade and/or feedback.	Reviewing materials and seeking feedback.
Peer	Engaging in peer assessment and providing constructive feedback.	Providing constructive feedback for improvements in the future.	Providing feedback, common understanding, and sharing.

GMLE Assessment Framework
Developed based on Western and Northern Canadian Protocol for Collaboration in Education (2006).

Parent	Reviewing home-work and class-room projects. Providing for-mative insight assessment and constructive feed-back.	Reflecting on the final grade, score and/or feedback while identifying the future solutions and suggestions for improve-ment.	Participating in classroom activ-ities and open houses, and pro-viding feedback.
Global Com-munity and other stake-holders (e.g. Department of Education Accreditation agencies, local, national and interna-tional peers)	Providing prelim-inary, formative results. Posing a question, idea and/or a prob-lem to seek out common interests and projects such as posting an online survey.	Providing overall, summative results. High-light the results, statistics and/or comparative data.	Engaging in multi-cultural dialogue and providing constructive feed-back and alterna-tive points of view.

Designing Transdisciplinary Curriculum Projects through Journaling

In our teacher education programs, teacher candidates were asked to develop lesson plans. After being introduced to Universal Design for Learning (UDL) (CAST, 2015), Understanding by Design (UbD), growth mindset versus fixed mindset (Dweck, 2007), media literacy, global competency, and ped-agogy of plenty frameworks, as well as exploring UNESCO's Global Media and Information Literacy Assessment Framework, teacher candidates were first introduced to writing "smart objectives." They were given several lesson plan models and resources, such as the online Lesson Builder tool from the CAST website.[7] In addition, they were given twelve journal entries to com-plete during the course. Each journal exercise was connected to their cur-riculum project. They were given specific tasks to complete each week and confirm their progress with the instructor.

The purposes of the journal entries are: to encourage teacher candidates to experience *deep learning* on the topic or theme; to explore transdisciplinary connections to the theme or topic they plan to teach; to provide effective lesson planning steps; to reflect on those experiences; and to assess teaching techniques and integrate new media and technologies for global media literacy education. Teacher candidates were encouraged to write one journal entry each week related to the chosen topic or theme. After they write the first entry on their curriculum proposal, the order of the journal entries can be changed. They are also allowed to write more than one journal entry.

The table below lists the guidelines for the journal.

Table 13.2

Journal Entries: Curriculum Unit Project/ Lesson Planning (Deep Learning)

Frequently Asked Questions

What should be included in each journal entry?

Journal responses may include:

1. Accomplishments: What you accomplished each week (readings, responses in online discussions, etc.), where you are with your projects and assignments, etc.
2. Detective work: What you have discovered lately on TV, websites, blogs, listservs, etc. Please share a link.
3. Classroom practice: How you responded to the flipped classroom activities (reading materials, websites, online quizzes, and videos).

How long does the journal need to be?

Each journal entry is recommended to be one page, or a suggested length of 250–500 words.

Where should the journals be posted?

Please post your journals to your portfolio.

Week	Entries	Explanation
1	Curriculum (deep learning) and/or lesson plan proposal	1. Pick a topic, theme, or subject in a grade level that you want to teach related to your subject field (art/music, physical education/health, language arts, math/science, social studies, geography, world languages, or technology). 2. Write your proposal, including rationale and significance of the subject. See the guidelines below.

Week	Entries	Explanation
	Guidelines for your curriculum proposal Please cite all the resources that you used. Provide credits to the primary and secondary sources (print and nonprint material, electronic resources, and websites).	Briefly address these questions: 1. What is your chosen subject area, theme, or topic? 2. Who is your intended audience (grade level, age, gender)? 3. What standards are you planning to address? 4. What are the educational goal(s) and objective(s) and the expected outcome of the lesson? 5. What is the specific problem(s) or essential question(s) you will pose? 6. What tasks, projects, and/or assignment will the students accomplish? 7. Why do you want to teach this topic, title, or theme? 8. What teaching methods, strategies, and resources are you planning to use? 9. How do you plan to involve parents, local, national, or global community in your lesson plan? 10. What career skills or career options do you plan to introduce? 11. How do you plan to assess and evaluate students' learning? What type of assessment strategies do you plan to employ? 12. What type of media, technologies, and educational materials do you plan to use?
2	Textbook standards	1. Find a textbook or section of a textbook related to your topic. 2. Explore state, Common Core, and national (Specialized Professional Associations, SPA) standards such as ISTE. 3. Explore connections to other disciplines and subject fields.
3	Smart objectives	Write "smart objectives." Post at minimum one lower and one higher order skill-level objective for the lesson plan that you are planning to write in your curriculum proposal. See the formula and an example below, with font styles designating the different elements.

OBJECTIVE = SWAT + SPECIFIC PERFORMANCE **+ learning
outcome** + conditions or constraints + *criterion or standard.*
Students will be able to LIST **in their journals** at the end of the lesson *two
differences between urban and rural communities.*

4	Assessment Plan: How to assess student learning. Consider adaptation for ELL/ Special Education	For each objective, plan an assessment including diagnostic (e.g. pre-survey), formative, and summative assessment strategies. See sample below.	

Objectives	Assessments	Format	Adaptations
Obj. 1: At the end of the lesson, students will be able to identify all seven continents on a world map.	Pre-assessment diagnostic evaluations	Checklist: The day before the unit, students will play an interactive World Map Game locating the seven continents. Teacher will find out the common mistakes.	Repeat and modify instructions, as needed. Demonstrate and assist with cutting, gluing, etc. Provide model of a world with seven continents. Keep all activities high-interest and brief.
	Formative assessment	Students will rotate around different learning stations exploring seven continents. Examples include: 1. World map puzzle with continents; 2. Cut and paste activity placing continents on a world map; 3. Video clip or song about continents; 4. Book or article about continents.	Provide concrete models and assistance with fine motor tasks, as needed. Provide multiple explanations and model performances. Process writing (i.e. dictations) when needed. Provide verbal cues and plenty of wait time for Q&A.
	Summative post-assessment	Students will identify and write the name of the continents on a world map.	

5	Find a couple of **print** resources. Visit your local or school library to locate two articles, one from a popular magazine and the other from a scholarly journal, as well as one nonprint resource.	1. Search, read, and summarize an article in a popular magazine or newspaper (e.g. *New York Times, Time, Newsweek, Fortune, Smithsonian, National Geographic*) about some aspect of your topic. 2. Search a scholarly (peer-reviewed) journal in your subject field and read and summarize an article in a scientific or scholarly journal about some aspect of your topic. 3. Search, explore, and summarize one nonprint resource (e.g. educational website, music CD, DVD video, TedEd video) related to your project.
6	Find a **nonprint** resource.	Search, watch, review, and cite one nonprint resource related to your project (e.g. educational website, documentary film, music CD, DVD video, TedEd video, film on demand). Search, video, and summarize one nonprint resource related to your project (e.g. educational website, music CD, TedEd, PBS video).
7	Conduct an experiential learning activity (e.g. field trip, geocaching).	Explore and visit (field trip) a location (e.g. museum, natural site, food shelter, public library). Record how you felt, what lesson ideas you came up with, and what you learned.
8	Pick one: 1. Interview (have a conversation with) someone whose job is related to your topic. 2. Attend a lecture, seminar, or webinar on some aspect of your chosen topic.	After the interview or the lecture, post your notes in double-entry format. Suggestions: Seek another point of view on the subject on the Internet using weblogs, listservs, and global education networks related to your topic. Explore global learning networks such as Kidlink or iEARN for bringing together people from other parts of the world using webcams and other telecommunication tools.

9	Search one lesson plan, one learning object, and one WebQuest related to your topic.	Search, read, and respond to lesson ideas related to your topic. Find one lesson plan (e.g. Learner. org, http://www.globaled.org/curriculum3.html), WebQuest, or learning object (e.g. from Merlot. org) related to your topic. Read, adopt, and respond to one of the lesson ideas that is related to your topic.
10	Write lesson plan.	After collecting all the data and necessary information related to your topic, outline your lesson plan using the template provided in your own discipline. Make sure to list smart objectives, standards, and assessment plans. Suggested site: Lesson Builder at Cast.org to integrate Universal Design for Learning.
11	Integrate multicultural and multilingual aspects.	Explore ways in which you include multilingual and multicultural resources in your lesson plan. For instance, include multilingual children's books and posters. (Please see Picture 1: Multilingual Bingo Game that we developed in English, Turkish, Chinese, and Spanish.)
12	Write process paper, addressing the following points in your lesson plan and/or curriculum project.	1. **Civic Engagement**: What actions do your students plan to take to better the world? How does your unit relate to civic engagement? 2. **Motivation**: What type of motivational strategies do you plan to use? How do you relate the material to the students? (e.g. introduce the topic with fun facts, misconceptions, and/or current events) 3. **Educational materials**: What type of educational tools will you use? (e.g. slide presentation, websites, maps, graphics, cartoons, statistics, animations, video clips) 4. **Community Integration**: How do you connect your topic to the family, school (librarians), and world community? How does this topic relate to your students? Please make connections to: • Student as self-learner with individualized instruction • Multicultural education as a national perspective • Global literacy including international perspective on the chosen topic/theme for your curriculum.

12	Write process paper, addressing the following points in your lesson plan and/or curriculum project.	5. **Primary and Secondary Resources**: Add a reference or works cited section to your curriculum project. Make sure to list each picture, music, and lesson idea you used or adopted in your project in APA or MLA style. Use Worldcat (http://www.worldcat.org) or Citation Machine (http://citationmachine.net) for citing your resources.
13	After presenting your curriculum project and/or lesson plan, please write a self-reflection.	**Reactions to lesson presentation and future considerations**: Please respond to the suggestions and comments by your peers and the instructor. How will you alter your lesson? What should have or could have happened differently? **Fill out the self-assessment checklist**: Calculate your final grade.

Teacher candidates posted their journal entries to their e-portfolio portal. Each portfolio was linked to the common course site so that each student could view and comment on each other's websites, and the instructor could provide feedback under each journal entry. By incorporating the GMLE framework and journaling process, teacher candidates developed transdisciplinary and globally connected lesson plans. Their lesson plans were designed to prepare the new generation to develop critical media and 21st-century skills for the global world in which they live. Through their curriculum project, they experienced developing lesson ideas to address the needs of all their students (who e.g. speak different languages, are from different cultures, and learn best via different methods).

One of the diagnostic tools that we used in our classes was a "KWL" chart. Students were given this one page handout to write what they *know* about the topic, what they *want* to know, and (at the end of each class) one thing they *learned*. This KWL chart serves multiple functions, for instance, it can be used as a name tag when the paper is folded into three parts. We also used it as an attendance tool, and most importantly it can be used as a self-assessment tool to identify students' progress.

Teacher candidates experience the "jigsaw" method of assessment,[8] where the students are given freedom to research and present their own topic given by the instructor. The jigsaw method is a cooperative learning technique that was developed by Elliot Aronson and his students at the University of Texas and the University of California in 1971. Ellis (2001) believes in the jigsaw method "for bringing teaching, learning and assessment together." It promotes peer collaboration and "peer teaching [which] is one of the best ways to learn…" (p. 79).

In the global media literacy curriculum, students are encouraged to learn through a process where they are supported in questioning the questions, deconstructing the learning materials (e.g. textbooks), researching using advanced search tools and information literacy skills, and constructing their own projects and papers to share on their e-portfolios.

Table 13.3

Global Media Literacy Education Curriculum Framework
Deconstruct (Read Media): Explore global media literacy activities (deconstructing webpages, news, advertisement, and newspapers; POV (point of view) exercises; etc.)
Research (Use Media): Information literacy (library skills, researching Internet resources, etc.)
Construct (Write Media): Media production (create an oral history project, video documentary, website, webquest, weblog, or multimedia presentation). Students create media projects integrating new media and technologies.
Assess (Celebrate Learning Using Media): Assessment of learning and for learning methods. Students participate in assessment process. They can be encouraged to provide test questions. They assess their peers and use self-assessment checklist and rubrics.
Take action (Talk Back to Media): Social reconstructivist theory advocates change, improvement, and reforming society through education. Social reconstructivist perspectives claim that the learning environment is active, that assessment is based on creative work, and that education is relatively autonomous and can and does lead to social change. The role of education is to enhance students' learning through the interpersonal negotiation of meaning. Knowledge is socially constructed through language and interpersonal processes.

Prior to designing assessment for GMLE projects, here are a few questions to ponder.

Table 13.4

Planning GMLE Assessment: Questions to Consider

Design	What are the student learning outcomes? How can I assess learning that reflects critical thinking? What kind of artifacts do they need to create? How do they create their projects? What types of portfolio design, assessment strategies, and reflective practices are most conducive for my students to enhance their teaching?
Types of assessment	How can I include self, peer, in-class, or nationally and globally connected assessment? Is the assessment included a formative vs. summative adaptive assessment strategy? Are the students allowed to learn from their mistakes?
Print vs. nonprint format	What is the added value of publishing a portfolio in an electronic format? (When I look at a lot of paper-based portfolios, I see documents printed by laser printers, so the documents already exist in some type of electronic format.) Is it worth the extra effort to publish these documents in an electronic format?
Institutional/ program level decisions:	How do we take "compliance" or classroom mandated portfolios developed in the class, and transform them into life-long learning tools?
Technology	What are the role of new media and technologies? Does creating an electronic portfolio enhance students' multimedia development skills or learning? Does constructing an electronic portfolio develop global competencies and 21st-century skills and demonstrate achievement of both state and Common Core standards and the ISTE National Educational Technology Standards? Will multimedia skills gained from the process of developing electronic portfolios transfer to students' life-long learning process?
Adaptation and modifications for English language learners (ELLs)/Special Education	What adaptations and modifications do you consider not just for ELL and Special Education students but for all students? How can you design an assessment that challenges students based on their ability level? What type of computerized adaptive testing (CAT) can I use that tailors the assessment for the ability level of students?

In a project-based, globally connected learning and assessment model curriculum, teacher candidates were encouraged to learn through a process where they write questions and integrate new media and technologies into their media projects. When it comes to assessment, usually the instructor's role is to ask the questions, give the assignments, and judge the products, whereas the role of students is to produce successful outcomes. From a constructivist point of view, this is inappropriate in relation to students' learning. Therefore, alternative approaches to project assessment are critical, especially in teacher education programs. We explored and designed new assessment tools, templates, and strategies, so that we could reflect on our own learning process and teach our students how they need to take responsibility for their own learning.

Teacher candidates discussed the relationship between assessment practices and effective schools; how to conduct day-to-day classroom assessment; how to handle the demand for accountability; and how to clarify their achievement goals. In recent years, there are major breakthroughs in using technology in assessment, and our understanding of the effective use of assessment to benefit student learning. We have gained new insights into cognitive processes and have succeeded in connecting them to new assessment strategies that promise unprecedented achievement gains for students. Yet in districts, schools, and classrooms across the nation, educators still assess student learning the way their predecessors did 60 years ago. It may be because they have not been given the opportunity to learn about these new insights and practices.

This PAR study examined the role of assessment strategies, tools, and rubrics in global media literacy education. It explored the role of assessment in learning and teaching. It brings new understanding of the power of assessment in learning by aligning local, national, and international media and technology standards.

We examined the study used in Chris Worsnop's (1997) model of authentic media assessment, which consists of the content, environment, process, and performance of students. The study is about the work that students produce for teachers to mark, and educators' concern with being consistent in grading and having appropriate standards in their assessment. It was impossible to evaluate students' work without evaluating the classroom environment, media equipment, etc.

We emphasized the importance of studying assessment from process to product and outlining the elements of assessment in teacher education programs in order to gain different perspectives in our teaching and learning styles and strategies. It is about rethinking the relationship between assessment practices and effective teacher education curricula.

We experienced several difficulties and discovered unique characteristics of assessing new media projects such as videos and multimedia presentations. We explored the role of standards and integrating those with the GMLE framework; explored alternative assessment tools and strategies and the role of assessment in improving learning; and finally aligned our assessment with state and national standards. Most teacher candidates created their e-portfolios online, and some used paper-based portfolios. They received final exams online that we co-created together. We used self-assessment checklists (see a sample below), peer assessment, and portfolio assessment.

Reflected in our participants' reflections, self-assessments, projects, and presentations, teacher candidates evaluated websites, media projects, and presentations, observed and interviewed in-service teachers, and co-created new assessment tools and rubrics for their own curriculum projects.

To date, few scholarly studies have investigated the impact of assessment in global media projects. This PAR study attempts to fill the gap by outlining the natural links between the role of assessment in teacher education and educational assessment. In addition to increasing demand for developing authentic assessment methods and rubrics for multimedia projects, there is still a great need for research-based classroom materials. Teacher candidates explored various online tools (e.g. RubiStar, Quizlet) for creating rubrics and interactive online quizzes.

The overall aim of the media assessment is to enable educators to reflect on their teaching practice through formative assessment, encourage learners to reflect on their learning and make connections among subjects and disciplines across cultures and people, and cultivate a learning culture in the educational institutions that promotes social justice and provides culturally and linguistically responsive pedagogy.

Notes

1. https://www.photomath.net/en/
2. http://www.mobialia.com/apps/color-detector/
3. https://newsela.com/
4. http://opendyslexic.org/
5. https://www1.taskstream.com/
6. http://www.brightspace.com/
7. http://lessonbuilder.cast.org
8. https://www.jigsaw.org/#overview

References

CAST. (2015). *Universal design for learning.* Retrieved from http://www.cast.org

Dweck, C. S. (2007). *Mindset: The new psychology of success.* New York, NY: Random House.

Ellis, A. K. (2001). *Teaching, learning, and assessment together: The reflective classroom.* Larchmont, NY: Eye on Education.

Kohn, A. (2015). *Rescuing our schools from "tougher standards."* Retrieved from http://www.alfiekohn.org/standards-testing/

Programme for International Student Assessment (PISA). (2012). *PISA 2012 results.* Retrieved from http://www.oecd.org/pisa/keyfindings/pisa-2012-results.htm

Tucker, M. S. (2011). *Surpassing Shanghai: An agenda for American education built on the world's leading systems.* Cambridge, MA: Harvard Education Press.

UNESCO. (2013). *Global media and information literacy assessment framework: Country readiness and competencies.* UNESCO Communication and Information Sector. Retrieved from http://unesdoc.unesco.org/images/0022/002246/224655e.pdf

Western and Northern Canadian Protocol for Collaboration in Education. (2006). *Rethinking classroom assessment with purpose in mind.* Retrieved from http://www.wncp.ca/media/40539/rethink.pdf

Worsnop, C. M. (1997). *Assessing media work.* Mississauga, Canada: Wright Communications.

Additional Readings Used by Teacher Candidates

Barrett, H. (2004–8). *My online portfolio adventure.* Retrieved from http://electronicportfolios.org/myportfolio/versions.html

Barrett, H. (2010). Balancing the two faces of e portfolios. *Educação, Formação & Tecnologias, 3*(1), 6–14. Retrieved from http://eft.educom.pt

Beck, R., & Bear, S. (2009). Teacher's self-assessment of reflection skills as an outcome of e-folios. In P. Adamy & N. B. Milman (Eds.), *Evaluating electronic portfolios in teacher education.* Charlotte, NC: Information Age Publishers.

Black, P., & Wiliam, D. (1998, November). Inside the black box: Raising standards through classroom assessment. *Phi Delta Kappan, 80*(2), 139–48.

Crooks, T. J. (1988). The impact of classroom evaluation practices on students. *Review of Educational Research, 58*(4), 438. Retrieved from http://search.proquest.com/docview/214114484?accountid=14872

The Gordon Commission. (2013). *To assess, to teach, to learn: A vision for the future of assessment: Technical Report.* Retrieved from http://www.cse.ucla.edu/colloquium/GC_Report030513_Report.pdf

Looney, J. W. (2009). Assessment and innovation in education. *OECD Education Working Papers, 24.* Retrieved from http://dx.doi.org/10.1787/222814543073

Petersen, N. (2008). *Case studies of electronic portfolios for learning.* Retrieved from http://wsuctlt.wordpress.com/2008/03/14/case-studies-of-electronic-portfolios-for-learning/

Robinson, K. (2006, February). Do schools kill creativity? [Video]. Retrieved from http://www.ted.com/talks/ken_robinson_says_schools_kill_creativity.html

Figure 13.1: Multilingual Bingo Game in English, Turkish, Chinese, and Spanish.

Bingo -宾果游戏- **Bingo** – Tombala

<u>Directions:</u> Walk around the room and get acquainted. A person can sign your sheet only once. Go for it!

路线：在房间里到处走和大家相互认识。一个人只可以在你的表上签名一次。大胆试试吧！

Direcciones: Caminar alrededor del cuarto y conseguir conocimiento. Una persona puede firmar tu hoja una vez solamente. ¡agalo!

<u>Talimat:</u> odanın içinde yürüyün ve hakkında bilgi almak. Bir kişi sadece bir kez sac kayıt olabilirsiniz.

Find someone who ...　　找到的人是...	Encontrar a alguien que...	O kişiyi bul...
Calls himself or herself a globally competent, scientist or a researcher. 谁认为他或她自己是一个有能力的国际科学家或研究员。 **¿Te considera un mundo competente, un científico o un investigador?** Kendini küresel yetkili, bilim adamı ya da araştırmacı gören kişi. NAME/ 名称/ NOMBRE/ İSİM: _____	Was born in another state or country and lived OR traveled in another country more than a month. 一个人出生在另一个州或另一个国家，或在另一个国家居住超过一个月。 **Nació en otro estado o país y vivido o viajado a otro país por más de un mes.** Başka bir devlet veya eyalette doğmuş veya bir aydan fazla başka bir ülkede yaşamış biri. NAME/ 名称/ NOMBRE/ İSİM: _____	Created a digital video/digital story and uploaded to YouTube or another website. 有人曾经做过一个数字视频/数字的故事，并上传到 YouTube 或其他网站。 **Ha creado un video / historia digital y ha subido a YouTube u otro sitio web.** Bir dijital video / dijital hikaye oluşturulan ve YouTube veya başka bir web sitesine yüklemiş biri. NAME/ 名称/ NOMBRE/ İSİM: _____
Has the same birthday month or birth year as you. 有人与你同年或同月出生 **Tiene el mismo cumpleaños o hayan nacido en el mismo año suyo.** Sizinle aynı doğum günü ayı veya doğum yılı olan biri. NAME/ 名称/ NOMBRE/ İSİM: _____	Speaks another language (does not have to be fluent). 会说另一种语言（不一定要流利）。 **Habla otra lengua (no tiene que ser fluido).** Yabancı dil bilen biri (akıcı olmak zorunda değildir). NAME/ 名称/ NOMBRE/ İSİM: _____	Can say the word "health," "global," or "education," in another language. 有人可以用另一种语言说"健康"，"全球"或"教育"。 **¿Puede decir la palabra "salud," o "educación" en otro idioma?** Başka bir dilde "sağlık," ve ya "eğitim" diyebilen biri. NAME/ 名称/ NOMBRE/ İSİM: _____
Practices dance, exercise, or sports. 有人练习舞蹈，做体育锻炼或各种运动。 **Danza, ejercicio o deportes de las prácticas.** Dans, egzersiz veya spor yapan biri. NAME/ 名称/ NOMBRE/ İSİM: _____	Plays a musical instrument. 有人演奏乐器。 **Reproduce un instrumento musical.** Musik aleli çalubilen biri. NAME/ 名称/ NOMBRE/ İSİM: _____	Loves outdoors and nature. 有人爱户外活动和大自然。 **Amors al aire libre y naturaleza.** Açık havayı ve doğayı seven biri. NAME/ 名称/ NOMBRE/ İSİM: _____

Table 13.5. Self-Assessment Checklist.

	Self-Assessment	Checklist		Points	DUE
Pre-Survey	Yes (1)		No (0)		WK 1
Portfolio (Draft)	Beyond Expectations (3)	Needs Improvement (2)	Satisfactory (1)		WK 2
Weekly Reflections/ Process Paper Curriculum Journals	Completed all + timely submission (2–10)	Satisfactory. Each reflection, 2 points	No evidence (0)	20	WK 2–11
Curriculum Proposal Project (CP)	Meets Expectations (3)	Satisfactory (2)	Needs Improvement (1)		WK 3
CP Lesson Plan	Excellent + timely submission 10	Meets Expectations (9–8) Satisfactory (7–6)	Needs Improvement	10	WK 7/8
Assignments (5 pts each)	Submitted all 7 assignments on time and showcased technical skills (20)	Satisfactory (19–1)	No evidence 0	35	WK 5–14
Final Project (e.g. Digital Storytelling)	Completed a digital story (10)	Satisfactory (9–1)	No evidence 0	10	WK 7
Quiz	Completed all. 1 quiz, 5 pts each		No evidence (0)		WK 13
Lesson Plan Presentation	Meets Expectations. Completed presentation (5)	Satisfactory (4) Needs improvement (3–2)	No evidence (0)	5	WK 13/14
Post Survey Self-Assessment + Final Reflection	Completely answered each section.		No evidence (0)	5	WK 15
E-portfolio	Meets Expectations (5)	Satisfactory (4–3)	Needs Improvement (3–1)	5	WK 15
Attendance Participation Disposition	Missed less than 1 and actively participated in class and online (10)	Missed less than 2 and actively participated in class and online (9)	Missed more than 3	10	WK 1–15
Total				100+	

14. *Practice to Action: World Savvy Teachers*

MELDA N. YILDIZ

"A democratic civilization will save itself only if it makes the language of the image into a stimulus for critical reflection, not an invitation to hypnosis."
—Umberto Eco, 1976

Introduction

Situated within the context of global media literacy education, this chapter highlights areas from theory to practice, in taking action in teacher education programs. In order to develop culturally and linguistically responsive pedagogy, the chapter first outlines social reconstructivist theory, the role of social justice in education, and participatory action research (PAR) methodology for developing a curriculum that leads to transformative, collaborative, and inclusive projects. Second, it makes the natural connections between the Global Competency Matrix and the global media literacy education framework and their common focus on taking action while advocating for and contributing to social change on local, national, or global levels. Third, the chapter outlines global media literacy education activities and resources for educators that aid in re-thinking and re-designing curricula, while preparing students for the cyber world and ethics. Finally, it provides the role of heutagogy, as opposed to pedagogy, in teacher education and professional development that promote transformative leadership skills, edupreneurship, and lifelong learning among educators.

> Good teachers possess a capacity for connectedness. They are able to weave a complex web of connections among themselves, their subjects, and their students so that students can learn to weave a world for themselves. [...] The connections

made by good teachers are held not in their intellects but in their hearts—meaning hearts in the ancient sense, as the place where intellect, emotion and will converge. (Palmer, 1998)

In light of Palmer's observations, teacher education programs need to prepare future teachers to be more interconnected with local, national, and global issues and more able to use new media and technologies. They need to be able to differentiate facts from propaganda. They need to be able to connect knowledge integrating history, culture, and languages, while dismantling myths and misconceptions, and rethink the role of education for developing economies and the power of learning and teaching for developing a peaceful world.

The role of teachers in fostering global competence and 21st-century skills is critical, yet many teachers have not themselves developed this competence or taken formal training on the subject. As the Longview Foundation (2008) has argued, the critical role of teachers "in internationalizing P–12 education has never been clearer, yet today's educators rarely begin their careers with the deep knowledge and robust skills necessary to bring the world into their classrooms." While the tremendous influence of globalization, the interconnectedness of global economies, and the importance of intercultural communication have been outlined for some time, minimal attention has been given to how to make teacher preparation programs more transformative, reflective, and innovative. Knight (2003) emphasizes the importance of "infusing and embedding the international and intercultural dimensions into policies and programs to ensure that the international dimension remains central, not marginal, and is sustainable."

From the perspective of educational policy, educational reform has been linked to national economic competiveness in the global economy. K–12 curriculum has been criticized for being an inch deep and a mile wide (Schmidt, McKnight, & Raizen, 1997). According to the latest report funded by the OECD for the Programme International Student Assessment (PISA, 2012), U.S. students performed below average in math among the 65 nations surveyed. The current trends in global competition require higher standards, with deeper understanding of the content and application of knowledge to real life settings. Preparing the next generation of global citizens for the second half of the 21st-century workforce demands world savvy educators. In essence, we need to cultivate world savvy teachers who develop transdisciplinary and transformative curricula.

As the world flattens (Friedman, 2005) and our U.S. population includes a broad range of diversity, many of our teacher candidates are likely to work abroad or in school districts that serve children from diverse backgrounds and international students who require skills in a developing global curriculum that is innovative and transformative.

Participatory Action Research

In this chapter, we share our teacher candidates' experiences and reactions to global media literacy activities. Through the use of participatory action research (PAR) methodology, the teacher candidates were engaged in a participatory dialogue and semester-long curriculum, to design activities to rethink the role of culture while developing a culture of learning that goes beyond the classroom walls. For example, in our participatory action research (PAR) projects in teacher education courses for elementary education majors, teacher candidates were given a "Draw a Scientist" task. Just like the previous studies indicated, our teacher candidates mostly drew a picture of a White male.

This action research study focused on teacher candidates' perceptions and experiences of engaging in dialogue on the world savvy teacher model. Teacher candidates engaged in redefining the professional identity and translating it into classroom practice, as well as interviewing in-service teachers about their lived experiences before, during, and after engaging in action research, at the same time as conducting a self-study on their own teaching practices through the lens of global education.

As transformative education intersects with race, class, gender, and sexual orientation, the global media literacy education (GMLE) framework can be used as a tool for social justice education. Borrowing and extending the work of critical theorists, particularly Henry Giroux and Paulo Freire, our study explored the transformative critical pedagogy of teaching and learning in the 21st century.

Here are the some of the research questions that guided the PAR study: Given the requirements and limitations of pre-service teacher education programs and the reality of the classrooms,

- Is it possible to introduce participatory action research to teacher candidates in a way that will empower them professionally and prepare them to be reflective and transformative leaders in global education?
- What are the pedagogical and transformative perspectives of in-service teachers and teacher educators, in relation to the teaching practices that they find essential in preparing future transformative educators with 21st-century skills and global competencies?

- What are the teacher educators and teacher candidates' (participants') personal experiences and reactions in the global media literacy activities and heutagogical curriculum model?
- What skills, assessment methods, strategies, and tools do we need to provide to our teacher candidates (undergraduates) to improve their 21st-century skills (e.g. media literacy, information literacy skills) and global competencies?
- How can educators prepare students for the symbol-rich culture in which they live and function, as informed and productive citizens in a democratic society?
- What are the advantages and challenges in fostering transformative thinking and critical autonomy among learners, while implementing transformative critical education, global competencies, and visionary leadership theory in teacher education?
- What common problems and discoveries do the participants share during the process of developing their global competencies and preparing inclusive and globally connected curriculum projects?
- What are the effective and research-based teaching strategies and transformative resources that are recommended by the participants?
- What innovative suggestions and innovative teaching models do the participants provide, in order to improve assessment in higher education?
- How do we design and implement community-based, globally connected, and effective instruction models with limited resources and equipment, and prepare them for the global economy?
- What does it mean to be a world savvy educator teaching in a media-rich, globally connected world culture?
- Why study media and integrate global education into the P–20 curriculum?
- How do we design effective instruction integrating media literacy and global education into the P–20 curriculum?

What Does a World Savvy Teacher Look Like?

We explored three key topics in order to develop a world teacher educator model: the wide range of meanings associated with social justice and media literacy education in teacher education; the impact of developing project-based, globally connected, linguistically and culturally responsive projects on teacher candidates' global competencies and 21st-century skills; and the ways in which they respond to transdisciplinary, globally connected, culturally and linguistically responsive curriculum through developing media literacy skills for K–12 students.

For the last 15 years, we have worked with in-service and pre-service teachers, highlighting certain characteristics for a globally competent educator. We developed the table below to summarize our collective thoughts. We questioned what globally competent individuals should possess—what skills, characteristics, and abilities they need to acquire, and how to learn, collaborate, and engage with globally significant issues. In order to inspire our students to become globally competent, we argued that educators must develop these skills, core concepts, attitudes, values, and attributes in themselves and cultivate ways to foster them in students.

Table 14.1

What are the characteristics for a globally competent educator and student?		
Characteristics	Educators will be able to:	Students will be able to:
BE AWARE and INVESTIGATE THE WORLD (The "what" of learning).		
Observant	* pay close attention to the details for each learner (e.g. gestures, verbal and nonverbal feedback). * affirm each student and accept each student's unique learning preferences. * be self-aware of micro-affirmations and micro-inequalities and their power in teaching (Rowe, 2008).	* investigate the world beyond their immediate environment. * demonstrate respect and passion for other cultures and languages. * listen actively and attentively. * engage in inclusive and reflective dialogue. * stay engaged in new opportunities, ideas, and ways of thinking.

Research-oriented	* check alternative points of view from multiple resources. * liberate themselves from a textbook format. * integrate critical, creative thinking and problem-solving skills into teaching and learning. * deconstruct the learning material by rethinking, reframing the questions, analyzing, and synthesizing relevant evidence that leads to further exploration and study.	* differentiate facts from propaganda. * question the questions. * read between the lines. * form opinions based on research, exploration, and evidence.

ANALYZE and RECOGNIZE PERSPECTIVES (The "how" of learning).

Explor-atory	* seek cultural resources and experiences in local, national, and global contexts, as well as grant opportunities to enrich the classroom experience. * provide resources from multiple points of view.	* recognize their own and others' perspectives. * seek opportunities to travel and study abroad.
Globally con-nected	* speak the languages of the classroom, integrating multicultural perspectives, multilingual resources, and materials using multimedia tools and software.	* study at least one foreign language. * say a few words (thank you, hello) in several languages, as well as in sign language. * value diversity as an asset, not a deficit. * show self-awareness about identity and culture.

REFLECT and COMMUNICATE IDEAS (The "why" of learning).

Connective	* connect past to future and local to global in preparing students to be future change agents. * create lessons that are transdisciplinary, innovative, and transformative. * make connections between topics and units while connecting disciplines and subject fields.	* communicate their ideas effectively with diverse audiences. * experience oral history projects, interviewing local, national, and global people and documenting their stories and experiences. * develop 21st-century skills that connect disciplines.
Networked	* constantly seek guidance from experienced educators (take time to listen to their wisdom) and immerse themselves in contemporary youth culture. * find ways to connect the youth culture to the classroom curriculum.	* collaborate with others while solving problems and working on projects. * share knowledge in the class and the community, as well as online, while encouraging multicultural, multilingual, multimedia dialogue.
Transformative	* expand the learning spaces beyond the wall of the classroom. * examine appropriate tools, frameworks, and strategies to communicate and collaborate effectively. * provide new media and technologies and innovative resources and opportunities to students, to co-develop, co-create, and co-present projects with other learners around the world. * practice "pedagogy of plenty" in the classroom while integrating social reconstructivist theory.	* continue learning beyond the classroom. * demonstrate fluency in media and new technologies. * collaborate with peers and scholars around the world. * reflect on the learning material, while making connections and meaning about its relationship to other subject fields.

TAKE ACTION (The "what if" of learning).

Maker/ Edupreneur	* create a learning environment that focuses on ethics, innovation, entrepreneurship, and transforming self and society. * repurpose and curate tools and materials into cost effective, environmentally friendly education resources. * design learning modules that are personalized, learner-centered, situated, collaborative, and ubiquitous.	* translate their ideas and findings into appropriate actions to improve conditions. * co-create new meanings and develop innovative projects.
Life-long learner	* attend conferences, workshops, and webinars regularly. * participate in local, national, and/or international organizations. * commit to the process of continuous learning and reflection.	* demonstrate interest and passion for learning for life. * show willingness to rethink and relearn, and demonstrate resiliency in new settings and situations.
Change Agent	* develop lesson plans that integrate global education topics: social justice, human rights, and global patterns of injustice and inequality. * question provided curricula while challenging the myths and misconceptions. * assess the impact of advocacy and actions taken to inform policy.	* translate ideas, concerns, and findings into appropriate and responsible individual or collaborative actions to improve conditions. * seek challenges to dismantle ambiguity and unfamiliar situations. * do not take anything for granted. * act ethically. * share the responsibility, serve community, and take personal or collaborative action. * advocate for human rights, social justice to improve injustice and inequality locally, regionally, or globally.

Personal Story

In our first action research study, we shared our personal stories. First, we discussed the importance of being self-aware and self-reflective for developing a world savvy teacher model. We believe our teaching philosophies have been shaped by our professional and personal experiences. It is crucial to know who we are, and what our life and educational experiences are prior to the study. Below is a personal except:

> I grew up in Turkey, immigrated to the U.S. in 1992, and became an American Citizen in 2004. I work harder each day because I feel responsible and fortunate. I am the only person who went to a four-year college in my family and among all my relatives. I owe so much to the people of the world who are less fortunate. I had limited access to books and educational materials while I was growing up in Turkey. That's why I do not take anything for granted. During my junior year at Bogazici University in Istanbul, I have taken an educational technology course that changed my life and inspired me to explore new technologies further to improve my teaching skills. Later, I came to the U.S. to study instructional technology and multicultural education.

> Since September 2001, I have been developing and teaching transdisciplinary teacher education courses as well as womens and Asian studies courses as an affiliate faculty. I was just hired as an ABD to teach educational technology courses. It was my first week. I was preparing my syllabi in the copying room when I witnessed the collapse of the World Trade Center through the window of the university. The scream of one of our graduate students in that room is still in my ears: "Let's get rid of Palestinians and Muslims." Later that year, I learned a term "passing." I questioned myself: "Do I want to be 'passing' because I was not wearing traditional Muslim women clothing?" Instead, I chose to share my experiences. I was invited to be in various panels and presentations that fall semester, and I realized how little I knew about Arabs, Arab Americans, and Muslim traditions around the world. It was the semester to rediscover my belief and my role as an international faculty member, an immigrant woman who needed to provide an alternative point of view to my colleagues and students.

Myths and Misconceptions: Hidden Biases

Psychologists at Harvard, the University of Virginia, and the University of Washington developed "Project Implicit"[1] to measure our unconscious and hidden biases. Our teacher candidates signed up for Project Implicit. They identified and examined their own hidden biases. We discussed the first step, which is to understand where our myths and misconceptions are coming from. In order to prevent discrimination in our classrooms and "micro-inequalities," we argued that first we need to figure out the foundation of our stereotypes and prejudices. Teacher candidates read articles and explored lesson ideas from Tolerance.org and Rethinking Schools.

Participants experienced several eye-opening moments. One was in response to an article by Kelley (2012) called "10 Facts You Need to Know about Immigrant Women." Another occurred after they watched a documentary called "Mickey Mouse Monopoly." (Sun et al., 2002). It inspired a great discussion on how media portray immigrants and people of color by giving them certain negative roles or accents. We watched a clip from CBS called "Yeh-Shen" (Keeshan et al., 1992). It is a based on a Cinderella story from China. In the clip, all the good characters in the children's cartoon speak English very well, and their features are depicted as more Caucasian; by contrast, the stepmother and evil sisters speak English with a heavy Chinese accent and their facial features are colored yellow with extremely slanted eyes. One of my students developed a lesson plan using this video. She wanted to demonstrate how she integrated international story and created a multicultural project. When I pointed out the accent and facial features, all participants agreed how we may be doing a disservice to multicultural education if we do not deconstruct images and sound with our students. This video opened such a lively discussion. Almost all students had a story to share about their experiences being discriminated against or oppressed in university because of their background or accent. One student told us how one of the faculty confused names, calling George "John," and commented on how all Asians look alike. Another student told us how her communication instructor insisted that she could not get an "A" in the course because of her accent. One student confessed how he avoided taking classes with international professors because of their accents. I asked them about the British accent. Participants agreed that someone with a British accent can be considered smarter than someone who speaks with a Chinese or Spanish accent.

Visualization in Education

Eisenberg (2008) cites Ben Shneiderman, who is a computer science professor and a pioneer in information visualization: "The great fun of information visualization is that it gives you answers to questions you didn't know you had."

I was invited to be on a panel for International Women's Day in 2003. It was a couple of weeks before the start of the Iraq War. One of the colleagues in the audience said: "I support the war." After a couple of my colleagues whispered into my ears that war is good for the economy and for lowering gas prices, I realized how the power of images created a picture that blinded us as a nation. As a media educator, I decided to use a visualization exercise with the audience to discuss the power of media with my teacher candidates, especially when they have certain myths and misconceptions that need to be discussed in our lessons.

I asked the audience to indulge me for a visualization exercise, and they agreed. I asked them to close their eyes and tell me the first image that comes to their mind when I say "the Iraqi people." Once they opened their eyes, I asked them to draw a picture of what they saw or describe in writing the image they visualized. When they were ready to respond, I told them my prediction for what I they did not see. I said: "I bet none of you saw a pregnant woman." They all nodded. I continued: "A mother nursing her baby? A family eating dinner?" The audience nodded again. They started to tell me what they saw, mostly men with beards, turbans, or with a gun in a desert. This is called a commutation test in semiotics.

According to Daniel Chandler (2014), the commutation test is a way to challenge our perception or feelings about a particular sign (text or visual). We will reread our knowledge or understanding by transforming certain aspects of the signifier such as color, shape, angle, gender, or height, by substitution, transposition, addition, or deletion of the signifier to add, delete, or replace it with another. For example, in this visualization exercise, the audience was challenged to alter their image of an Iraqi person with a different gender.

While I was working as a media specialist in a high school, I had an interesting incident. Teachers were required to save students' progress reports on a floppy disk, and then upload the file to the registrar's office through a school wide information system. One day, one of the teachers told me that the registrar received her file without any data. She was sure she followed all the directions in the manual, and even the computer said, "OK." However, she forgot to upload her file, since she saw "0K" next to her name, and the date it was sent. It took us a while to find out which step she missed and why she thought she was right. When she saw "0K" (zero kilobytes), she thought it meant "OK," that her message had been transmitted safely to the registrar's office.

When I attended a presentation given by a dance teacher, Luana, at the National Association of Multicultural Education conference in the fall of 1996, she talked about the differences in art and dance among cultures, and gave interesting examples, even encouraging us to dance and present ourselves through dance. Through dance and movement, humans define themselves. In Western culture, the dance, especially ballet, includes upward movements. It is as if the dancers are trying to reach to the sky. In Africa, the dancers dance toward the earth. For instance, whirling dervishes (Sufi) try to reach to the sky (God) with one hand, and the other hand points to the earth. The movement in dance reflects cultural differences. As one teacher pointed out, African American students walk as if they are reaching to the ground. Some may interpret this as an attitude toward a system or teacher, but as the speaker pointed out, it may be related to the student's culture.

The teachers' role in education is critical and important. For Paulo Freire (1972), "education must begin with the solution of the teacher-student contradiction, by reconciling the poles of the contradiction so that both are simultaneously teachers and students." Although it is almost impossible to understand each and every student's background and culture and their inter-pretation of the signs and symbols, as Sloan (1995) suggests, "we can use our various interpretations of signs as a starting place for discussion of our often opposing value systems, to create interesting juxtapositions, and to investi-gate others 'personal structures' to broaden our own experiences."

Freire's (1972) notions of "dialogue" in education insist on breaking the "contradiction" of the teacher-student relationship (p. 72). He was critical of the "banking education," wherein learners are asked to file and silently absorb the deposits that they are imparted from the oppressor. Srinivasan (2006) adds: "Liberating education consists in acts of cognition, not transferals of information." Today, various tools such as instant messaging, webcams, and digital voice recorders bring multicultural voices into the classroom and lib-erate teachers and students from a textbook format. The curriculum can be redesigned based on the needs and aspirations of the students.

In the millennium, we are going to be surrounded by more and more images from bulletin boards to the Internet, from advertisements and ban-ners to book covers. The Internet and new technologies create new images, icons, symbols, and metaphors to study, for us to make sense of cyberspace.

> The mass media [...] play a critical role in the social construction of knowledge concerning race and ethnicity. [...] For the full flourishing of multicultural edu-cation, scholars need to develop more sophisticated ways to explore and assess media-based multicultural knowledge construction. (Cortes, 1995)

Since the new generation is spending more time with mass media, their interpretation of the world is mainly based on images they have seen. As writer Walter Lippmann says, "whether right or wrong [...] imagination is shaped by the pictures seen. [...] Consequently, they can lead to stereotypes that are hard to shake."

Participants discussed the importance of encouraging our students to be the producers of media, instead of consumers of media. The more they deconstruct media and its messages, the more likely they are to interpret and act on issues such as race, gender, and immigration. Len Masterman (1985) considers media literacy education to be a crucial step toward "participatory democracy." Masterman adds: "Media Education is both essential to the exercising of our democratic rights and a necessary safeguard against the worst excesses of media manipulation for political purposes."

Participants outlined the importance of studying signs and symbols in teacher education, in order to gain different perspectives on our teaching styles and strategies. Without an understanding of media languages and grammars, we cannot hope to achieve a contemporary awareness of the world in which we live (McLuhan & Fiore, 1967).

After several visualization exercises, a number of teacher candidates said they learned more from this than from the content of the course. One participant said: "This class became the dinner table discussion. I cannot stop talking about it with my family." Another wrote: "More than learning the class material, this course helped me reflect on my own biases and how to develop pedagogy of plenty for my classroom." They found the online activities and resources engaging and helpful. As one said: "I cannot watch TV without my new media literacy eye. The videos we watched helped me to question the statistics, graphs and charts."

Lessons Learned

In December 2011, I was contracted to teach in Myrtle Beach, South Carolina. It was my first teaching assignment in a Southern state. I think I may have received the assignment because most instructors did not want to use air transportation after September 11. The aim of the course was to teach media literacy and media production skills to educators. It was one of the most memorable teaching experiences for me, as well as for the participants. We compared media coverage and stories and discussed how they may be distorted or skewed by word choices, and we discussed the use of graphics and images. Teachers told me they could not figure out my background. They all knew I was coming from New Jersey. Finally, one asked me if I am a "damn Yankee," as a joke. They tried to guess. Most of them thought that I might be Hispanic. Looking back, how strange it must have been for these teachers when I introduced myself. They all looked puzzled when I told them I am from Turkey. In that class, we taught each other global literacy skills. For example, they taught me what "Bible Belt" means. The teachers told me they do not have any friends from a Middle Eastern background.

When we were talking about the role of media in presenting points of views, one teacher said that all the national news stories are mostly related to the Northeast in reference to September 11. She continued to explain: "For instance, we had a huge forest fire, [but] it never made it to national news." Our classroom discussion got richer every time we shared our points of view from various corners of the world. I asked the students if they have been to New York City. Only a couple of them said they had. I realized proximity makes a big difference, when experiencing events or understanding the scale. Some who may only have seen a skyscraper on TV may think that the World Trade Center towers were just a couple of large buildings. I told the class that I was at the World Trade Center attending a professional training seminar a few weeks prior to September 11. That day we all learned about the role of proximity in experiencing an event, and how cultures and background affect the way we see.

Another discussion was a dialogue on going to war in Afghanistan. Most of the participants were clearly against war. They started sharing their viewpoints on the cost of war. We were speechless when one participant raised her hand and told the class, "my husband just left for active service in Afghanistan." Participants all paused and reflected on how it is sometimes easy to have a strong point of view on an issue, until it touches us at home.

In another teacher education course focusing on curriculum design, the teacher candidates reflected on their curriculum project. One of the pre-service students in the course summarized it in her final reflection:

> "This course has taught me a great deal about teaching. This course more than anything taught me to be passionate about my teaching, and to stay true to my belief that I can make a difference. [...] I learned a great deal about how to integrate technology into the classroom. While teaching in some ways has become robotic (input worksheets, output, supposed student achievement), there are many ways to use technology to form a creative lesson and inspiring classroom environment to engage students in what they are learning. In addition, I have learned a great deal about incorporating every content area [a transdisciplinary approach] and learning style into a unit. By doing this you enable students to see the connections within their world, and enable higher order thinking among students."

Another student in the class highlighted the importance of self-set pacing. He said, "I found this class very interactive and freeing. I enjoyed the different opportunities to create and personalize the work assigned. Through creating lesson plans based on multimedia and multicultural aspects, I learned that incorporating these aspects creates lessons that are more engaging and innovative." When the teacher candidates were given access to new technologies, they all developed innovative and transdisciplinary lesson plans that integrated media literacy and global education. They admitted that they struggled at the beginning to let go of the fear of failure, or getting a low grade. They constantly referred to our lessons as "MM" (Multimillion dollar) lessons. I reminded them that for the million-dollar teacher, getting an "A" should not be their only goal. Ultimately the biggest test is to secure a teaching position upon graduation. Teacher candidates toward the end of the study were more inclined to focus on developing MM lessons integrating maps, math, and media, as well as creating activities that are multicultural and multilingual, using multimedia resources. In their teaching philosophy statement and self-study reflections, most of the teacher candidates outlined the importance of being life-long learners and future educational entrepreneurs (edupreneurs) and leaders in their communities.

Considerations for the Future

With the increasing need for globally competent and world savvy K–12 educators who can teach for global competence and prepare the next generation to be globally informed and active citizens, as well as competitive in the global market, there are vast amounts of educational resources for educators. In addition to MOOCs, online conference, webinars, unconferences, and podcasts, here are several organizations that educators can explore to receive formal training and experience.

In addition to online organizations and resources such as Global Teacher Education,[2] teachers will be able to attain a formal Global Competency Certificate,[3] which is currently available through collaborative work between the Teachers College at Columbia University, World Savvy, and the Asia Society. The World Savvy Classrooms program provides professional development and consulting for middle and high school educators who want to align state and national standards, in a way that establishes real-world connections to the material. For middle and high schools, the World Savvy organization provides fully funded youth exchange opportunities both within and outside of the United States. The Asia Society is a leading global nonprofit organization that partners with educational institutions to ensure that our rising generation is ready for the interconnected world, and to provide resources to promote global competency in education, while informing policy and practice.

Conclusion

By actively involving teacher candidates in producing media (e.g. wikis, blogs, and digital stories) and using online collaborative tools (e.g. VoiceThread, CommunityWalk) for integrating global issues and resources, we were able to ensure that they understood the conventions of the medium, developed innovative projects, gained alternative points of view on world issues, gained global competency skills, and renewed their interest and commitment to global education through globally connected projects. As they became the producers of their own online media and blended learning projects, they developed 21st-century skills, and became informed consumers and citizens of the world.

We related our classroom discussions to current public debates and movements that narrowly frame the educational issues in the United States and reframe multicultural education from another point of view, by reworking "heutagogy" to broaden our perspectives, to address equity and social justice in a global dimension, not in isolation. In our innovative, transdisciplinary projects, pre-service teachers had a chance to deconstruct the media and develop leadership and critical thinking skills, while also gaining 21st-century skills. Through their rediscovery process, they explored, designed, and created the strategies, curricula, and programs for improving P–12 students' outcomes, and they gained alternative points of view on integrating global literacies into their teaching and developed culturally and linguistically responsive curricula.

Borrowing and extending the work of critical theorists, particularly Paulo Freire (1972, 2005), we continue to explore the transdisciplinary approach to teaching and learning and explore the heutagogy curriculum design model in teacher education. In recent years, there have been major breakthroughs in educational research that provide new insights into cognitive processes and have succeeded in connecting them to new educational strategies and technologies that provide inclusive and transformative education models and promise higher achievement scores for students (Darling-Hammond, 2006; Ladson-Billings & Tate, 2006). Yet in districts, schools, and classrooms across the nation, educators still teach and assess their students in the ways they were taught. It may be because they have not been given the opportunity to learn about these new insights, research, and practices in their teacher education programs.

In our PAR, pre-service teachers were given the opportunity to be a bricoleur (Levi-Strauss, 1998), where they are the author as well as the cast, collector, and the director of their curriculum projects. The content of their knowledge is co-constructed by their peers, teacher education faculty, and in-service teachers, while collaborating with the local and global community. We treated our teacher candidates as creators of their own knowledge, our future colleagues, and most importantly our research collaborators. They experienced the impact and power of 21st-century literacy skills and its promising implications for global education. They were told to produce knowledge, not just regurgitate the information. Once the students were shown the CNN news story about a teacher from South Carolina who made a million dollars selling her lesson plan ideas,[4] they were more engaged in creative and innovative lesson planning.

From showcasing digital portfolios (Google Sites) to posting online reflections and journals (Wordpress); from co-writing books (Wikibooks) to co-producing digital stories (VoiceThread) and classroom videos (EDpuzzle); from co-creating interactive maps (Google Earth) to collecting data (GPS) to solve community-based issues, new technologies were used for educational and lifelong learning environments. We used social interaction software to develop opportunities and support "open-source learning" practices and tools, and to promote exchanges, connections, and collaboration among teacher candidates who share common ideas and interests.

Teacher candidates in the study put together lesson plans and shared their projects and resources on their electronic portfolios. They created blogs and used social media to advocate for culturally and linguistically responsive curricula for P–20 classrooms. Based on our findings, we developed a gallery walk,[5] outlined lists of documentaries, cartoons, infographics, and online E-Race-ing resources for teacher educators and P–20 teachers, and invited other teacher candidates and faculty to explore our research and provide feedback.

Through our PAR, teacher candidates explored global education resources; argued the challenges and advantages of integrating media literacy and global education into K–12 curriculum; developed skills in deconstructing existing curricula and digital resources and media messages; examined the process of integrating new media as a tool for teaching and learning; integrated the use of media in an instructional context in order to develop global understanding; explored lesson plans, assessment tools, and curriculum guides that incorporate new media and technologies across grades and subjects; co-developed the GMLE framework; and experienced how a critical approach to the study of new media combines knowledge, reflection, and action to promote educational equity, and prepares the new generation to be socially responsible members of a multicultural, democratic society.

Notes

1. https://implicit.harvard.edu/implicit
2. http://globalteachereducation.org
3. http://globalcompetencecertificate.org/founding-partners

4. http://schoolsofthought.blogs.cnn.com/2012/09/28/teacher-earns-a-cool-mil
   lion-by-selling-lesson-plans
5. http://galeri.wikispaces.com/Immigration

References

Chandler, D. (2014). *Semiotics for beginners*. Retrieved from http://visual-memory.
co.uk/daniel/Documents/S4B/the_book.html

Cortes, C. E. (1995). Knowledge construction and popular culture: The media as multicultural educator. In J. A. Banks & C. A. McGee Banks (Eds.), *Handbook of Research
on Multicultural Education* (pp. 169–83). Retrieved from http://eric.ed.gov/?id=
ED382705

Danesi, M. (1994). *Messages and meaning: An introduction to semiotics*. Toronto, Canada:
Canadian Scholars' Press Inc.

Darling-Hammond, L. (2006). Constructing 21st-century teacher education. *Journal of
Teacher Education, 57*, 300–14. doi: 10.1177/0022487105285962

Eco, U. (1976). *A theory of semiotics*. Bloomington: Indiana University Press.

Eisenberg, A. (2008, August 30). *Lines and bubbles and bars, oh my! New ways to sift data*.
Retrieved from http://www.nytimes.com/2008/08/31/technology/31novel.
html?_r=0

Freire, P. (1972). *Pedagogy of the oppressed*. London, UK: Penguin Books.

Freire, P. (2005). *Teachers as cultural workers: Letters to those who dare teach* (D. K. D.
Macedo & A. Oliveira, Trans.). Boulder, CO: Westview Press.

Friedman, T. L. (2005). *The world is flat: A brief history of the twenty-first century*. New
York, NY: Farrar, Straus and Giroux.

Keeshan, R., Louie, A.-L., CBS Inc., & Fox Video (Firm). (1992). *Yeh-Shen: A Cinderella story from China*. S.l.: CBS Video. Retrieved from https://www.youtube.com/
watch?v=SEvB6h6lOw4

Knight, J. (2003). Updated internationalization definition. International Higher Education, 33, 2–3. Retrieved from http://www.bc.edu/content/dam/files/research_
sites/cihe/pdf/IHEpdfs/ihe33.pdf

Ladson-Billings, G. J., & Tate, W. (2006). Education research in the public interest: Social
justice, action, and policy. New York, NY: Teachers College Press.

Lévi-Strauss, C. (1998). *The savage mind*. London, UK: Weidenfeld & Nicolson.

Longview Foundation. (2008). *Teacher preparation for the global age: The imperative for
change*. Silver Spring, MD. Retrieved from http://www.longviewfdn.org/index.
php/download_file/force/10

Luke, C. (1994). Feminist pedagogy and critical media literacy. *Journal of Communication
Inquiry* [Special issue on "Critical Media Pedagogy"], *18*(2), 27–44.

Mangan, J. W. (1981). Learning through pictures: A study of cultural and cognitive
aspects of visual images. Thesis (Ed.D.). University of Massachusetts.

Masterman, L. (1985/2001). *Teaching the media*. New York, NY: Routledge.

McLuhan, M., & Fiore, Q. (1967). *The medium is the message*. Singapore: HardWired.

Palmer, P. J. (1998). *The courage to teach: Exploring the inner landscape of a teacher's life*. San Francisco, CA: Jossey-Bass.

Programme for International Student Assessment (PISA). (2012). *PISA 2012 results*. Retrieved from http://www.oecd.org/pisa/keyfindings/pisa-2012-results.htm

Rowe, M. (2008, March). Micro-affirmations and micro-inequities. *The Journal of the International Ombudsman Association, 1*(1), 45–48.

Schmidt, W. H., McKnight, C. C., & Raizen, S. A. (1997). *A Splintered Vision: An Investigation of US Science and Mathematics Education*. Dordrecht, Netherlands: Kluwer Academic Publishers.

Sloan, K. J. (1995, February 8). *Icon or symbol: A teacher's moral dilemma*. Retrieved from http://php.indiana.edu/~ccolon/Semiotics/kjsloan1.html

Srinivasan, R. (2006). Where information society and community voice intersect. *The Information Society, 22*(5), 355–65.

Sun, C.-F., Picker, M., Fordham, M., Mizell, L., Berkower, R., Inouye, N., & Media Education Foundation. (2002). *Mickey Mouse monopoly*. (DVD). Northampton, MA: Media Education Foundation.

Part 4
Take Action

15. Global Education Resources

MELDA N. YILDIZ AND BELINHA S. DE ABREU

"If we cannot bring our own cultural contest into perspective, then we cannot take the perspective of culturally-different others. And when we cannot take the perspective of others, we cannot imagine their reality, we cannot be competent in the intercultural communication demanded by multicultural societies and global intentionalities."

-—Milton Bennett, 2004

This final chapter provides a compilation of resources from organizations all over the world that consider the value of global media literacy education. The list is not exhaustive nor necessarily inclusive, but as comprehensive as possible, to give the reader insights and ideas for further thinking in this area. The sites provided have been used widely by teachers, researchers, and activists for the purpose of learning or moving forward the conversation on global media literacy. *Note: Many of the summaries provided were reproduced from the organization's websites in order to keep the information intact and be true to their foundational purpose.*

Resources

Action Coalition for Media Education (ACME)
http://www.acmecoalition.org

Offers a bi-annual conference and a discussion listserv for members. Local chapters have occasional meetings and regional conferences in Northern California, Vermont, Missouri, New York, and New Mexico.

Alliance for Civilizations
http://www.unaoc.org

A United Nations initiative created in 2005 under the initial sponsorship of the governments of Spain and Turkey. Currently, there are 77 member states and 13 intergovernmental organizations associated. Their goal is to develop a variety of programs and initiatives that encourage international cross-cultural dialogue around four main areas: media, youth, education, and migration.

American Film Institute
http://www.afi.com

A national institute providing leadership in screen education and the recognition and celebration of excellence in the art of film, television, and digital media. The site offers information on the conservation of films and more.

American Museum of the Moving Image
http://www.movingimage.us

A truly wonderful and interactive museum that advances the public understanding and appreciation of the art, history, technique, and technology of film, television, and digital media. They are collectors and preservers of moving-image related artifacts, screening significant films and other moving-image works and presenting exhibitions of artifacts, artworks, and interactive experiences. They offer a number of educational programs for students and teachers.

Amnesty International
https://www.amnesty.org

A global movement of more than 7 million people who take injustice personally. They campaign for a world where human rights are enjoyed by all. They consider themselves independent of any political ideology, economic interest, or religion. The site provides numerous resources that would be valuable to the educational classroom.

Asia Society
http://asiasociety.org

Asia Society is the leading educational organization dedicated to promoting mutual understanding and strengthening partnerships among peoples, leaders, and institutions of Asia and the United States in a global context. Across the fields of arts, business, culture, education, and policy, the Society provides insight, generates ideas, and promotes collaboration to address present challenges and create a shared future.

Avaaz
http://avaaz.org/en

Avaaz—meaning "voice" in several European, Middle Eastern, and Asian languages—launched in 2007 with a simple democratic mission: organize citizens of all nations to close the gap between the world we have and the world most people everywhere want. This organization empowers millions of people from all walks of life to take action on pressing global, regional, and national issues, from corruption and poverty to conflict and climate change. They use the Internet as a model for combining individual efforts rapidly into a powerful collective force.

Baltic Sea Project
http://www.unesco.org/new/en/education/networks/global-networks/aspnet/flagship-projects/baltic-sea-project

This is probably the world's longest running, multi-country school project in support of both environmental education and intercultural learning. Since 1989, 300 associated schools in nine countries around the Baltic Sea have taken part in the flagship Baltic Sea Project to combine environmental education with intercultural learning. It seeks to raise the awareness of students on environmental problems in the Baltic region and to help them understand the scientific, social, and cultural aspects of the interdependence of people and nature. Both in the classroom and in the field, students study water quality, coastal observation, and environmental history. Countries participating in the project include Denmark, Estonia, Finland, Germany, Latvia, Lithuania, Poland, Russian Federation, and Sweden.

BoomWriter
http://www.boomwriter.com

A transdisciplinary, collaborative, literacy-focused project for children grades 3–12. The BoomWriter's focus is to engage students in project-based learning that fosters critical thinking and 21st-century skills, while engaging in collaborative writing projects with other students in the school or around the world. Founded in 2010, it works in over 20 different countries.

Cable Impacts Foundation
https://www.ncta.com/cableimpacts

As the cable industry's foundation dedicated to social responsibility, Cable Impacts leverages cable's resources—including its platform, technology, and content—to empower consumers and enhance communities. The foundation's work targets the advancement of education, increasing broadband adoption, and providing parents with the tools and resources to help their children appropriately and effectively use media.

The Center for Global Education
http://www.globaled.us

An international research and resource center that provides support for international learning at colleges and universities, offering to faculty, staff, students, and parents information and resources about a variety of issues, including integrated international learning, health, safety, diversity, and the impact of study abroad on student retention and success.

Center for Innovation in Engineering and Science Education (CIESE)
http://www.ciese.org

A host for collaborative, project-based science activities, such as the Human Genetics Project, Global Water Sampling Project, and the Noonday Project, around the world for elementary through high school students. Their mission is "to catalyze and support excellence in teaching and learning of science, technology, engineering, mathematics (STEM) and other core subjects through innovative, research-based instructional strategies and use of novel technologies."

Center for Media Literacy
http://www.medialit.org

The Center for Media Literacy provides the educator with a wide selection of teaching tools carefully evaluated for their quality and importance to the field. They are dedicated to a new vision of literacy for the 21st century: the ability to communicate competently in all media forms, as well as to access, understand, analyze, evaluate, and participate with powerful images, words, and sounds that make up contemporary mass media culture.

The Centre for Excellence in Media Practice
http://www.cemp.ac.uk/about

This organization has developed a range of online tools that are now widely used in education and industry. The Centre provides postgraduate courses, which are catered to those working in media education. It also aims to influence media education research through projects, publications, and conferences.

Centre for the Study of Children, Youth and Media
http://www.cscym.zerolab.info

A research center based at the Institute of Education, University of London. They undertake funded research projects and consultancies, provide conferences and public seminars, organize networks of researchers and practitioners, contribute to the Institute's MA Media program, supervise doctoral research students, and work with other institutions, nationally and internationally.

Children Now
http://www.childrennow.org

A national organization for people who care about children and want to ensure that they are a public policy priority. The website provides a number of resources about children, but also specifically about media education.

Civic Media Project
http://civicmediaproject.org

The Civic Media Project (CMP) is a collection of short case studies from scholars and practitioners from all over the world that range from the descriptive to the analytical, from the single tool to the national program, and from the enthusiastic to the critical.

CNN Student News
http://www.cnn.com/studentnews

A 10-minute, commercial-free, daily news program for middle and high school students. This show is produced by the journalists and educators at CNN and is available free of charge throughout the school year. The site includes a media literacy question of the day, useful quizzes, and classroom exercises.

Cyberschoolbus
http://cyberschoolbus.un.org/

A website created by the United Nations with the mission to promote education about international issues. The site provides resources, curricula, quizzes, and games.

Edutopia
http://www.edutopia.org

A George Lucas foundation that empowers and connects teachers, administrators, and parents with innovative solutions and resources.

ePals
http://www.epals.com

In terms of global learning, this organization is offering a classroom matching service through the use of a virtual workspace optimized for collaborating, creating, and sharing educational content. They provide a safe platform to use their Web 2.0 communication tools, including email, blogs, wikis, forums, media galleries, and much more. There is a cost for this service.

Facing the Future
https://www.facingthefuture.org/default.aspx

This organization focuses on global issues and sustainability to promote critical and creative thinking, systems thinking, problem-solving, decision-making, collaboration, and cooperative learning. They tend to build global awareness and a sustainable world by taking on big issues like poverty, energy, and climate change. Facing the Future is a nonprofit organization that provides educators with the tools and resources they need to inspire their students' interest in global issues.

Fairness and Accuracy in News Reporting (FAIR)
www.fair.org

A news watchdog organization, publishing a bi-monthly magazine (EXTRA!) dedicated to analysis and commentary on the news.

Family Online Safety Institute (FOSI)
http://www.fosi.org

This organization works to make a safer online world for kids and their families by identifying and promoting best practice, tools, and methods in the field of online safety. They also have a strong grounding in the belief in and respect for free expression, which they promote through the development of public policy, technology, education, and special events.

Federal Communications Commission (FCC)
www.fcc.gov

An independent United States government agency, the FCC was established by the Communications Act of 1934 and is charged with regulating interstate and international communications by radio, television, wire, satellite, and cable. Their interest in children and media has been covered regularly by the media. Their website provides up-to-date information on the most current issues and problems in the media environment.

The First Amendment Center
http://www.firstamendmentcenter.org

Offers one-stop access to information about the First Amendment. The center serves as a forum for the study and exploration of free-expression issues, including freedom of speech, press, and religion, and the rights to assemble and to petition the government. They also offer a variety of programs for students, teachers, journalists, lawyers, and the general public.

Flat Stanley Project
http://www.flatstanley.com

In terms of giving students a global look at the world while teaching about technology and media literacy, this could be one of the best sites for younger children. The Flat Stanley project was started by a Canadian educator in 1995 and was based on the book by Jeff Brown and Scott Nash. Students make paper "Flat Stanleys" and begin a journal with him for a few days. Then Flat Stanley and the journal are sent to another school where the students there treat Flat Stanley as a guest and complete the journal. Flat Stanley and the journal are then returned to the original sender. Students can plot his travels on maps and share the contents of the journal. Some teachers prefer to use e-mail only, but with new digital technologies other formats may be used.

Free the Children
http://www.freethechildren.com/about-us

An international charity and educational partner that believes in a world where all children are free to achieve their fullest potential as agents of change. They work domestically through We Day and We Act to educate, engage, and empower youth to become active local and global citizens. Through their holistic and sustainable development model—Adopt a Village—they work to remove barriers to education and to empower communities to break the cycle of poverty.

The Freedom Forum
http://www.freedomforum.org

A nonpartisan foundation that champions the First Amendment as a cornerstone of democracy. The Forum provides programs and other sources of information that would be useful for the classroom. Furthermore, the Freedom Forum is the main funder of the operations of the Newseum in Washington, DC, the First Amendment Center, and the Diversity Institute.

Global Buddy
http://www.globalbuddy.org

Connects schools in developed and developing countries to promote cultural understanding and global friendships. Students can interact with peers around the world through video calls, text chats, and interactive activities. This organization is student-run, based on the principle of peer support—students reaching out to students.

GlobalEd 2
http://globaled2.com/about-globaled-2

GlobalEd 2 is a problem-based learning (PBL) simulation that capitalizes on the multidisciplinary nature of social studies as an expanded curricular space to learn and apply science literacies, while simultaneously enriching the curricular goals of social studies. It is designed to cultivate a scientifically literate citizenry by grounding science education in meaningful socio-scientific contexts related to the world in which students currently live. It is implemented in grades 7–8 social studies classrooms, and facilitated by the social studies teachers. GlobalEd 2 is mediated by technology to enhance communications and learning. Each simulation consists of three phases: research, online interaction, and debriefing, spanning 14 weeks in the fall semester.

Global Education Conference Network
http://www.globaleducationconference.com

A global education community initiative, involving students, educators, and organizations around the world. The organization holds a weeklong free online conference in a webinar format once every year in November and presentations are archived for future use. The conference is intended to connect classrooms across the world and recognizes diversity and educational access for all. The organization's wiki houses many curriculum-based global education efforts.

Global Learning and Observations to Benefit the Environment (GLOBE)
http://www.globe.gov

One of the U.S.-government-sponsored programs to promote collaborative inquiry-based science investigations and to bring together students, teachers, and scientists around the world to study the dynamics of Earth's environment on local, regional, and global scales. It is a worldwide, hands-on, and K–12 science-focused project that has over 112 participating countries collaborating on GLOBE activities, such as Earth Day projects. GLOBE's mission is "to promote the teaching and learning of science; enhance environmental literacy and stewardship; and promote scientific discovery."

Global Math Stories
http://www.globalmathstories.org

This collaborative tool makes global connections in mathematics education, and was created by Chadd and Jenny McGlone of Chapel Hill, North Carolina. Stories of life from around the world have been submitted by users, along with questions meant to facilitate further exploration into the stories' mathematical content.

Global Nomads Group (GNG)
http://gng.org

Fosters dialogue and understanding among the world's youth by bringing the world to the classroom via interactive technology, while connecting students around the world to collaborate on projects, creating media and changing communities on global issues. Founded in 1984, GNG is a nonprofit education organization. GNG currently includes semester and year-long virtual exchange programs between students in North America and their peers in sub-Saharan Africa, Central and Southeast Asia, the Middle East, and North Africa.

Global Oneness Project
http://www.globalonenessproject.org

Offers free multicultural stories and accompanying lesson plans for high school and college classrooms with award-winning collections of films, photo essays, and articles exploring cultural, social, and environmental issues with a humanistic lens. Aligned to National and Common Core Standards, their curriculum content contains an interdisciplinary approach to learning and facilitates the development of active, critical thinking. All content and resources are available for free with no ads or subscriptions.

Global Partnership for Education
http://www.globalpartnership.org

The only multilateral partnership devoted to getting all children into school for a quality education. Established in 2002, it is comprised of 60 developing countries, donor governments, international organizations, the private sector, teachers, and civil society/NGO groups.

Global Schoolhouse
http://www.globalschoolnet.org

The mission of this organization is to support 21st-century learning and improve academic performance through content-driven collaboration by connecting schools around the world.

Global SchoolNet Foundation
http://www.globalschoolnet.org/gsnabout/aboutservices.cfm

Produces interactive, collaborative content, and tools that are web-based or on CD-ROM. Offers consulting services to schools, universities, businesses, and government organizations. Provides professional development and training materials focused on successful implementation of collaborative learning. Provides conference keynote presentations and workshops for public and private school districts in Africa, Asia, Australia, Canada, Europe, South America, and throughout the United States that excite, inform, and inspire.

Global Voices
http://globalvoicesonline.org

A borderless, largely volunteer community of more than 800 writers, analysts, online media experts, and translators. This organization has been leading the conversation on citizen media reporting since 2005 by curating, verifying, and translating trending news and stories you might be missing on the Internet, from blogs, independent press and social media in 167 countries.

iEARN
http://www.iearn.org

With over 30,000 schools and youth organizations in more than 130 countries this organization seeks to empower teachers and young people to work together online collaboratively around the world. In order to participate in any of their over 150 projects, educators must select a project and meet up with their counterparts online.

iKeepSafe
http://www.ikeepsafe.org

Provides families with all the tools, education, and resources they need to stay safe online and to implement an Internet safety strategy in their classrooms and homes. Furthermore, they assist educators in integrating the essentials of cyber-safety, cyber-security, and cyber-ethics (C3 concepts) into existing technology and literacy standards and curricula through the C3 Matrix.

International Media Literacy Research Forum
http://www.imlrf.org

A global look at media literacy from the research and public policy perspective. The Forum provides a platform to improve understanding of the emerging issues; promote innovative methodologies; and facilitate dialogue between researchers, policy makers, practitioners, and regulators worldwide. The Forum is currently supported by leading organizations in the United States, Australia, Canada, Europe, Ireland, New Zealand, and the United Kingdom, with more countries expected to follow.

International Society for Technology Education
http://www.iste.org

One of the top membership associations for educators and educational leaders who work on improving teaching and learning through the effective use of technology in PK–12 and teacher education. Their mission statement explains: "ISTE advances excellence in learning and teaching through innovative and effective uses of technology." They are also the home of NETS and ISTE's annual conference and exposition. They represent more than 10,000 members worldwide.

Internet Movie Database
http://www.imdb.com

A major database of movies, TV shows, and actors and actresses. The site keeps track of box office hits, upcoming movies and events, conferences, and various pieces of information that can be useful in the classroom.

Internet Movie Script Database
http://www.imsdb.com/scripts

Considered one of the best and biggest collections of movie scripts available anywhere on the web. The site lets you read or download movie scripts for free.

Journey North: A Global Study of Wildlife Migration and Seasonal Change
http://www.learner.org/jnorth

A free, Internet-based program supported by the Annenberg Foundation. The project aims to engage students and citizen scientists around the globe in tracking wildlife migration and seasonal change. Participants share field observations and explore interrelated aspects of seasonal change.

Kaiser Family Foundation
http://www.kff.org

A nonprofit, privately operated foundation focusing on the major health care issues facing the nation. The Foundation is an independent voice and source of facts and analysis for policy makers, the media, the health care community, and the general public.

Kidlink Project
http://kidlink.org

The purpose of the Association is "to promote a global dialogue among the youth of the world." The Association emphasizes electronic telecommunications, but also supports communications in other forms and media. The Association works to achieve its objectives through several educational projects belonging to the "The Kidlink Project." The projects are created and developed through an international collaboration of volunteers and are offered to schools, organizations, and youth around the world for free.

KIDPROJ
http://www.globalclassroom.org/projis.html

KIDPROJ is a forum enabling teachers and youth group leaders to provide projects for children through the Kidlink network. KIDPROJ has been set up for the exchange, among schools, youth, and youth groups, of curriculum-based activities and other projects of an educational or informative nature. KIDPROJ encourages adults and students to participate in global dialogue to reach greater multicultural understanding and to enhance learning opportunities.

LinkTV: Know the News
http://www.linktv.org/knowthenews

Compare news coverage from around the world, test your knowledge of how news is shaped, and shape some yourself. Know the News is part of the national satellite channel Link TV's Global Pulse News Service. Global Pulse, Mosaic, and Pulso Latino contrast and analyze news coverage produced by more than 70 national broadcasters. Know the News is funded by the John S. & James L. Knight Foundation.

Making Curriculum Pop
http://mcpopmb.ning.com

A resource-sharing community for educators interested in best practices and teaching with and about popular culture.

Media Awareness Network
http://www.media-awareness.ca.eng

A Canada-based website created for educators, parents, and community leaders. The site provides numerous lessons on the media focusing on both the elementary and secondary levels. They also serve as an extensive resource on Internet issues.

Media Education Foundation
http://www.mediaed.org

The mission of this organization is to produce and distribute documentary films and other educational resources to inspire critical reflection on the social, political, and cultural impact of American mass media.

Media Education Lab
http://mediaeducationlab.com

The lab resides at the University of Rhode Island and advances media literacy education through research and community service. They emphasize interdisciplinary scholarship and practice that stands at the intersections of communication, media studies, and education.

Media Literacy Clearinghouse
http://www.frankwbaker.com

The mission of this site is to assist K–12 educators who want to teach standards that include nonprint media texts, learn more about media literacy, further integrate it into classroom instruction, and assist students to read the media and become media-aware, while also assisting educators in locating appropriate resources.

MediaSmarts
http://mediasmarts.ca

A Canadian not-for-profit charitable organization for digital and media literacy whose vision is for children and youth to have the critical thinking skills to engage with media as active and informed digital citizens. They have been developing digital and media literacy programs and resources for Canadian homes, schools, and communities since 1996. Through their work, they provide adults with information and tools so they can help children and teens develop the critical thinking skills they need for interacting with the media they love.

National Association for Media Literacy Education (NAMLE)
http://www.namle.net

Formerly known as the Alliance for Media Literate America, it sponsors the bi-annual National Media Education Conference and has a monthly email newsletter for members.

National Model United Nations
http://nmun.org/ncca.html

A nonprofit organization that advances understanding of the United Nations and contemporary international issues. They work to "positively affect the lives of participants and prepare them to be better global citizens through quality educational experiences that emphasize collaboration and cooperative resolution of conflict." Their work is comprised of civically engaged people who strive for peaceful, multi-lateral conflict resolution and equitable, sustainable human development. Cooperative, hands-on, experiential learning allows students to confront a range of topics with the perspective of their assigned country or organization. Through these experiences—during preparation, in committee sessions, and even in hallway caucuses—students develop an appreciation of differing viewpoints, experience the challenges of negotiation, see the rewards of cooperation, broaden their world view, and discover the human side of international relations and diplomacy.

National Telemedia Council
http://www.nationaltelemediacouncil.org

The NTC sponsors occasional international videoconferences of media literacy educators, with numerous U.S. downlink sites. More importantly, it publishes *The Journal of Media Literacy*.

New Media Consortium
http://www.nmc.org

The NMC is an international, not-for-profit consortium of learning-focused organizations dedicated to the exploration and use of new media and new technologies.

New Mexico Media Literacy Project
http://www.nmmlp.org

A group that provides training and materials in support of media literacy. Their mission is to cultivate critical thinking and activism in media culture.

Newsela
https://newsela.com

An innovative way to build reading comprehension with nonfiction that's always relevant: daily news. This site can adapt news for different reading levels.

Newseum
http://www.newseum.org

A wonderful and interactive museum of news information. Provides a behind-the-scenes view of how and why news is made. The hands-on exhibits trace five centuries of news gathering. The Newseum educates the public about the value of a free press in a free society and tells the stories of the world's important events in unique and engaging ways. It is located on Pennsylvania Avenue in Washington, DC, and it is worth taking students in groups or individually.

Nordic Information Center for Media and Communication Research (NORDICOM)
http://www.nordicom.gu.se/en

A knowledge center for the area of media and communication research, a cooperation between the five countries of the Nordic region—Denmark, Finland, Iceland, Norway, and Sweden. NORDICOM's work aims at developing media studies and at helping to ensure that research results are made visible in the treatment of media issues at different levels in both the public and private sector.

NOW (PBS)
http://www.pbs.org/now/series

PBS's weekly newsmagazine that engages viewers with documentary segments and insightful interviews that probe the most important issues facing democracy, including media policy, corporate accountability, civil liberties, the environment, politics, social responsibility, and foreign affairs. A number of resources are available to educators fitting a variety of classroom styles.

Oxfam International
https://www.oxfam.org

Their vision is a just world without poverty, a world where people are valued and treated equally, enjoy their rights as full citizens, and can influence decisions affecting their lives. The purpose of the organization is to help create lasting solutions to the injustice of poverty. They are part of a global movement for change, empowering people to create a future that is secure, just, and free from poverty. They use a combination of rights-based sustainable development programs, public education, campaigns, advocacy, and humanitarian assistance in disasters and conflicts. The site provides lessons and resources organized by grade level.

The Paley Center for Media
http://www.paleycenter.org

This museum can be found in New York City and Los Angeles, California. It is a collector of media artifacts, with a collection of nearly 150,000 television and radio programs and advertisements. The New York location offers on-site classes, videoconferencing classes, and workshops for educators. Field trips with students are encouraged. They also have a scholar's room where researchers can go to study these media and their programs.

The Partnership for 21st Century Learning
http://www.21stcenturyskills.org

This organization offers a vision for 21st-century learning that can be used to strengthen American education. They provide a framework for learning that, as they indicate, "presents a holistic view of 21st century teaching and learning that combines a discrete focus on 21st century student outcomes (a blending of specific skills, content knowledge, expertise, and literacies) with innovative support systems to help students master the multi-dimensional abilities required of them in the 21st century." There are four elements to their framework: (1) core subjects and 21st century themes; (2) learning and innovation skills: creativity and innovation, critical thinking and problem solving, communication and collaboration; (3) information, media, and technology skills: information literacy, media literacy, ICT literacy; and (4) life and career skills.

The Pauline Center for Media Studies
http://www.daughtersofstpaul.com/mediastudies

Promotes media mindfulness and media literacy education in schools and faith communities. They have a number of resources available, including a special interest topic of film.

PBS Kids: Don't Buy It!
http://pbskids.org/dontbuyit

A media literacy website for young people that encourages users to think critically about media and become smart consumers. There are several activities on the site that provide users with some of the skills and knowledge needed to question, analyze, interpret, and evaluate media messages.

Peace Corps
http://www.peacecorps.gov

As the preeminent international service organization of the United States, the Peace Corps sends Americans abroad to tackle the most pressing needs of people around the world. Peace Corps volunteers work at the grassroots level toward sustainable change that lives on long after their service—at the same time becoming global citizens and serving their country. When they return home, volunteers bring their knowledge and experiences—and a global outlook—that enriches the lives of those around them.

Pew Internet and American Life Project
http://www.pewinternet.org

As the site indicates, this is "a nonpartisan, nonprofit 'fact tank' that provides information on the issues, attitudes and trends shaping America and the world. The Project produces reports exploring the impact of the Internet on families, communities, work and home, daily life, education, health care, and civic and political life."

Project Look Sharp
http://www.ithaca.edu/looksharp

Provides materials, training, and support to help teachers integrate media literacy into their classroom curricula. As their site indicates, their primary goals are: to promote and support media literacy education at the community, state, and national levels; to provide teachers with ongoing pre-service and in-service training and mentoring in media education; to work with teachers to create new or revised teaching materials and pedagogical strategies that incorporate media literacy and enhance classroom practice; to develop and publish curriculum materials that infuse media literacy into core content; to evaluate the effectiveness of media literacy as a pedagogical approach to education; to develop a model for including media literacy in the school curriculum at all grade levels and in all instructional areas; and to show how media literacy can help teachers address new and existing learning standards.

Reach the World
http://www.reachtheworld.org

This organization makes the benefits of travel accessible to classrooms, inspiring students to become curious, confident global citizens. Enabled by their digital platform, classrooms and college student travelers explore the world together. They provide direct programming to school, after-school and summer school sites in New York City, and online programming to sites nationwide. The National Geographic Society Education Foundation named RTW a Model Program in Geography Education and the HP Catalyst Initiative named RTW a world innovator in STEM+ education.

Salzburg Academy on Media and Global Change
http://www.salzburgglobal.org/index.php?id=103

The mission of Salzburg Global Seminar is to challenge current and future leaders to solve issues of global concern. To do this they design, facilitate, and host international strategic convening and multi-year programs to tackle systems challenges critical for the next generation. Originally founded in 1947 to encourage the revival of intellectual dialogue in post-war Europe, they are a game-changing catalyst for global engagement on critical issues in education, health, environment, economics, governance, peace-building, and more. They work with carefully chosen partners to drive social change in the areas of imagination, sustainability, and justice. Salzburg Global connects the most talented people and the most innovative ideas, challenging governments, institutions, and individuals at all stages of development and all sectors to rethink their relationships and identify shared interests and goals.

Skype
http://www.skype.com/intl/en-us/home

Known for allowing people to make free calls all over the world. In education circles this tool is now used for virtual author and museum visits. This platform is known for its simple telecommunication platform that only needs Internet access.

The Society for Information Technology and Teacher Education (SITE)
http://site.aace.org

An international association that provides conferences, books, and journals in the field of teacher education. It is dedicated to the advancement of the knowledge, theory, and quality of learning and teaching at all levels with information technology.

TakingITGlobal.org (TIG)
http://www.tigweb.org

An online community that connects youth to find inspiration, access information, get involved, and take action in their local and global communities. A non-governmental organization, TIG's stated mission is to "provide opportunities for learning, capacity-building, cross-cultural awareness, and self-development through the use of Information and Communication Technologies." Teachers and students around the world have a chance to connect and collaborate with one another through various telecommunication tools.

Teach for All
http://teachforall.org

The goal of this organization is to expand educational opportunity around the world by increasing and accelerating the impact of national organizations that are cultivating the leadership necessary for change.

Tree of Life Web Project (ToL)
http://tolweb.org/tree

A collaborative effort of biologists and nature enthusiasts from around the world. On more than 10,000 websites, the project provides information about biodiversity, the characteristics of different groups of organisms, and their evolutionary history.

UNESCO: Media Literacy
http://www.unesco.org/new/en/communication-and-information

UNESCO's action to provide critical knowledge and analytical tools, empowering media consumers to function as autonomous and rational citizens, and enabling them critically to make use of the media.

UNICEF
http://www.unicef.org

A premier and leading humanitarian and development agency working globally for the rights of every child, beginning with safe shelter, nutrition, protection from disaster and conflict, and also including protections for traversing the life cycle: prenatal care for healthy births, clean water, sanitation, health care, and education.

Voices of Youth
http://www.voicesofyouth.org

Offers inspiring, original insight and opinion from across the globe—from young people, for young people. Countering disheartening headlines about today's young generation, the Voices of Youth community proves that young people *are* making a difference, each and every day. But making a difference docsn't have to be boring, and this site brings in new, honest views and stories, written and filmed by international youth bloggers.

World Wise Schools
http://www.peacecorps.gov/wws

The website provides free cross-cultural learning materials including videos, lesson plans, podcasts, publications, and much more. In addition to the online learning materials, WWS also enables educators to connect their classrooms with current and returned Peace Corps volunteers.

All these resources seek to help U.S. educators to promote cultural awareness, broaden perspectives, and encourage service among their students.

Y-Pulse
http://www.ypulse.com

A website that describes the opinions and behavior of tweens, teens, collegians, and young adults in order to provide news, commentary, events, research, and strategy for marketing, brand, and media professionals. They are heavily involved in social networking and provide a weekly newsletter to subscribers.

Afterword: Media Literacy Goes Global

ALICE Y. L. LEE

Half a century ago, media educators called for "media literacy [to go] into the classroom." Today, media literacy has to go global. The 21st century is an era of transformation. We have witnessed great social and technological changes in the new millennium, and media literacy also has had a paradigm shift. The notion of media literacy no doubt has incorporated a global dimension. This book, *Global Media Literacy in a Digital Age,* is a timely academic exploration on this new development.

In the past two decades, scholars and researchers have identified a number of future-shaping forces in our world (Castells, 2000; Friedman, 2006; Gratton, 2011; Tvede, 2010), and these forces are definitely related to the development of media literacy. The key elements include technological development, social transformation, and the rise of the Net generation. Taking all of these new social drivers into account, authors of this book magnificently place media literacy in context historically, socially, and educationally, for scrutiny within a wider field of globalization.

Global Connections: From Web 1.0 to Web 3.0

De Abreu aptly states, "The world is globalized." This is certainly associated with the advancement of communication technologies in recent years. When Internet use started to become popular in the 1990s, the world entered its Web 1.0 era. People around the globe began to be connected in a global village that Marshall McLuhan (1962) envisaged. As more people went online and had more power than ever to go global as individuals, Friedman (2006) argued that "the world is flat" and individuals had become the driving force of globalization.

The most important technological change that caused the paradigm shift of media literacy is the Internet applications of Web 2.0. In this new era, we see the emergence of "we media," including blogs, wikis, citizen journalism sites, social media (e.g., Facebook), media sharing sites (e.g., YouTube), and microblogging services (e.g., Twitter, Weibo). The content of "we media" is not produced by media professionals in traditional media organizations, but by regular people who are amateurs. It has upset existing social relationships, power structure, and the rules of the game in communication. It has blurred the boundary between communicator and audience, and brought "user-generated content" into the mainstream of social communication. Moreover, the social networking sites have further connected people around the world. As everybody becomes a global prosumer, media education has to cultivate both critical media consumers and responsible media producers. The basic assumptions, goals, and pedagogy of media education have changed accordingly (Lee, 2007). Hence, media education has shifted from a "receiver paradigm" to a "global participatory paradigm." Media Education 1.0 evolved into Media Education 2.0. Media literacy has become increasingly important in the Web 2.0 era.

It is worth noting that the continued development of digital media has led human society to go through the "triple revolution," which refers to the rise of social networking, the capability of the Internet to empower individuals, and the real-time connectivity of mobile devices. With the advanced Internet and mobile technologies, people in the world have become "networked individuals" (Rainie & Wellman, 2012).

The rapid growth in global mobile media makes it mandatory for us to look at human communication in a new light. The mobile phone has moved beyond being a communications technology (Goggin, 2011). Mobile movies, mobile music, mobile TV, and mobile gaming have changed the landscape of entertainment media. The prevailing mobile news apps and microblogging have led to what Hermida (2010) described as "ambient journalism." This new model of para-journalism is like an always-on "awareness system," enabling global audiences to receive instant, short, and fragmented information from various sources around them (p. 298). With the popularity of the iPhone and tablets, applications like WhatsApp, Telegram, Twitter, and WeChat have revolutionized the way people communicate not only locally but also globally. As the mobile Web is connecting the world in an unprecedented way, it does not only have impact on global North (the developed countries) but also on global South (the developing countries) (Goggin, 2011). Now the world has become a single, globalized society, and people in different parts of the globe have joined and become "mobile publics," in open mobile networks

(p. 171). Meanwhile, IT experts have already reminded us that Web 3.0 is just around the corner. It is predicted that in 2016, we will be moving into the Web 3.0 era (Tsoi, 2011). By that time the super computer of the Web will further connect global citizens and provide efficient information services, as it will be a "read-write-execute Web." There are several characteristics of Web 3.0, including worldwide database connection, networking computing, wireless access, semantic Web, and artificial intelligence applications. This new, global, and networked environment will pose a number of challenges to media and information users, such as how to manage information overload, deconstruct the huge amount of information coming from different channels, and constructively use communication power in the networked society. In the foreseeable future, communication development will cause a further paradigm shift in media education. Global media literacy will become essential to making sense of global connections.

Knowledge Society and World News Literacy

UNESCO always pays great attention to the impact of digital media on individuals and the global community. In particular, when the world is transforming from an industrial society to a knowledge society, this international organization is concerned about how to build a knowledge society that is inclusive, pluralistic, equitable, and participatory. In a knowledge society, most members are knowledge workers, and the reception, production, and transmission of information and knowledge will be essential in all sectors (Drucker, 1988).

In the new society, what kind of literacy skills should be cultivated for knowledge workers? In the view of UNESCO, people should be capable not only to access information, but also to transform it into knowledge that empowers them to improve their livelihoods and contribute to social development. Therefore, UNESCO is promoting media and information literacy (MIL) education at the global level. MIL is a holistic concept integrating media literacy, information literacy, and ICT skills (Lee, 2013; UNESCO, 2013). Apart from publishing a resource document *Media and Information Curriculum for Teachers* (Wilson et al., 2011), UNESCO also developed a global framework on MIL indicators (UNESCO, 2013). If members of a society are not able to master information well and their MIL level is low, the society may not be able to transition to a knowledge society smoothly. The MIL indicators can remind governments of different countries to put more educational resources on MIL training. In addition, UNESCO and United Nations Alliance of Civilizations (UNAOC) have worked together to set up an MIL university network and establish an international clearinghouse on MIL. Empowerment of people through media and information literacy is considered "an important prerequisite for fostering equitable access to information and knowledge, and promoting free, independent and pluralistic media and information systems" (UNESCO, 2014, p. 1). It is nice to see that a chapter in this book provides details of this worldwide collaboration on MIL initiatives.

Information for all and education for all are basic human rights in a knowledge society. In recent years, there is a global open educational resources movement. With the advancement of ICTs and new educational technologies, education is no longer limited to the classrooms. Online distance learning is more and more common. Education is moving from a vertical model that emphasizes teaching, to a horizontal model that encourages active collaborative learning. It is expected that many young people will learn from global curricula outside the school settings. In fact, a major channel for them to acquire knowledge and understand major world issues is the news media. It is thus important to equip youngsters with MIL skills so that they can become media- and information-literate and be capable of conducting self-learning through various information platforms.

The First Global Generation

Many young people do not read newspapers, but they still remain informed. They get news from various online means. Young people are digital natives. According to Tapscott (2009), these youngsters are the first global generation. They are living online and reaching out to the world. Their media habits are different from those in previous generations. They are active in social media and are enthusiastic mobile device users. They belong to the mobile generation and get connected to the world through the mobile Web. They have a strong sense of social justice and are regarded as a force for social transformation.

In recent years, many Net Geners are active in social movements. Friedman (2014) called them the "square people," saying that "they are connected to one another either by massing in squares or through virtual squares or both, and united less by a common program and more by a shared direction they want their societies to go" (p. 1). These people were seen in the squares of Tunis, Cairo, Istanbul, Beirut, Tehran, Moscow, Taipei, and Hong Kong. Today, the young people on the one hand have tools such as the Internet and social media to see the world and understand their community. On the other hand, they also have tools to collaborate, voice their opinions, or take collective action. In order to understand how global activism incidents were conducted and how they were represented by the news media, it is necessary to apply critical media literacy skills for analysis and evaluation.

This book has produced a comprehensive overview and penetrating analysis of the issues of global media literacy. It systematically discusses the media literacy education framework and articulates the importance of world news literacy. More importantly, it also includes practitioner responses and assessment. This book provides innovative assessment strategies for assessing global media literacy projects. It discusses the nurturance of world-savvy teachers and examines how they can integrate action into their teaching practices.

Taken together, the four parts of the book provide a well-timed introduction and inspiring explication of the study of global media literacy. The authors together successfully bring media education into the 21st century, for a new generation of students, scholars, and media educators.

Alice Y. L. Lee, PhD
Head & Associate Professor
Department of Journalism
Hong Kong Baptist University
Hong Kong

References

Alice Y. L. Lee, PhD Head & Associate Professor Department of Journalism Hong Kong Baptist University Hong Kong

Castells, M. (2000). *The rise of network society.* Oxford, UK: Blackwell Publishers.

Drucker, P. F. (1988). The coming of the new organization. *Harvard Business Review, 66* (1), 45–53.

Friedman, T. L. (2006). *The world is flat: The globalized world in the twenty-first century.* London, UK: Penguin Books.

——. (2014, May 13). *The Square People, Part 1.* Retrieved January 5, 2015, from http://www.nytimes.com/2014/05/14/opinion/friedman-the-square-people-part-1.html

Goggin, G. (2011). *Global mobile media.* London, UK: Routledge.

Gratton, L. (2011). *The shift: The future of work is already here.* London, UK: Harper Collins Publishers.

Hermida, A. (2010). Twittering the news: The emergence of ambient journalism. *Journalism Practice, 4*(3), 297–308.

Lee, A. Y. L. (2007). *The paradigm shift of media education in a participatory media environment: The impact of "YouTube phenomenon."* Paper presented at the Research Summit of the Alliance for a Media Literate America, June 22–4, 2007, St. Louis, USA.

——. (2013). Literacy and competencies required to participate in knowledge societies. In UNESCO (Ed.), *Conceptual relationship of information literacy and media literacy in knowledge societies.* Paris, France: UNESCO.

McLuhan, M. (1962). *The Gutenberg galaxy: The making of typographic man.* Toronto, Canada: University of Toronto Press.

Rainie, L., & Wellman, B. (2012). *Networked: The new social operating system.* Cambridge, MA: MIT Press.

Tapscott, D. (2009). *Grown up digital: How the net generation is changing your world.* New York, NY: McGraw-Hill.

Tsoi, A. (2011). When the post-80s generation meets Web 3.0. A speech presented at the Distinguished Speakers Seminar held on April 2, 2011 at the School of Communication, Hong Kong Baptist University, Hong Kong.

Tvede, L. (2010). *Supertrends: Winning investment strategies for the coming decades.* Chichester, UK: Wiley.

UNESCO. (2013). *Global media and information literacy assessment framework: Country readiness and competencies.* Paris, France: UNESCO.

——. (2014). *Media and information literacy.* Retrieved April 11, 2015, from http://www.unesco.org/new/en/communication-and-information/media-development/media-literacy/mil-as-composite-concept/

Wilson, C., Grizzle, A., Tuazon, R., Akyempong, K., & Cheung, C. K. (2011). *Media and information literacy curriculum for teachers.* Paris, France: UNESCO.

Appendix A: Glossary and Key Terms

Acceptable Use Policies (AUP): AUP is a document with a set of rules developed by schools and school districts to prevent potential legal action, to inform parents of the use of new media and technologies in the school, and to provide guidelines for educators and students.

Assistive technology: Technology tools that enable individuals with a disability to access curriculum or to accomplish daily activities with minimal assistance.

Avatar: An avatar is a representation of a person or character in graphical form in 2 or 3 dimensions. A user may create and use an avatar in his or her likeness while participating in digital spaces, such as online games, virtual worlds, or Internet communities. There are applications that allow users to create customized avatars as characters that can speak using computerized or recorded speech.

Badges: Digital badges are typically icons that represent a skill or achievement that has been earned. Badges may be earned from various websites or awarded by others. People usually display their badges online in a digital community, blog, game, or other online space to share their skills and accomplishments for public recognition.

Banking education: In the banking concept, education is considered an act of depositing knowledge, in which the students are the depositories and the teacher is the depositor. Paulo Freire first uses it in his book *Pedagogy of the Oppressed*. Students are considered empty containers and the role of teacher is to deposit knowledge into the students' containers. The banking model of education generates a "Pedagogy of Poverty" in the classroom, where the students are consumers of knowledge not producers.

Bricoleur/ Bricolage: A term used for the construction or creation of a work from a diverse range of things that happen to be available, or a work created by such a process. It is in essence building by trial-and-error and is often contrasted to engineering (theory-based construction). A person who engages in bricolage is called a bricoleur and usually invents his or her own strategies for using existing materials in a creative, resourceful, and original way.

Critical autonomy: Len Masterman, the author of *Teaching the Media*, calls critical autonomy an ability to "think and choose for oneself." Without this fundamental media literacy skill, one cannot read and deconstruct a media text for himself or herself, make autonomous judgments about elections, and be a productive, critical, democratic citizen. Critical autonomy is the process by which a member of the audience is able to read a media text in a way other than the preferred reading. It is also used to describe the ability of media literacy students to deconstruct texts outside the classroom.

Culturally and linguistically responsive curriculum: A pedagogical approach taking into consideration the learners' characteristics, having high expectations for all the students, providing student-centered instruction, connecting with families and their experiences, and reshaping education based on the needs of the students. This is a curriculum that recognizes the importance of the students' cultural, heritage, and language background in education. It is a "Pedagogy of Plenty" model that is based on providing student-centered instruction and valuing the students' culture and language as an asset not a deficit.

Distributed learning: Distributed learning can occur anytime, anywhere, in multiple locations, using one or more technologies. Learners complete courses and programs at home or work by communicating with faculty and other students through various forms of computer-mediated communication and Web-based technologies. Learners participate in classroom activities at their own pace and at a self-selected time.

Edupreneurship: Educational Entrepreneur

English Language Learner (ELL): ELL is an English language learner who is learning English as foreign language (EFL), or a English as a second (ESL) language in addition to their native language.

Gallery Walk: Gallery Walk is based on a museum approach to teaching. It can be collection of artifacts (i.e. maps, pictures, posters, books, interactive games, audio and video clips) designed to present the particular topic to the audience. In the classroom, students walk around the classroom and explore a particular topic, theme, or project as if they were in a library or museum. They seek answers to guided questions by themselves or in groups.

Geocaching: Geocaching is a worldwide, outdoor hide-and-seek activity in which participants navigate and locate hidden containers called geocaches, using mobile phones or Global Positioning System (GPS) devices.

Geographic Information System (GIS): GIS may also stand for geographical information science or geospatial information studies. It is a system for managing, storing, manipulating, analyzing, and presenting all types of geographical data.

Global competency: Global competency is a life-time process of developing skills—critical thinking and problems skills, to research, cope, and communicate on global issues, knowledge—of world history, geography, culture, people, events, values, and attitudes. Global competency considers new ideas and ways of thinking, self-awareness about identity and culture, sensitivity and respect for differences and multiple perspectives, and behaviors in order to seek out multiple opinions and perspectives and take informed action on global issues.

Global Positioning System (GPS): GPS is a satellite navigation system that is maintained by the U.S. government with satellites orbiting the Earth. It is accessible anywhere in the world with a GPS device or a GPD built into mobile phones, and is used from military to agriculture, seismology to education. It gives the coordinates of a particular location, as well as information on time, weather, and altitude on the Earth's surface.

Heutagogy: Heutagogy is a life-long learning process that is self-directed and self-organized by a learner. Stewart Hase of Southern Cross University in Australia coined the term. Even though heutagogy is built on andragogy (education that focuses on adult learners), given the current proliferation of online, open-education resources, students at every level, including the elementary, have access and the ability to engage in the autonomous educational experiences of heutagogy.

Learning communities: Learning communities are informal learning environments. Emphasis is on authentic and collective learning. Learning communities are formed by groups of people who work together on projects, support one another, and engage in socio-cultural experiences.

Micro-affirmations: The term was coined by Mary P. Rowe in the 1970s. Rowe defined micro-affirmations as "small acts, which are often ephemeral and hard-to-see, events that are public and private, often unconscious but very effective, which occur wherever people wish to help others to succeed." In the context of education, educators and students sends micro-messages to each other. These messages can be in many different forms and gestures. It could be a gesture of inclusion, an attentive way of listening, respecting students' culture and language, paying close attention to the students' needs, or affirming another's point of view. Micro-affirmations assist educators in providing constructive, formative, and subtle feedback to their students, so that they can improve their learning. They can create a safe and positive learning environment for the students, and improve productivity.

Open learning: Open or flexible learning is a type of online education where the focus is on learning rather than teaching. It is student-centered, addresses local needs and requirements as opposed to standardized curriculum, and provides choices for students in meeting their educational goals.

Participatory Action Research (PAR): In Participatory Action Research projects, participants collaborate and co-design a research study. They are all part of a research team that seeks to investigate the issues by trying to change them. They participate (in society and democracy), take action (engaging with experience and history), and conduct research (contributing to objective thought and the growth of knowledge), both collectively and individually.

Participatory culture: Participatory culture, as opposed to consumer culture, is a new term describing a cultural climate in which each person acts as a contributor or co-producer. With the advent of Web 2.0, the Internet was no longer a static place. Instead, it turned into a dynamic environment where each participant becomes a part of the meaning-making process.

Pedagogy of Plenty: As opposed to "Pedagogy of Poverty," "Pedagogy of Plenty" describes a rich learning environment with high-quality resources, and exposes students to an inquiry-based and critical-thinking approach to instruction that emphasizes meaningful work and leads to higher academic outcomes and success in life.

Primary source: Documents, video, or other material created in the past at the time of events.

Project Based Learning (PBL): This is an instructional model, in global education, that addresses the development of global competence and awareness of cultural perspectives through ongoing opportunities for cross-cultural interactions, mediated by the use of technology as an integral part of the learning process. According to the Buck Institute for Education, Project Based Learning (PBL) allows students' "voice and choice," integrates 21st-century skills (such as collaboration and communication), and assesses authentic academic content. It also creates high-quality, authentic products and presentations. PBL addresses the development of global competence through ongoing opportunities for cross-cultural collaborative interactions, mediated by the use of technology.

Read/write web: This term refers to the new era of Internet, sometimes used to describe "Web 2.0." Users will be able to contribute and publish content on the web actively, in addition to reading or searching for information passively.

Social Media Software (SMS): This is a free and open-source web service that integrates wikis, chat, blogs, tagging, media sharing, social bookmarking, RSS, and other read/write web tools. SMS provides teachers and learners with an integrated set of social media that each course can use for its own purposes, and includes curricular material: syllabi, lesson plans, resource repositories, screencasts, and videos.

Social reconstructivist theory: This advocates change, improvement, and reform of society through education. Social reconstructivist perspectives claim that the learning environment is active, that assessment is based on creative work, and that education is relatively autonomous and can and does lead to social change. The social reconstructivist paradigm represents knowledge as socially constructed through language and interpersonal social processes. The role of education is to enhance students' learning through the interpersonal negotiation of meaning.

Third place: The sociologist Ray Oldenburg coined the term "third place," or great good places, to describe the public spaces used for informal social interaction outside of the home and workplace.

Transdisciplinary/Transdisciplinarity: "Transdisciplinary" signifies a unity of knowledge beyond, across, and between disciplines. This approach gives equal weight to each discipline, and allows research study to span disciplinary boundaries, while focusing within the framework of disciplinary research. Jean Piaget introduced the term in the 1970s.

21st-century skills: This term generally refers to the core competencies such as reading, writing, and arithmetic, as well as digital literacy, critical thinking, communication, collaboration, global competencies, and problem-solving skills necessary for students to thrive in the 21st century. It is outlined by the Partnership for 21st Century Skills (http://www.p21.org/) as the teaching and learning skills required to have subject-specific knowledge, use 21st-century tools to foster learning, connect learning to the real world, and use assessments that measure 21st-century learning.

Unconference: Also called an OpenSpace conference, this is a more informal conference event driven by its participants. Once the location and date are identified, participants gather to volunteer to lead sessions. Topics are identified based on the talent and interest of the attendees, and the focus throughout is on interpersonal connection and collaboration.

Universal Design for Learning (UDL): UDL is a curriculum-design framework used extensively in the field of special education. It was first introduced by the Center for Applied Special Technology (CAST). It is designed according to brain-based education research that promotes flexible learning environments that can accommodate individualized learning. UDL lessons aim to provide alternative methods, tools, and resources for each learner in the classroom, to optimize access to learning by reducing obstacles such as physical, cognitive, intellectual, and organizational barriers.

Appendix B: Applications and Tools

Translation Applications

- Google Translate: https://translate.google.com
- Translator Speak and Translate: https://play.google.com/store/apps/details?id=com. voicetranslator.SpeakAndTranslateFree&hl=en
- WordLens: http://wordlens.com/

Blogging Sites

- Blogger: https://www.blogger.com
- Edublog: https://wordpress.com/
- Glogster Edu: http://edu.glogster.com/?ref=com
- KidBlog: http://kidblog.org/home/
- SchoolTube: http://www.schooltube.com/
- VoiceThread: http://voicethread.com/
- Voki: http://voki.com/
- Wordpress: https://wordpress.com/

Collaboration Tools

- AirMedia: http://www.crestron.com/products/airmedia_mobile_wireless_hd_presentations/index.html?from=www.crestron.com%2Fairmedia
- Google Docs: http://www.google.com/docs/about/?gclid=COb06v73xsUCFceRHwodnLYAFQ
- Google Hangouts: http://www.google.com/+/learnmore/hangouts/
- Microsoft Office 365: http://products.office.com/en-us/student/office-in-education
- PenPal Schools: https://penpalschools.com/

- Smart Board 8000 series interactive flat panels: http://smart tech.com/Home+Page/TSolutions/Business+Solutions/Prod ucts/8000+series+interactive+flat+panels
- Smart Table: http://techcrunch.com/2008/10/21/smart-table-you-know-for-kids/

Creation Tools

- Camtasia: https://www.techsmith.com/camtasia.html
- Captivate: http://www.adobe.com/products/captivate.html
- Comic Creator: http://www.readwritethink.org/files/resources/interactives/comic/
- Google Sites for Education: https://www.google.com/edu/train ing/get-trained/sites/introduction.html
- Kid Pix: http://www.mackiev.com/kidpix/index.html
- MinecraftEdu: http://minecraftedu.com/
- Office Mix: https://mix.office.com/
- Project Spark: http://welcome.projectspark.com/
- Prezi: https://prezi.com/
- Sway: https://www.youtube.com/watch?v=Jw-g6IuBVJE&feature= youtube

Current Event Tools

- Time for Kids: http://www.timeforkids.com/
- C/NET: http://www.cnet.com/
- DoGo News: http://www.dogonews.com/
- Flipboard: https://about.flipboard.com/
- Kids Go Global: http://www.kidsgoglobal.net/
- Kids Post: http://www.timeforkids.com/news
- National Geographic: http://kids.nationalgeographic.com/
- PBS NewsHour for Kids: http://www.pbs.org/newshour/extra/
- The Learning Network: http://learning.blogs.nytimes.com/

Learning Management Systems

- Blackboard: http://www.blackboard.com/
- Edmodo: https://www.edmodo.com/
- NEO: https://www.neolms.com/
- Twiducate: http://www.twiducate.com/

List of Contributors

Maria Boos

Dr. Maria Boos is the E-Portfolio Coordinator at the Center for Teacher Education at the University of Cologne (Germany). Before that she worked as a research assistant in the work group "Theory and Design of Teaching and Learning in the Classroom" at the Ruhr-University Bochum (Germany). She has been teaching courses on media literacy for four years and has written about media education in Germany and the United States. She received her PhD at the University of Paderborn in 2014. In her dissertation she used quantitative and qualitative research methods to examine the media-related participation activities of soap opera fans from 35 different nationalities. Based on theoretical foundations of fandom research and concepts of media literacy and participation, she developed a model of media-related participation activities of soap opera fans on the Internet.

Victoria Brown

Dr. Victoria Brown is the assistant provost for eLearning at Florida Atlantic University. She is responsible for the administration of the University's Center for eLearning. Before working at the Provost's Office, Dr. Brown taught instructional technology in the College of Education at Florida Atlantic University and the Adrian Dominican School of Education at Barry University. She also has 10 years of experience teaching in K–12 special education classrooms. She received her bachelor's and master's degrees from Central Missouri State University and her doctorate from the University of West Florida. Her research interests are in the field of cognition and attention deficit and hyperactivity in distance learning environments and multimedia. She received a Meritorious Service Medal for her work with online professional development and was named Distance Educator of the Year for Higher Education by the Florida Distance Learning Association.

Belinha S. De Abreu

Belinha S. De Abreu, PhD, is a media literacy educator and Assistant Professor of the Practice in the Department of Educational Technology at Fairfield University in Connecticut. Her research interests include media literacy education, new media, visual and information literacy, global perspectives, critical thinking, young adults, and teacher training. Dr. De Abreu's focus is on the impact of learning as a result of media and technology consumed by K–12 students; providing students with viable, real-life opportunities for engaging in various technological environments; and encouraging students to be creative and conscious users of technology and media. Dr. De Abreu's work has been featured in Cable in the Classroom and *The Journal of Media Literacy*. She is the author of *Media Literacy, Social Networking, and the Web 2.0 World for the K–12 Educator* (Peter Lang, 2011) and the co-editor and author of *Media Literacy Education in Action: Theoretical and Pedagogical Perspectives* (Routledge, 2014). She serves as the Vice President for the National Telemedia Council, and organized the first international Media Literacy Research Symposium at Fairfield University. Follow @belmedia.

Jennifer Fleming

Dr. Jennifer Fleming is an associate professor in the Department of Journalism and Mass Communication at California State University, Long Beach. Dr. Fleming's research explores the conceptual and practical intersections between media literacy, news literacy, and journalism education. She has participated in dozens of academic conference presentations on these subjects, and her work has been published in *Journalism & Mass Communication Educator*, *Handbook of Research on Media Literacy in the Digital Age*, *UCLA Journal of Education & Information Studies*, and *Journal of Broadcasting & Electronic Media*. She received a PhD in education from the University of California, Los Angeles. Previous to her academic career, Dr. Fleming worked at CTV, Canada's largest private broadcaster. At CTV National News, she contributed as a writer and producer to the country's most-watched news and current affairs programs, CTV National News with Lloyd Robertson, and Canada AM.

Silke Grafe

Silke Grafe is a professor of Education and Chair of School Education at the Julius-Maximilians-University of Würzburg. Her research interests include media literacy and ICT in an international perspective, influence of learning theories and instructional design on learning with technology, media literacy and ICT in teacher education and professional development, and design of online learning environments. She has been working on the projects "Initial Teacher Education and Professional Development: Reflective Learning with Multimedia," funded by the Ministry of School, Science, and Research (North Rhine-Westphalia) and "Media and Information Technologies in Education: Development of an eLearning Environment in Initial Teacher Education," funded by the University Network Multimedia, among others. One of her current projects funded by the Federal Ministry of Education and Research (BMBF) focuses on developing and validating measures of pedagogical media competencies of students in initial teacher education. Silke Grafe was a member of the expert group of media literacy of the German Federal Ministry of Education and Research, and a member of the EMEDUS European Expert Group of Media Literacy Education.

Petra Hesse

Petra Hesse is an associate professor of human development. Her research interests are children's emotional development and emotional education, children's political socialization and political education, and children's media and media literacy education. She has written for a variety of European and American publications: *Psychosozial, Telemedium, International Journal of Mental Health, Young Children*, and *Contemporary Psychological Review*. In graduate school, she co-edited a monograph on emotional development and co-authored several book chapters on emotional development. As a post-doctoral fellow, she wrote about children's fears of nuclear war. Since her arrival at Wheelock College, she has written about children's enemy images in different cultures, about German adolescents before and after reunification, and about children's reactions to 9/11. She produced a videotape and wrote several articles and book chapters about political messages on children's television. She is currently working on several projects about teacher training, in media literacy and in emotional and political education.

Richard Hornik

Richard Hornik is Director of Overseas Partnership Programs for the Center for News Literacy at Stony Brook University, where he has been a lecturer since 2008. He just concluded a semester as the inaugural Daniel K. Inouye Visiting Scholar at the University of Hawaii, and was a visiting lecturer at the

University of Hong Kong in 2012. During his 24 years at *TIME*, he was news service director and served as bureau chief in Warsaw, Beijing, and Hong Kong. He was executive editor of *AsiaWeek* and interim editor of the *Harvard Business Review*, where he is now a contributing editor. Hornik co-authored *Massacre in Beijing: China's Struggle for Democracy* (Warner Books, 1989) and has written for *Foreign Affairs*, Smithsonian, *The New York Times* and the *Wall St. Journal.* He has been Journalist-in-Residence at the EastWest Center in Honolulu, a Knight International Press Fellow, and a Woodrow Wilson Visiting Scholar. He is a member of the Council on Foreign Relations and has an MA in Russian Studies from George Washington University and a BA in Political Science from Brown.

Vanja Ibrahimbegović-Tihak

Vanja Ibrahimbegović-Tihak is a media and digital literacy educator, researcher, and advocate. For the last five years she has been pioneering the development of media literacy in Bosnia-Herzegovina, with several other fellow practitioners. She conducts media literacy trainings for teachers, students, and youth activists throughout the region. Her research interests are related to teachers' competencies for teaching media literacy, and media literacy education in general. Vanja is a communications specialist and a former journalist with extensive experience in project management within CSOs. She holds an MA in the field of democracy and human rights, and a BA in journalism.

Masato Kajimoto

Dr. Masato Kajimoto is an assistant professor at the Journalism and Media Studies Centre (JMSC) at the University of Hong Kong. Dr. Kajimoto specializes in international news literacy education, multimedia storytelling, and social media in journalism. He heads the Asia Pacific Digital Citizens Project at JMSC that aims to guide the future generation of discerning media audiences. His latest research and publications have focused on the influence of social and political climate on the pedagogical design and implementation of news literacy curricula in Asia. He recently designed and taught a Massive Open Online Course on news literacy on edX, titled "Making Sense of News." His other research interests include digital communication data mining, learning analytics, stereotype studies, and narrative analysis. Before beginning a career in teaching and research, he worked as an online reporter and a web producer for CNN International.

Kelly McNeal

Kelly McNeal is an associate professor of urban education at William Paterson University in Wayne, New Jersey. She is also Director of the Masters in Middle Level Education Program and teaches undergraduate classes in the Department of Middle and Secondary Education. Dr. McNeal received her PhD in language, literacy, and learning from Fordham University, and her areas of research include literacy, standards-based education, and urban education. At present she is the Program Chair for the American Educational Research Association's Urban Learning Teaching and Research Special Interest Group (SIG). She was previously the editor and associate editor of the *Journal of Urban Learning, Teaching, and Research* and has been published in the *Journal of Adolescent and Adult Literacy*.

Michael RobbGrieco

Michael RobbGrieco, PhD, is the director of Curriculum and Technology Integration for K–12 schools in the Windham Southwest Supervisory Union in Vermont. Mike has a background in teaching high school English and ESOL, and is an experienced teacher educator, media artist, and researcher. His research interests include history of media literacy, educational affordances of remix practice, new theories of agency in media education, and using humorous media to teach savvy media use. He is an affiliated faculty member of the Media Education Lab at the University of Rhode Island, and an associate editor of the *Journal of Media Literacy Education*.

Kristine Scharaldi

Kristine Scharaldi is an educational consultant and professional development provider based out of New Jersey. She offers expertise, resources, and pedagogies to support educators and students in digital-age learning environments from preschool through higher education. Her areas of interest and specialization include educational technology, mobile learning, global education, mind-brain-education, Universal Design for Learning, and 21st-century skills. She presents workshops and conference sessions regionally and internationally. Kristine Scharaldi is co-founder of Unite to Educate, an initiative that aims to advance education in our modern world through research, publication, curriculum development, collaboration, and online instruction. She earned a master's degree in computing and education from Teachers College, Columbia University and a bachelor's degree in sociology from Rutgers

College at Rutgers University. She has worked as a teacher, instructional coach, and staff developer.

Jennifer Tiede

Jennifer Tiede is a research assistant and PhD student in the Department of Educational Sciences at the Julius-Maximilians-University of Würzburg. She focused on media pedagogy during her teacher education studies and wrote her master's thesis on a media pedagogical topic. Her PhD thesis is also concerned with media-related teaching strategies. She is currently working in a BMBF-funded project that develops and validates measures of pedagogical media competencies of students in initial teacher education. Her main activities are developing the test instrument for measuring pre-service teachers' pedagogical media competencies, organizing and conducting an international survey, and establishing contact and holding interviews with international fellow researchers. Her research interests focus on media education from an international perspective, media pedagogical competencies of pre-service teachers, game-based learning, and gamification.

Rob Williams

Rob Williams, PhD, teaches new/digital and social media, communications, and journalism courses at the University of Vermont, Saint Michael's College, Champlain College, and Sacred Heart University. The co-founding president and current board co-chair of the Action Coalition for Media Education (ACME at www.smartmediaeducation.net), he is the author of numerous articles and book chapters about media education, lectures widely on topics and issues related to digital media literacy education, and has consulted with a number of organizations, including the College for America, PH International, and the U.S. State Department. His books include *Most Likely to Secede: What the Vermont Independence Movement Can Teach Us about Reclaiming Community and Creating a Human Scale Vision for the 21st Century* (Vermont Independence Press, 2013) and *Media Education for a Digital Generation* (Routledge, 2016).

Melda N. Yildiz

Melda N. Yildiz is an educational consultant and co-founder of Unite to Educate, an initiative that aims to advance education in our modern world through research, publication, curriculum development, collaboration, and online instruction. Yildiz served as the first Fulbright Scholar in Turkmenistan. Since 1994, she taught Media Literacy Education, Multimedia Production, Women's Studies, Asian Studies, and Global Education to P–16 educators and teacher candidates. Yildiz worked as a Media Specialist at Northfield Mount Hermon School, taught video and media production to grades 9–12, and published and presented work featuring educational media, global education, media literacy, education semiotics, and multicultural education in many national and international conferences. She received her EdD from University of Massachusetts in math and science and Instructional Technology. She received an MS from Southern Connecticut State University in Instructional Technology. She majored in teaching English as a foreign language at Bogazici University, in Turkey.

Index

CRITICAL ISSUES
FOR LEARNING AND TEACHING

Shirley R. Steinberg
General Editor

Minding the Media is a book series specifically designed to address the needs of students and teachers in watching, comprehending, and using media. Books in the series use a wide range of educational settings to raise consciousness about media relations and realities and promote critical, creative alternatives to contemporary mainstream practices. *Minding the Media* seeks theoretical, technical, and practitioner perspectives as they relate to critical pedagogy and public education. Authors are invited to contribute volumes of up to 85,000 words to this series. Possible areas of interest as they connect to learning and teaching include:

- critical media literacy
- popular culture
- video games
- animation
- music
- media activism
- democratizing information systems
- using alternative media
- using the Web/internet
- interactive technologies
- blogs
- multi-media in the classroom
- media representations of race, class, gender, sexuality, disability, etc.

- media/communications studies methodologies
- semiotics
- watchdog journalism/investigative journalism
- visual culture: theater, art, photography
- radio, TV, newspapers, zines, film, documentary film, comic books
- public relations
- globalization and the media
- consumption/consumer culture
- advertising
- censorship
- audience reception

For additional information about this series or for the submission of manuscripts, please contact:
    Shirley R. Steinberg
    msgramsci@gmail.com

To order other books in this series, please contact our Customer Service Department:
    (800) 770-LANG (within the U.S.)
    (212) 647-7706 (outside the U.S.)
    (212) 647-7707 FAX

Or browse online by series:
    www.peterlang.com